The War against Paris 1871

D1339899

THE
WAR AGAINST PARIS
1871

ROBERT TOMBS
Fellow of St John's College, Cambridge

CAMBRIDGE UNIVERSITY PRESS

Cambridge
London   New York   New Rochelle
Melbourne   Sydney

Published by the Press Syndicate of the University of Cambridge
The Pitt Building, Trumpington Street, Cambridge CB2 1RP
32 East 57th Street, New York, NY 10022, USA
296 Beaconsfield Parade, Middle Park, Melbourne 3206, Australia

First published 1981

British Library Cataloguing in Publication Data
Tombs, Robert
The war against Paris 1871.
1. Paris (France) – History – Commune, 1871
I. Title
944'.36081   DC316   80–42024
ISBN 0 521 23551 0
ISBN 0 521 23551 0 hardcover
ISBN 0 521 28784 7 paperback

Transferred to digital printing 2003

Contents

Illustrations

Preface

vvvvvvvvvvvvvvvvvvvvvvvvvvvvvvvvvvvvvvvvvvvvvvvvvvvvvvvvvvvvvvvvvvvvvvvvvv

During the preparation of this book I have been fortunate in benefiting
from the valuable advice and criticism of several historians and friends
whom I am glad to have the opportunity of thanking here. Dr J. P. T.
Bury and Dr C. M. Andrew were most generous with their time and
counsel. Dr Jonathan Steinberg has been kind enough to follow progress from an early stage and offer encouragement and constructive
criticism. Dr John Keiger of Salford University, Mr Albert Vaiciulenas,
of Queens' College, Cambridge, and Dr Iain Hamilton, of Durham
University, soothed the birth pangs and did much to bring some order
out of chaos in the days when we were a nest of singing birds in the 3rd
arrondissement. The shortcomings, and the opinions expressed, are
mine.

The late Jacques Millerand, whose recent death Cambridge historians have special reason to lament, gave me the benefit of his vast
knowledge and generous hospitality. Professor Louis Girard and Mr
William Serman, of the University of Paris, guided me through the
administrative maze. Generous financial assistance from the British
and French governments and the British Institute in Paris made re-
search possible. My thanks are due to the staffs of the Service Historique de l'Armée, who bore a heavy burden with patience and forti-
tude, of the Archives de la Préfecture de Police, and of the archives of
the Ministère des Affaires Etrangères. Elizabeth Wetton of the Cambridge University Press has been unfailingly helpful and encouraging.

I am particularly grateful to the Master and Fellows of Trinity Hall,
and the Master and Fellows of St John's College, for their hospitality
during the preparation of this work. Without my parents it would
never have been written, and the task would have been a less happy
one without Isabelle, my wife, and the many Parisian friends who
have given me a glimpse of the life of the city.

Acknowledgements

The contemporary drawings are reproduced by kind permission of the Illustrated London News Picture Library. Photographs are from the Commune Collection, Sussex University Library, and the portraits from the Bibliothèque de la Ville de Paris were kindly provided by Dr A. Rifkin.

Glossary

action d'éclat – a 'brilliant action' in battle

capitulards – insulting nickname for advocates of surrender

chasseurs à cheval – light cavalry

chasseurs à pied – light infantry

compagnies de guerre or *de marche* of National Guard – active service units liable for service outside the city walls

compagnies sédentaires of National Guard – home defence units

Conseil de Discipline – regimental disciplinary tribunal

Conseil de Guerre – formal court martial

cour martiale – informal 'drumhead' court martial

franc-tireurs – irregular units, guerrillas

fuséen – Communard fire-raiser (imaginary)

Garde Mobile – part of the National Guard, composed of men of military age, liable for wartime service alongside the regular army

libérables – men due for demobilization

mairie – 'town hall' of an *arrondissement*

mitrailleuse – machine gun (introduced 1866)

National Guard – citizen militia used for internal order and home defence

outranciers – nickname for advocates of a fight to the finish

perceur – nickname for advocates of 'breaking out' (at Metz)

pétroleuse – female Communard fire-raiser (imaginary)

prévôt – provost-marshal: gendarmerie officer commanding military police

prévôté – summary tribunal and military police detachment commanded by *prévôt*

refractaire – man avoiding National Guard service

régiment de ligne – regular infantry regiment (*lignard* – infantryman)

régiment de marche – regiment formed in wartime from reserves, depot troops etc.

Glossary

régiment provisoire – temporary regiment formed from mixed detachments

sédentaires – men of *compagnies sédentaires* (above)

zéphirs – nickname of men of *infanterie légère d'Afrique,* penal units

zouaves – elite infantry of North African origins and French
recruitment

To my parents

Wars and rumours of wars

The war against Paris began on 11 April 1871 when units of the French army opened the first siege trench on the Châtillon plateau about a mile and a half south of the city walls. Five and a half weeks of trench digging, bombardment and skirmishing among the ruins of the suburban villages followed until, on 21 May, the army entered Paris and in a week of street fighting put a bloody end to the revolutionary Paris Commune, and left the city strewn with the bodies of thousands of its citizens and the rubble of many of its most famous monuments.

The sequence of events preceding this tragedy seemed in retrospect to lead so inevitably to it that many supposed it to have been planned, either by a government intent on crushing once and for all the troublesome revolutionaries of Paris, or by the revolutionaries themselves in a plot to ruin France and destroy the society they abhorred.

The first of these events was the catastrophic Franco-Prussian war. Declared on 19 July 1870 following a period of nervous rivalry with Prussia, and under pressure from a jingoistic public, the war produced during its first weeks a series of astounding defeats for France. They culminated in the trapping of one army (155,000 men under Marshal Bazaine) in the fortress of Metz on 19 August, and the capture of a second (130,000 men under Marshal de MacMahon) at Sedan on 1 September, and with it the Emperor Napoleon III himself. On 4 September, when the news reached Paris, a huge crowd invaded the parliament, where the fall of the Empire was proclaimed. A provisional republican Government of National Defence, composed of the solidly republican Deputies of Paris, took power.

There followed a period of patriotic fervour in which all classes and parties joined. Nowhere was this stronger than in Paris, which was surrounded by a German army on 20 September. But four months of siege, hunger, cold and disappointment for Parisians, of struggle, bloodshed and suffering for the new armies raised by Léon Gambetta in the provinces, and of almost unbroken defeat for all, shattered the patriotic union of the early days. The now detested government in Paris signed an armistice on 28 January 1871. Electors in the provinces returned a huge conservative majority to a new National Assembly to vote a peace settlement; Parisians returned a predominantly radical deputation, including men in favour of continuing the war.

In Paris, still surrounded by German troops, the armistice left the population in arms and determined, if not to continue the war alone, at least to resist the authority of those it considered responsible for the defeat and who, furthermore, seemed intent on overthrowing the new Republic. During the siege, political life in Paris had flourished into numerous clubs and committees, which had taken on a revolutionary tone. The National Guard itself, the citizen militia expanded during the war to 320,000 men, had become politicized, and in February 1871 many of its battalions joined a Fédération Républicaine de la Garde Nationale with the intention of protecting the Republic and the rights of Paris, if necessary by resistance to the new National Assembly.

The monarchist majority in the National Assembly, which met in Bordeaux on 12 February, and the new provisional government which it chose, headed by the veteran statesman Adolphe Thiers, were convinced of the need to bring Paris back under their authority and to end the agitation there, which was so damaging to the prestige of the government both at home and abroad, and which compromised post-war economic recovery. This, then, was the crisis bequeathed by the Franco-Prussian war: Paris, angry at its defeat, devoted to the Republic and to its own newly won liberty; a National Assembly at Bordeaux looking forward to a restoration of the monarchy and determined to assert its own authority and that of France over the capital; and both sides disposing of armed forces – the National Guard of Paris and the regular army.

Wars, particularly unsuccessful ones, have frequently been the occasions of civil strife. But the conflict of 1871 can be traced back further. The Parisian republicans of 1871 knew themselves to come from a long line. In 1789 their forefathers had taken the Bastille; in 1792 they had created the revolutionary Commune of Paris, pressed forward the revolution, punished traitors and defended the first Republic against foreign invaders. Within living memory, during the Three Glorious Days of July 1830, the people of Paris, fighting in the streets and from their houses, had overthrown the Bourbon monarchy by force of arms. In February 1848, King Louis-Philippe too had succumbed to their

2

power. In September 1870 they had proclaimed the Republic for the third time. These were the moments of triumph; but republicans saw their saga as one of continual betrayal and defeat. In 1830 they had been cheated of the fruits of the revolution; in 1848, disappointed by the failure of the government they had set up to change the lot of working men; in June of that year, massacred by the bourgeois militia; on 'Deux Décembre' 1851, crushed by the *coup d'état*. For two decades since then, they had been oppressed by the Empire with the consent of conservative rural voters, and denied control even of their own municipal affairs. Finally, they felt that they had been unsupported in their resistance against the Prussians by those same provincials, who had elected a reactionary 'Assembly of rustics' and demanded peace at any price. If all Parisians considered their city to be the centre of civilization, republicans felt it to be a city of heroes and martyrs, and to keep the flame of the Great Revolution alive they intended to keep Paris free from the reactionary hordes outside, both Prussian and French.

Recent history had marked the stones of Paris as well as the minds of its citizens. Its population had been growing rapidly since the 1820s, and never more quickly than during the two decades of the Empire. Realizing the need for modernization, and wishing to create a capital worthy of the new France, Napoleon III had commissioned Georges Haussmann, as Prefect of the Seine, to transform the city. The old centre was gutted to make room for boulevards, squares and public buildings. Suburban villages were annexed and, their population swollen by thousands of poorer families pushed out from the centre by demolitions and rising rents as well as by new immigrants from the provinces, they became huge working-class settlements on the northern, eastern and southern edges of the city. These districts, the most populous of which were Montmartre and Belleville, were dismal, half-finished urban wastes of railway yards, factories, quarries, building sites, workshops and jerry-built housing, short of schools, churches, transport services and urban facilities of all kinds, even water.[1] With an almost entirely working-class population – and a discontented and sometimes unruly one at that – they provided an atmosphere in which radical organizations, both political and, in the form of the wartime National Guard, military, could develop. Class war was written in the geography of the capital.[2] It had intensified during the late 1860s, when a relaxation of the authoritarian Empire coinciding with an economic recession produced an overflowing of political protest and industrial conflict. Although there was certainly a long step from protest to revolution, it was at this time that many of those who were to lead the insurrection of 1871 won influence among the working class. They confirmed and increased their influence during the siege when, through popular clubs, committees and newspapers and in the ranks of the National Guard itself, a revolutionary leadership emerged.

Those who were to combat the insurgents in 1871 were similarly conscious of the past, with the word Commune evoking less agreeable memories – 'there is blood on that word'.[3] The provinces had their own memories of Paris, under whose heavy yoke they had often chafed, and of the turbulent politics of the previous eighty years. The revolutionary 'Terror' had been carried from the capital. Three times during the nineteenth century its citizens had changed the form of government, and although the provinces generally acquiesced, there had been times when Paris had gone too far. The hated 45 centimes tax had come from there in 1848 – to feed the Parisian workers in idleness, it was said. Rumours of 'red terror' had come from the capital in June of that year, and the provinces had sent an army of volunteers to help to suppress it. Most recently, the prolongation of the disastrous war against Germany, with the burdens it imposed on the country, had been seen as the fault of the republican Parisian regime; the provinces had responded by electing an 'Assembly of rustics' with a large majority of conservative rural notables – men they knew and trusted, for the moment, to do what was necessary. These men, feeling that the country was at last with them, were in no mood to trifle with Paris or to make concessions to the 'spirit of revolution'. Any weakness would, in their view, merely prolong the political and social sickness with which Paris was infecting France. 'France knows', cried a royalist deputy, 'that ten times in eighty years Paris has sent her governments ready made, by telegraph', causing national decadence and now defeat and 'the dismemberment of her territory. She knows this, and she wants no more of it.'[4] Such feelings were to fuel the war against Paris.

The new government did not completely share this view. Thiers himself was soon to accept the Republic openly, and his most important ministers were republicans of long standing. But they were republicans of the centre, who fought the extreme Left in Paris in order, as they saw it, to defend a 'sensible' republic against a lunatic fringe supported by the riff-raff and manipulated by outside forces. Some had won their spurs in 1848, helping to suppress the workers' insurrection in June of that year, when intellectuals and middle-class repub-

4

licans had been the most determined opponents of the rebels. And, in the words of Thiers's Minister of Public Instruction, Jules Simon, 'June 1848, March 1871 – the same struggle'.[5] These republican politicians, who had taken part in the legal opposition to the Empire, had felt themselves overtaken by new men of the extreme Left during the late 1860s, preaching 'anti-liberal practices and doctrines . . . we had known [them] by name for two years; we had guessed their existence, we had felt them there, for more than six years'.[6] This rivalry was immeasurably intensified during the Prussian siege, when the failures of the Government of National Defence, whose leading members continued in office under Thiers, had provoked two unsuccessful putsches by Left-wing National Guards, in October 1870 and January 1871. The second attempt had ended in bloodshed. At the end of the war, the 'Jules' (Favre, Ferry and Simon), formerly the leaders of the republican party in Paris, were execrated by workers and bourgeoisie alike: 'Never have I seen a more profound unpopularity than theirs', noted one observer.[7] This antagonism between moderate and Left-wing republicans was of the utmost importance. The discredit of the moderates in Paris greatly increased the influence of the Left there, while the fact that the counter revolution was to be led, as in June 1848, by prominent republicans made it difficult for the insurgents to convince potential allies outside their walls that they were fighting to defend the Republic.

The outcome of the struggle between Paris – represented by its popular leaders and its dissident National Guard – and the legal government, elected by the National Assembly, depended on the army. The army had never taken the political initiative, but its reaction to events had been decisive. While it invariably obeyed orders, it sometimes had a choice of orders: in 1851 it had obeyed the orders of the President, Louis-Napoleon, rather than those of the Assembly. In 1870, Marshal Bazaine, besieged in Metz, decided that his obedience was due not to the new Government of National Defence, but to the Emperor. However much officers sought to shelter behind their orders, in times of political upheaval they might be forced to make a choice, for above and beyond passing regimes, as Marshal Bazaine was reminded at his trial for treason, 'France remained'.[8] But even when they had no doubts as to whose orders they should obey, there were degrees of enthusiasm in executing them. In both 1830 and 1848, the hesitancy of officers and men when called upon to fire on revolutionary crowds in Paris had brought about the fall of the existing regime, and those officers who had obeyed orders too enthusiastically risked finding themselves punished later for their misplaced loyalty. In June 1848, the army had helped to crush the revolt, but precautions had been taken not to expose the troops too much, and the brunt of the fighting had been borne by the citizen militia, the National Guard. The army had an uneasy relationship with the population. While a majority of officers were of humble origin, long years of service removed them from contact with their fellow citizens and made the army the undisputed centre of their lives. The same was true of the men. Although the majority were originally conscripts, seven years of service followed for many by reenlistment made them a race apart. This was encouraged by successive regimes, which moved units regularly round the country to prevent them from developing ties with the community. The army had its moments of popularity, after its victories in the Crimea and Italy, for example, when triumphant troops were cheered by the workers as they paraded through the streets of Paris. But in the 1860s, it had frequently been used to control strikes, and so its role as the ultimate support of an authoritarian regime could not be forgotten. The coming of war in 1870 naturally increased its popularity until defeat brought forth a chorus of accusations of ineptitude, cowardice and even treachery against the regulars and especially the officers. At the same time, the war brought an influx of new elements whose attitudes were often different from those of the old army.

Given the precedents of the previous eighty years, the fall of the Empire and the turmoil caused by the German invasion brought thoughts of civil war into the minds of many. Rumours of strife and anarchy outside had been rife among the troops besieged in Metz, and towards the end of the war, among the troops still fighting, 'very often, in our conversations concerning the political conditions of our poor country, we had foreseen a civil war'.[9] In February, rumours that civil conflict had already broken out in Paris swept Bordeaux, where the National Assembly was sitting. Many in Paris too felt the danger, and in the early days of the insurrection a republican deputy was to warn of 'fatal June Days' in the offing, and fresh catastrophe for the workers of Paris; the revolutionaries, for their part, feared another 'Deux Décembre'.[10]

The insurrection began on 18 March when the government, using the small number of troops at its disposal, and hoping to avoid serious conflict by a sleight of hand, tried to capture by surprise the artillery of the Paris National Guard as a first step towards its disarmament and the restoration of order in the city. The attempt failed in the face of generally non-violent resistance from the local inhabitants and the National Guard. The government and military command, fearful that the army might disintegrate and fraternize with the crowd, as in February 1848, ordered a general retreat to Versailles, seven miles south-west of the city. There followed a week of confused attempts to negotiate a way out of the impasse, but no true compromise was acceptable either to the Right in the Assembly, determined to resist revolution at all costs, or to the Left in Paris, convinced that revolutionary victory was within its grasp. Negotiations broke down when quasi-legal elections were held in Paris on 26 March for a municipal government, the Commune, which rivalled the authority of the national government now in Versailles. The rupture became irreparable when fighting broke out in the western suburbs on 2 April. The army began its siege on the 11th, and fighting steadily intensified over the next five weeks until it culminated in the Bloody Week, *la Semaine Sanglante*, from 21 to 28 May.

This war is the subject of the present book, which describes it from the viewpoint of the government and army of Versailles. The army was the key to victory. On 18 March, its failure to seize the National Guard cannon and its willingness to fraternize with the crowd permitted the revolutionaries to seize control of Paris. Its change of attitude over the following weeks condemned the revolution and led to one of the bloodiest repressions in the history of Europe. How and why this change took place is a question that has been posed before but never answered. This seems to be due in part to a false assumption that the troops used by the government were merely the hardened 'praetorians' of the Imperial Army aided by fanatical or docile peasants – the *chouans* and *ruraux* of Communard propaganda – whose attitudes and responses were predictable and obvious. It will be argued that this is far from the truth. The rank and file, as the government realized, continued to show a disturbing reluctance to take part in the civil war – an attitude shared even by some of the officers. The need to take account of the half-heartedness of many of their troops affected the policies of the government and high command throughout the crisis. Other considerations – of parliamentary politics, public opinion and diplomacy – had to take second place to the immediate demands of the military situation. This, of all the problems facing the government, was the least amenable to the kind of circumvention by parliamentary and diplomatic manoeuvring at which Thiers was so dextrous. The most important decisions taken by the government – to begin disarming the National Guard on 18 March, to evacuate the city, to begin hostilities on 2 April and to undertake a long siege of the capital – followed calculation of the military balance between themselves and the dissidents and the dangers and possibilities it offered. The attitude of the German government, whose troops were still hemming Paris in on two sides, was influenced by the same calculation.

The major theme of this work is therefore the organization of the army, its morale and its use in combat. Several questions suggest themselves. How was the army brought to fight the insurgents in April and May after its failure in March? Was it merely a matter of creating a physical distance between the troops and the civilians and 'blooding the pack'; were the soldiers of March replaced by others who did not share their doubts and scruples; and what was the importance of circumstance, persuasion, propaganda and compulsion? Who were the soldiers of Versailles: the long-service regulars of the Imperial Army, peasants with a traditional hatred of Paris and its subversive ideas, or simply a cross-section of the whole population? Was the conflict the reflection of a division between town and country and a repetition of the great uprising against the capital that took place in June 1848? To what extent was the final bloodshed, in which perhaps 20,000 people were killed in the space of a few days, engendered by the heat of combat, and to what extent was it a deliberate purge? What was in the minds of those responsible for the slaughter?

An attempt to answer these questions requires an imaginative reconstitution, from orders, letters, police reports, memoirs and newspapers, of the experience of fighting in the 'terrible year' of 1870–1. First, the defeat by Germany, and the strain it placed on the morale, organization and loyalties of the army. Second, the weeks following the armistice, during which the government and its troops were confronted with the rejection of their authority in Paris, which finally brought the army face to face with the population of the city, in a mission which the troops barely understood and in a political situation which divided and confused public opinion. Third, the weeks of the French siege of Paris, during which the army was involved in a growing conflict while being exposed to intensifying (and increasingly one-sided) propaganda and constantly stricter discipline. Finally, the nightmare of the battle of Paris, in which psychological strain far exceeded physical danger for the troops, while the High Command had decided to crush the revolution without mercy. The author has never seen bloodshed, never heard the proverbial shot fired in anger, and never been subject to military discipline. For the imaginative task demanded here, these are weighty handicaps. It has had to be attempted, however, for otherwise there can be no understanding of the behaviour of the army of 1871 and all that stemmed from it.

Much has stemmed from it, and the wider significance of the events of 1871 should also be borne in mind during the course of this study. For the Commune has become one of the great myth-making events of modern French history, along with the taking of the Bastille, the June Days, the Dreyfus Affair, the Popular Front, the defeat of 1940 and the occupation, and the 'revolution' of May 1968. Indeed, in the imagination of many it is greater than these.[11] For the French Left in particular, it is the tragic and heroic culmination of the struggle of the workers of Paris, the furthest development of the French revolution, and the first step, unique in history, towards a new kind of revolution. In the words of a Secretary-General of the French Communist Party,[12] 'The Commune is a great epic for the working class. Every advancing movement needs an epic behind it. If it had not existed, what would we have? The Commune is ours. It is the first government of the dictatorship of the proletariat.' This is the classic Marxist–Leninist doctrine: that the Commune was 'essentially a working-class government . . . the political form at last discovered under which to work out the economic emancipation of labour'.[13] Because of this view of the immense importance of the Commune in world history, the first and direct effect of its defeat in 1871 – that of putting a violent end to the series of Paris insurrections of the nineteenth century – was superseded by the opposite effect of helping to perpetuate the spirit of revolution, if not as a practical programme, at least as a mental attitude.

The evidence presented here, while not primarily concerned with the Commune, and not at all with its ideological interpretation, cannot but have some relevance to the question. First, it bears on the essentially epic nature of the myth, according to which the working-class, almost as one man, defends the city and the revolution to the death. But it will be seen, to put it brutally, that Paris was a walkover for the army when once it could pluck up the courage to attack. On both sides, the rank and file dragged their feet, leaving a determined minority on Right and Left to carry on a crusade which had a marked air of *déjà vu*. Second, it bears on the equally important idea, proposed by Marx and developed by Lenin, that the Commune could and should have succeeded, had it not made certain identifiable errors, of which the most

9

serious was failing to have taken the offensive at the very beginning. It will be seen that, for purely military reasons, an offensive was almost certain to fail, as the disastrous attack of 3 April shows. Third, it bears on the question of responsibility for the civil war, which traditionally has been placed entirely on a bourgeois government eager to crush the troublesome workers of the capital. It will be argued that the government and the army were far too uncomfortably aware of their own weakness and the unreliability of their forces to provoke a violent confrontation, or even to accept one with confidence. This being the case, it is clear that the insurgents themselves, and certain of their leaders in particular, share some of the responsibility for the final tragedy, for their revolutionary ardour was not untainted with intolerance, nor their courage with irresponsibility. As far as Paris is concerned, the argument of this book supports the judgment of Marx – not his fiery polemics in *The Civil War in France*, but the sober opinion of later years: 'the Paris Commune . . . was merely the rising of a city under exceptional conditions . . . with a modicum of common sense, however, it could have reached a compromise with Versailles useful to the whole people – the only thing that could be attained at the time'.[14] But common sense was lacking, and Paris paid the price.

2

A defeated army

The stunning defeat by Germany in 1870 transformed the organization of the French army and enfeebled its morale. Any attempt to understand the behaviour of officers and men during the civil war that followed must take this into account. The inability of the government forces to prevent or suppress the Paris insurrection in its early stages in March stemmed from the disorganization that the war and the armistice created, and from the disillusionment, doubt, conflicting loyalties and divided interests that the defeat engendered. At the same time, the bitterness that came to be felt as the civil war progressed, especially by the officers, which added so greatly to the horrors of the conflict, also owed much to the shock of defeat, and to the conviction that the acts of the insurgents were sorely aggravating the country's woes. 'It needed the kind of savagery created by six months of war or captivity', wrote an officer a few years later, 'for [the army] to have undertaken the second siege of Paris with the fury that we know.'[1]

The army that emerged from the Franco-Prussian war was a far less homogeneous force than its peacetime predecessor. As well as the regular army of long-term conscripts, volunteers and professional officers, nearly all made prisoner at Sedan and Metz, there had been formed by the Government of National Defence new armies of young recruits in the north, the east and on the Loire, commanded by a mixture of regulars and improvised officers of various origins. Cut off from these by the siege was the Army of Paris, which had spent the war in the defence of the capital. The new armies, as will be seen, had had a very different view of the war from that of the regulars, and this affected their reactions to the political agitation in Paris and to the ensuing civil war.

The first to suffer defeat in 1870 was the regular Imperial Army, the glorious and brilliant victor of Sebastopol, Magenta and Solferino, the inheritor of the prestige of Jena and Austerlitz. Officers and men, a handful of pessimists notwithstanding, had been thoroughly convinced of their superiority over what they had supposed to be a horde of conscripted amateurs: lumbering beer-drinking peasants led by bespectacled lawyers and oculists.[2] Most expert and amateur opinion held a similar view. The main reason for this self-confidence, which rendered the shock of defeat all the more demoralizing, was the wide experience of warfare that the army enjoyed: it was an army of old campaigners, from top to bottom. For instance, General Du Barail, later Minister of War, looking back over forty years' service, could recall with pride his beginnings as a trooper of Spahis, the only Frenchman in a squadron of Algerians, and his first night in the barrack-room disturbed by the nibbling of bed-bugs and the rustling of rats. Although a growing number of men of good family and education embarked on a military career during the Second Empire, filling most of the senior ranks – a frequently resented trend – the surest way to rapid promotion was still the *action d'éclat* on the battlefield. This applied not only to those rising from the ranks, such as Du Barail, Marshal Bazaine (thirty-two campaigns, wounded six times, mentioned in dispatches fourteen times), or General Félix Douay (wounded twice, mentioned in dispatches three times); but also to those enjoying every advantage of background and education. Marshal de MacMahon, for example, who was to direct the war against Paris, was a rich aristocrat who did well at the military academy of Saint Cyr, but his brilliant career – from captain to general in eleven years – was made campaigning in Africa, where he was nicknamed 'le petit lion'. At regimental level too there was wide experience of combat. In the 2nd infantry regiment in 1870, for example, all the field officers and captains, twenty-two out of twenty-four lieutenants, and thirteen out of twenty-five second-lieutenants had seen active service.[3]

Though the benefits of combat experience were felt many times during the war of 1870, the drawbacks of a system in which 'on tombe et retombe incessament de la bagarre à la routine'[4] were even more evident. The emphasis on *bagarre* (fighting) and the consequent neglect of all but the most superficial aspects of *routine* had encouraged an intellectual laziness on the part of the High Command which caused the French army to be outclassed strategically in 1870. Complacency was encouraged by victories in the Crimea and Italy, where the generals' *coup d'oeil* and the troops' fighting spirit compensated for the lack of thorough preparation. Colonial soldiers, while practised in minor tactics, had no occasion to widen their experience of large-scale operations, combat against European troops or the organization of a European campaign. In administration and planning, trust was placed in *le système D* – muddling through. The training of units based in France had lost touch with reality. When the new Colonel Du Barail arrived fresh from the African light cavalry to command a regiment of *cuirass-iers* permanently based at Versailles, he found that the men spent many of their waking hours burnishing their helmets and breastplates in an unending battle against raindrops and rust. With African practicality he carried out 'a minor revolution' – grease. There were other weaknesses in the metropolitan army far less easy to remedy. Large formations were trained in convoluted manoeuvres learnt from the manual and perfected on the parade ground. Discipline was unthinking obedience to the rule-book: great stress was placed on such matters of smartness and drill while slackness developed in the less visible but more essential aspects of the profession. Worst of all, no initiative was tolerated. Early in the war a young officer saw Prussian scouts allowed to approach an infantry column without a shot being fired at them: 'No doubt people were waiting for someone to give the order, and no one thought of it. We were so used then to doing nothing without an order.'[5]

All initiative was thus reserved for generals whose high rank, often the reward for gallantry in the field or of honourable old age, came to seem a dignity rather than a function. Many commanders were in reality resting on their laurels and enjoying an early retirement. In the provinces territorial commanders 'reigned' over several departments, treated with 'honours reserved today for heads of state'.[6] This encouraged a haughty, violent and autocratic manner. Olympian generals concerned themselves little with the welfare of their men; their duty was to give them an example of bravery in battle, frequently leading them into action sword in hand: between 4 August and 2 September 1870, sixteen generals were killed and forty-five wounded. But otherwise, they were often nowhere to be seen. The example was followed down the line. Lieutenant Patry complained that his regiment was never visited by senior officers: he did not even know the name of the corps commander, he had never seen the brigade or divisional commanders, and rarely saw even his colonel; as a result, officers and men understood nothing of events. Yet, though annoyed by their superiors' negligence, the subalterns themselves used to leave their men when on outpost-duty and spend the night playing cards at a nearby inn.[7] This system of remote commanders and ignorant, passively obedient subordinates meant that in case of disaster all the blame was rightly or wrongly laid on the commanding generals. The blind confidence they demanded was shattered, with demoralization and disobedience the result.

With the grip of the High Command loosened by defeat, the divisions within the army were exposed. Even before the war they were noticeable: the rank and file a mixture of reluctant conscripts, hardened mercenaries and ambitious volunteers aiming at a commission; and the officer corps including ex-rankers of modest origin, high flyers from the military schools looking towards the staff and a general's stars, and wealthy young men-about-town idling away a few years in a fashionable regiment. Even in peacetime there was friction between them, and rival cliques often took the form of political *clientèles*.[8] The majority of subaltern officers were veteran ex-rankers, and although they formed (in the opinion of the Prussians)[9] the backbone of the army, few had any prospect in peacetime of rising above captain. Men trained at the military academies held most of the senior positions: about two-thirds of captains and below in the Line and Cavalry came from the ranks, but only about a quarter of commandants and one-eighth of Generals of Division.[10] Loyalty to the regiment was strong: it was not uncommon for officers to serve twenty or thirty years with the same unit. In the ranks too there was a high proportion of veterans: at the beginning of 1870 more than one-third of the soldiers had served for more than seven years. These were the archetypal troopers of the old French army, in whose affections, as Marshal Bugeaud said, the regimental colours had replaced the village steeple. Many were a doubtful asset, however, indisciplined and physically past their best, 'often weakened by debauchery and drunkenness'.[11]

This old army, with its strengths and weaknesses, discontents and loyalties, was transformed after the outbreak of war in July 1870: 61,000 reservists, 112,000 men of the Second Portion (those not called up in peacetime), and 60,000 recruits of the Class of 1869 were called to the colours.[12] Lieutenant Patry's company of 70 men was brought up to 110 by reservists and recruits. Some of the former were veterans of the Crimea and Italy, but Patry was disappointed in his hope that they would provide moral support for the others, for they did their best to find safe jobs at base: 'the reservists are reserving themselves', quipped a *zouave* sergeant at Sedan.[13] The new arrivals lacked not only martial ardour but also that sense of discipline that the best regular units maintained to the end. This was the army that met an inglorious end at Sedan and Metz; all but two regiments were taken prisoner. It was an odd amalgam, particularly the officer corps; and the exigencies of the war had added further disparate elements, while at the same time increasing the strains acting on it.

Men of all ranks were aware of things that had gone wrong – contradictory orders, faulty supply, inadequate equipment, strategic blundering – and they produced their own diagnoses and criticisms. Indignation was heightened by the knowledge that the fighting soldiers had done their duty: 'the gallantry of the French has been as great as can be conceived', wrote a British observer, 'but they have always been outmanoeuvred'.[14] Heavy casualties increased the bitterness: at Reichshoffen, for example, the *cuirassiers* suffered dreadful losses, as did the 2nd *zouaves*, of whom 33 officers and 1,500 men fell.[15] The first objects of the army's anger were its own commanders. 'Nos généraux sont des c— !', judged one NCO,[16] and such feelings were not confined to the ranks. 'Never have military operations been more stupidly conducted', noted an officer of the Guard,[17] and a Line battalion commander told his officers that 'we are going to the devil with people who have no notion of what large-scale war is, and who are afraid, because they do not feel up to fighting the Prussians, and they know very well that they will all be beaten one after the other, because they are all ignorant and frightened'.[18] At Saverne, after the battle, drunken soldiers shouted insults at their generals resting in a café. No action was taken; the generals, as demoralized as their men, remained silent.[19] There were more serious reproaches than that of ineptitude: 'I heard for the first time the word treason, and it was not the ordinary soldiers who pronounced it.'[20] A Guards officer noted, after Bazaine failed to attack the outnumbered Prussians outside Metz on 31 August, 'It is no longer a suspicion, now it is a certainty either of utter incapacity or of criminal intent.'[21]

At Metz, where the Army of the Rhine, consisting of most of the regular units, was besieged, these suspicions increased further when the news of Bazaine's negotiations with the enemy became known. Patriotic agitation among the civilian inhabitants spread to the army. A movement to oppose Bazaine's policy attracted the support of a number of senior officers, including General Clinchant and his ADC Captain Cremer; Generals Deligny, Aymard, de Courcy, Péchot and Besson; Colonels d'Andlau, Lewal, Davoût and Boissonet. Among the organizers were Colonel Leperche, ADC to General Bourbaki, and Captain Rossel of the Engineers.[22] At first they hoped to overthrow

Bazaine, but later limited their ambitions to the organization of a last-minute breakout through the German lines, hence their nickname of *perceurs*. The plot, an open secret, provoked bitter controversy. The motives of the participants were mistrusted and many deplored the effect of their insubordination on the cohesion of the army. 'France is tearing herself apart at this very moment, under the gaze of the triumphant enemy', reflected General Du Barail; 'the army must not imitate France.' The elderly General Changarnier declared to General Clinchant, 'I would rather see the army perish than save itself by indiscipline!' For others, the choice was less plain, and so more painful. General Lapasset was dissuaded at the last moment by his superiors from joining the attempted breakout: 'God alone knows what I suffered.'[23] The *perceurs* provoked much interest among junior officers, though not all were impressed by their public meetings: one found them like the 'stormy sessions of our legislative assemblies', and Lieutenant Patry, at first favourable, was put off by the political opinions expressed; although 'quite ready to give my life for the honour of the flag . . . I admit that no political party seemed to me to deserve such a sacrifice'.[24] Finally, Clinchant, who was to lead the sortie, was headed off by Marshal Bazaine, and the troops involved were disarmed. Only a few arrived at the rendezvous, where a general tried in vain to calm the atmosphere. Colonel Leperche rode off in uniform through the German lines, and a large number of other officers managed to escape, often in disguise, including General Clinchant, Captain Cremer and Captain Rossel. This act of 'disobedience' was severely criticized by the disciplinarians, and created a deep division between those who had resigned themselves to being prisoners and those who escaped to serve in the armies of the National Defence.

One aspect of the controversy was political: many of the most notable *perceurs* and escapers were republicans, or were at least willing to accept and serve under the republican Government of National Defence; many of those who condemned their 'indiscipline' were opponents of the Republic and hence sceptical of its chances of winning the war. Clinchant, promoted to command the Army of the East, was well known after the war for his republican loyalties; Cremer, rapidly promoted to general, was suspected of sympathy with the Paris insurgents immediately after the events of 18 March; Rossel, promoted to colonel, served the Commune and became its War Delegate. The issue cannot simply be interpreted as one of patriotic republicans rebelling against the authority of defeatist conservatives, however: Leperche, for instance, was a fanatical Bonapartist. Nor did the *perceurs'* turbulent patriotism in general lead them into sympathy with the Commune, in spite of its warlike rhetoric: Clinchant commanded an army corps against it, with de Courcy as one of his brigadiers; Péchot and Besson were killed in action against it; and Leperche became one of its harshest enemies.

Anger and near-mutiny were thus caused by the failures of the High Command, but the generals were not the only objects of resentment. The imperial regime was likewise blamed. When Napoleon visited the army at Metz early in August, he was received in silence, and after the battle of Saint Privat 'There was a unanimous cry of malediction on the Emperor and Bazaine.'[25] MacMahon's troops had similar feelings, for the disastrous march to Sedan was blamed on the Emperor. Worse still than having started the war was having started it unprepared, and that this was the case soon became clear. The popularity of the regime evaporated. News of its fall left most men indifferent, even in the Imperial Guard. Wrote one officer to a friend, 'I voted for it in the last plebiscite, but that was because . . . I would never have supposed the Empire incompetent enough to undertake a war like this.'[26]

The Opposition and the Left in general were also blamed, even by those who served the National Defence, for their policies before the war and for some of their actions since its outbreak. Their hostility to the imperial government's military reforms was remembered: 'They were afraid of strengthening the Empire in strengthening France . . . the fall of a hated regime was worth a defeat.'[27] Lieutenant Patry recalled their election posters demanding the abolition of standing armies. Lieutenant Paul Déroulède had met the republican deputy Jules Ferry as the news of the first defeats reached Paris. 'Have you heard?' cried the exultant Ferry. 'The Emperor's armies have been beaten!' Déroulède was angered and revolted by 'this ambitious stoicism counting as nothing both the loss of the battle and our losses of men'.[28] Many soldiers in any case suspected that republican ideas were fundamentally damaging to the military spirit and therefore to the nation. This mistrust of the patriotism and good faith of the Left is important, for though many had abandoned the Empire, they still did not take the republicans at face value.

Politics aside, there was friction on a personal level between regulars and civilians, particularly the uniformed civilians of the Garde Mobile or the National Guard. The Mobiles of the Seine, for example, smartly uniformed, and with the girls they had brought from Paris, installed themselves comfortably at Châlons in August. 'We were enjoying ourselves very much', but it was unpleasant to meet there 'those ragged and demoralized soldiers who had escaped from our disasters. They hardly encouraged the patriotism of our Mobiles, and more than once we were obliged to silence them.' The regulars found this hard to stomach: 'Those gentlemen seemed glad to display their princesses and show off their luxury . . . Our uniforms were old and worn, they looked on us rather as ragamuffins, and then we were wretched losers, and therefore to be despised; no one in the streets or cafés dreamt of moving to make room for us, even in a distant corner.'[29] Naturally, many of the soldiers traded insult for insult. That the Imperial Army was frequently and unjustly blamed for the failures of the war by those who had been less exposed to its hardships led inevitably to a certain closing of ranks among the regulars. That some of the most vocal critics of the *capitulards*, as the defeated troops were called, were the leaders of the Paris Left and the 'red' National Guard made it all the less likely that the army would look with favour on a movement in which such people were prominent, or take seriously its patriotic claims.

Even with the best will in the world it was difficult for professionals to accept that amateurs could succeed where they had failed. General Lacretelle wrote to a friend that he no longer believed resistance possible. 'It is too late to make new armies . . . So I want peace as soon as possible . . . so that France can seize the first favourable opportunity.'[30] It followed therefore that those wishing to prolong a hopeless struggle were acting against the interests of France, probably for reasons of selfish ambition. For regular officers, another reason for wanting peace and a return to normality was that their own future as much as that of France hung in the balance, for those held prisoner in Germany were rapidly being overtaken in rank by the officers of the National Defence. Thus their future in the army was uncertain, and many must have feared the prospect of permanent unemployment and years on half pay. Rivalry between officers of the 'new' and 'old' armies became acute, and ill feeling was marked. The need to establish a claim to resume their places after the war provided an added incentive for the returning prisoners to distinguish themselves in the service of Versailles.

The officers and men of the new armies of the Government of National Defence interpreted events differently. There were among their commanders – Ducrot and d'Aurelle de Paladines for example – men whose scepticism about their chances of success and whose hostility to interference from republican politicians could hardly have been exceeded by their colleagues in Bazaine's Army of the Rhine. But the determination of the mass of officers and soldiers, many of them escapers from Sedan or Metz, to continue the fight, expressed a working acceptance of the Republic and a criticism of the old regular army by the very refusal to accept defeat as inevitable. Those who served in the provincial armies could claim to have defended the territory and honour of France when the Imperial Army had failed to do either, and to have persevered under the most unfavourable conditions at the risk of their lives, while the prisoners of war awaited the coming of peace in safety and sometimes even in comfort. There was therefore keen resentment among the officers and, it may be assumed, the more ambitious NCOs, when the prisoners of war claimed their old positions of primacy: General Faidherbe, the republican commander of the Army of the North, even suggested that the regular army should be replaced after the war by a militia in which National Defence officers would be given priority of employment.[31] This resentment was an important motive for the few who sympathized with the insurgents, and, no doubt, for the many who hesitated, if only momentarily, to act in what seemed to be an anti-republican *coup d'état* on 18 March.

The hasty organization of the provincial armies had demanded numerous promotions of officers to command them, not only in the Auxiliary Army (an assortment of Garde Mobile, mobilized National Guard and miscellaneous irregulars), which was understood to be temporary, but also in the regular army. Composite regiments – *régiments de marche* – had been formed, principally of new recruits, with a sprinkling of reservists, volunteers and veterans from the depots. They were officered by escapers of the regular army, men newly promoted from the ranks, experienced reservists, and cadets from the military schools. It was not clear whether such promotions – some spectacularly rapid – were temporary or permanent, for the regulations governing promotion had been suspended during the war as new armies were improvised, and many officers held their positions somewhat irregularly, on the personal authority of Léon Gambetta, the republican Minister of the Interior. Both obscure and prominent officers, irrespective of their previous political loyalties, therefore found their fortunes linked with his.[32] Their patriotic and republican ardour can only have been encouraged by the knowledge that their present status and future hopes depended on the continuation of the war and the firm establishment of the regime of 4 September.

But finally, after three months of hard and dispiriting winter campaigning, the army of the National Defence came to share with the old army the conviction that the war had been lost and that peace was desperately needed. Gambetta's acquiescence in the armistice was due to the inability of his armies, at least temporarily, to maintain the struggle. This decision was heartily endorsed by the rank and file, worn out by hopeless fighting in appalling weather. All the men in Patry's company – he had escaped from Metz and served with the Army of the North – voted for Thiers against Gambetta in the elections following the January armistice when Patry told them that Thiers stood for peace.[33] This change of view was one of the most important reasons why the insurrection which began on 18 March, ostensibly a patriotic movement of resistance to the Prussians and a treacherous government of *capitulards*, failed to attract the support of Gambettist officers, even in its early days when high hopes were still possible. 'For a moment it was possible to believe in the Commune', recalled Colonel Rossel. 'One wanted to believe it capable, honest, intrepid, to follow and obey it. That lasted one day.'[34] Clearly, there were few who still thought, like Rossel, if only 'for one day', of carrying on the war by means of a Parisian revolution. Rossel, however, had never held a combat command either at Metz or during the later part of the war when he commanded a training camp. He was out of touch with the bleak realities of the military collapse, unlike other Metz escapers such as his fellow *perceur* Cremer, to whom he wrote on 7 January: 'I do not know if you are still in the same mind as I am . . . I would like to avoid our running the risk of peace . . . I know very well that you will continue the war' – even if the armistice were signed.[35] By that time, after his experiences commanding an army corps in the east, nothing could have been further from Cremer's mind. In general, the Gambettist army had, so to speak, become Thierist, wanting peace, repair of the damage caused by the war and, for the amateur soldiers among them, demobilization. But many considered peace only as a tactical necessity, until France was strong enough to continue the war, which was not expected to be long delayed.

These regular 'provincial armies' provided most of the Versailles forces during the war against the Commune, and so they require closer examination. The rank and file were mostly very young men, without military experience, belonging to the Classes of 1870 and even 1871; that is to say, of twenty or twenty-one years of age and sometimes younger. They were drawn from depots all over France. These recruits had received little training, as facilities and instructors were lacking.[36] The practical experience of warfare which some had obtained towards the end of the campaign, as French resistance finally collapsed on all fronts, may have done more harm than good. Some regiments had been formed so late in the war that their men counted their military experience literally in weeks. Perhaps because they had avoided the débâcle of the winter campaign, these brand new regiments formed a large part of the force sent after the armistice to restore order in Paris.

The Army of Paris, which had defended the capital throughout the siege, contained elements of both the Imperial and the National Defence Armies. The only surviving infantry regiments of the old army, the 35th and 42nd *de ligne*,[37] had returned there after avoiding the trap of Sedan. They substantially retained their pre-war cadres, though the losses suffered in the ranks during the war had been made up with Parisian recruits. New regular *régiments de ligne* had been formed, comparable with the *régiments de marche* of the provincial armies, but they had the advantage of being altered and reorganized less frequently than the latter due, no doubt, to the circumstances of the siege. The remainder of the Army of Paris consisted of Mobiles and irregular units of various kinds, and of the National Guard of the Seine, 320,000 strong, composed of all other able-bodied men. The garrison had spent the bitter winter of the siege forlornly guarding the forts, trenches and ramparts of the city. Twice an attempt had been made to break through the German lines and join hands with the provincial armies trying to come to their aid. A four-day battle, from 30 November to 3 December, to the south-east of the city near Champigny, ground to a halt in frozen misery. On 19 January, a last effort to break out to the west was stopped by the deep Prussian defences on the Buzenval heights.[38] A week later, an armistice was signed. Its terms demanded the disarmament of the whole garrison, except for the National Guard and one regular division, for police duties, under General Faron of the Marines. This had nearly 12,000 men, in three brigades: General de la Mariouse's brigade (35th and 42nd *de ligne*); General Derroja's (109th and 110th *de ligne*); and General Daudel's (113th and 114th *de ligne*). These were among the most seasoned and solidly commanded troops in the garrison.

It has been asserted that by the end of the war the regular troops of the Army of Paris were on bad terms with the *outranciers* of the National Guard, who clamoured to continue the fight. The army had suffered heavier casualties and harsher conditions; their lower pay caused resentment; and the prolongation of the siege was blamed on the 'reds'. Whereas part of the National Guard, which had never been fully used, was ready to continue the resistance, the regular army was no longer capable of fighting. This was the opinion of all senior officers, and the civil authorities had no alternative but to bow to it and abandon their hope of one more sortie.[39] It is probable, therefore, that some hostility existed between troops and National Guards, though it may have been tempered by a shared hatred of the government and the generals for their failures during the war. Most observers have thought that such hostility as existed was diminished by the contacts formed between soldiers and Parisians during the weeks following the armistice when the troops reentered the city. Certainly there was little sign of enmity between the *lignards* and the crowds that opposed them on 18 March.

The events of that day, and of the weeks that followed, must be seen in the light of the army's mixed reactions to the war. Bonapartists, such as General Du Barail, while admitting the failures of the Empire and the High Command, reserved real criticism for the men of 4 September who had weakened France before the war, and who led a revolution 'which destroyed the Empire and aggravated our national disasters to an incalculable degree'.[40] The conservative General Montaudon agreed in seeing causes of defeat deeper than those of individual failings and errors: they lay 'in the very heart of the nation: in the hatred of parties . . .; in the false and tempting doctrines of independence, of well-being, of absolute liberty, of indiscipline, spread among all social classes, and lastly in the rather unwise choice of a number of leaders'.[41] The republican General Faidherbe, on the other hand, blamed the Empire – 'that immoral, corrupting regime' – and called upon republicans to make up for 'the failures and treasons of the imperial armies' and to 'wash the stains from our colours'.[42] These were the predictable reactions of men with well defined political beliefs. There were, however, many who considered themselves apolitical, and their reactions were less predictable. Patry, for example, who claimed to take no interest in politics and to have little enthusiasm for the Emperor, was nevertheless suspicious of the Republic: 'I foresaw no good for the interests of the army.'[43] Nevertheless he joined the Metz escapers and fought with Faidherbe. Some changed their allegiance totally. General de Gondrecourt, a former courtier and Guards officer, made a speech to his men soon after 4 September, reminding them that 'the grandeur of Rome dates not from the twelve Caesars, who brought about its decay, but rather from the period of the consuls and tribunes, the time when talent was not ignored'.[44] There was no single 'army view' of events, nor were later actions determined by previous party loyalties. It has been too often repeated that a Bonapartist army was brought back to crush the Commune and avenge 4 September: after Sedan the army was no longer Bonapartist.

On 18 March, in an obscure political situation, facing imminent civil war, when the cohesion of the army had been seriously weakened, it is understandable that officers and men hesitated to act. They, like many of their civilian compatriots, had often discussed the possibility of civil war, 'and every time this idea came to us, our greatest wish was not to be mixed up in it'.[45] Yet in May they crushed the Commune. Among the causes of this transformation – though it will be argued that it was a partial one – was another widely shared reaction to defeat: a belief in the need for discipline and national unity. Just as the failures of the siege only reinforced the Paris 'reds'' belief in the invincibility of the spontaneous force of the people in arms, so military men were convinced by their defeat that more rather than less of the traditional military virtues were needed. This conviction seemed to be confirmed by the Germans' success, ascribed to their superiority in these very virtues which the French army, 'long undermined by manifest indiscipline', seemed to lack. 'What a painful contrast! All my life I shall see that spectacle.'[46] There was a will to change shown by the remarkable shift in the attitude of the High Command after the war. No longer contemptuous of study and preparation, it produced numerous plans and reforms, such as those of Faidherbe or Ladmirault on recruitment and organization, and the fundamental changes made by Du Barail when Minister.[47] General de Galliffet, previously a mere swashbuckling man-about-town, totally ignorant of military science, devoted himself to asceticism, physical fitness and study, becoming in a few years one of the most capable corps commanders in the army.[48]

Army reform alone, however, was not regarded as sufficient. Though soldiers were ready, in private at least, to accept much of the blame for this defeat, they would not accept all of it. For it was not only that the French army had been beaten by the German army, but that French society had been beaten by German society. French military strength was limited to 'what was politically possible for a people which grudged every penny spent on the army, distrusted its own rulers and was deeply divided in itself'.[49] For an officer of Mobiles, 'the German soldier . . . represented for us the triumph of order over disorder, of organization over revolution'.[50] If France were to recover her position, changes and sacrifices would be necessary. 'First of all we must want it', wrote General Lacretelle to a friend:

we must manage to unite in a common idea, silence our stupid prejudices, our so-called political convictions which are never anything but personal calculation; we must reform our civil and military laws; we must decide to reestablish discipline in society first, to obtain it in the army afterwards; we need the suppression of universal suffrage, compulsory service, a firm hand at the Ministry of War and a very strong head to bear the crown. I do not believe in the Republic.[51]

France, in other words, would be obliged to imitate Prussia not only in her military but also in her social and political organization.

These beliefs were reinforced by a real depth of feeling which was obscured by the equanimity with which many officers and soldiers accepted defeat. There were flagrant cases of fraternization with the Prussians, and the readiness with which most captive officers gave their parole attracted comment. In most wars fighting soldiers tend to regard their opponents with far less bitterness than do civilians; and after the first reverses many soldiers regarded defeat as inevitable and thus to be faced philosophically and with dignity, comforted by the feeling of duty done. But deep feeling did exist. Déroulède and a brother officer read of the peace terms in a newspaper: 'After a fourth reading [he] snatched the paper roughly from my hands . . . tore it up, flung it to the ground without a word, and then, as if he were ashamed to be in the street, he said sharply, "Let's go in".'[52] Even Lacretelle, known for his ebullient good humour, admitted that his preoccupation with the defeat 'torments me night and day and leaves me not a moment of rest'.[53] Déroulède, abandoning the frivolous life of a Parisian man of letters, decided to remain in the army to prepare for revenge: 'I took the képi as one takes the veil',[54] a resolution that was to involve the republican patriot in civil war against other republican patriots in Paris. Rossel felt differently, though perhaps as strongly, writing to his family that he intended to leave the army, which had disgraced itself, and was considering emigration to the United States. The insurrection gave him fresh hope: he resigned his commission and left for Paris.[55]

Few of his former comrades shared his reaction. Although the armistice and the political crisis that followed the election of the National Assembly caused much heart-searching, hesitancy and indiscipline, in the long run nearly all officers remained loyal to the army: as an institution to which careers had been dedicated and on which future hopes rested; as a group of comrades with a shared experience of the war; as an expression of certain principles such as discipline, patriotism and national unity; and as the one enduring element of a nation apparently in decline. As Du Barail had said, 'the army must not imitate France'.

3

vuvuvuvuvuvuvuvuvuvuvuvuvuvuvuvuvuvuvuvuvuvuvuvuvuvuvuvuvuvuvuvuvuvuvuvuvu

Insurrection

Immediately after the armistice of 28 January, 'Paris was orderly and decent, and with a certain solemn, morose self-restraint mastering the tendency to demonstrate'.[1] Such calm could not be taken for granted. Three months earlier, on 31 October, there had been serious disorder when 'red' National Guards had invaded the Hôtel de Ville and temporarily held the government prisoner. Only six days before the armistice, on 22 January, small forces of National Guards had tried to repeat the performance, and were repulsed with some bloodshed by Breton Gardes Mobiles. The regular army, though ready to intervene, had not been involved. Moreover, the armistice, which disarmed all but one division of the army, 12,000 men under General Faron, left the National Guard, still over 200,000 men, with its arms.[2] The authority of the military and civil government was thus made, to say the least, precarious, depending on the forbearance of the 'red' battalions and the loyalty of the 'good' battalions – broadly speaking, those from working-class and middle-class districts respectively.

The shock of the armistice soon wore off, and the preoccupation of the starving population with food and fuel subsided. The public mood of guilty relief was replaced by one of righteous indignation, especially when it was realized that the German army was to make a triumphal entry into Paris on 1 March – a concession made by the government in return for retention of the fortress of Belfort. This was seen as an insult to the honour of the capital, as well as a threat to its security, and was the occasion of serious disorders and a rapid decline in the authority of the government. Minor agitation began almost at once: suspected Prussians were mobbed, army officers insulted and policemen attacked. Numerous public meetings were called, of which the most important were those concerning the National Guard, with the intention of creating an extra-legal organization to coordinate the action of its 280 battalions. After preliminary meetings on 15 and 16 February, a general assembly of delegates held on 24 February adopted statutes for a Federation, and elected a provisional executive commission, replaced on 3 March by a Central Committee. The Federation was to become the government's main rival in the city.[3]

Also on 24 February, which was the anniversary of the 1848 revolution, a huge demonstration took place at the July Column in the Place de la Bastille. This was the first in a series, made both by National Guard battalions and soldiers of the regular army. The violence of feeling displayed against the Prussians was enough to daunt those responsible for preventing a bloodbath; but the demonstrators showed that the French authorities were equally the object of their hostility, as was illustrated by the murder on 26 February of a policeman in plain clothes, Sous-Brigadier Vincenzini. He was caught spying on the demonstration at the Place de la Bastille, 'tried' and condemned by a show of hands, and then tied to a plank and thrown into the Seine. He was able to remain afloat until pelted with stones and pushed under the surface with boathooks. A large crowd was present, but those mainly responsible were soldiers: a gunner, Roche, of the 9th regiment, and several *chasseurs à pied*, said to be from the 17th and 23rd battalions. A local Commissaire of Police, Macé, tried to intervene, but was himself forced to seek refuge in the nearby Célestins barracks. The soldiers there, of the Military Train, refused to defend him, and he escaped the crowd by climbing over a wall. That evening, four regular battalions were sent to clear and occupy the Place de la Bastille, but they fraternized with the crowd and had to be withdrawn.[4] That same afternoon, soldiers guarding an artillery park at the Place Wagram had allowed National Guards to seize a large number of cannon, and to remove them from the zone the Prussians were to occupy, principally to the heights of Montmartre and Belleville[5] – a fateful act which was to provide the immediate cause of conflict. With less evident reason, 300 rifles had been taken by National Guards from the Gare de l'Est – outside the Prussian zone. That night, as the original armistice expired, the *rappel* (summons for the National Guard of a district to assemble) was beaten illegally at Belleville, the Faubourg du Temple and the Latin Quarter, and there was a march to the Champs Elysées to resist a rumoured Prussian entry. Simultaneously, the Sainte Pélagie prison was attacked, and 'red' leaders rescued. The troops on guard, of the 109th *de ligne*, made no resistance, and the officer in command was later placed under arrest for having 'let the prisoners escape'.[6] General Vinoy's inability to maintain order, due not only to the small number but also to the unreliability of his troops, could hardly have been more thoroughly demonstrated by a single day's events.

The following week the disturbances continued. Arms and ammunition were seized: three million cartridges from the Pantheon and more from rampart magazines on 27 February; arms from the Gare de l'Est and ammunition from the Rue de Flandre on the 28th; cannon from the ramparts of the 12th *arrondissement*, and 2,000 rifles from the Saint Antoine hospital on 2 March, the second day of the Prussian occupation. On the day the Prussians left, 3 March, powder was taken from a rampart bastion in the 13th *arrondissement*, and arms and ammunition from the police post at Les Gobelins, the occupants being forced to retire. The next day, on the other side of the city, twenty-nine howitzers and ammunition were taken at La Villette, and cannon at La Chapelle.[7]

The demonstrations at the Bastille were to continue until the departure of the Prussians, with the participation of units of the Mobiles of the Seine and a number of sailors. On 27 February the crowd marched to La Pépinière barracks, near the Gare Saint Lazare, to induce other sailors quartered there to join them. According to *Le Gaulois* (4 March), the commanding officer, wishing to avoid violence – his men were unarmed – gave permission for those off duty to leave the barracks with the crowd. Only about sixty did so, and most soon returned.

Not all the attention paid to the armed forces was so fraternal. The left-wing press, while praising the National Guard, 'was free with insults to the army . . . [which] was very sensitive to them'. Officers could not venture into the streets without the risk of insult. The attacks were not only verbal: 'They tore off our medals and . . . arrested us as Prussian officers when we went out in plain clothes.'[8] Belleville was particularly bad, and on 28 February had to be evacuated by the four regiments billeted there, both to protect the officers and to end fraternization between troops and civilians. On 4 March the detachment of the Garde Républicaine, the hated picked force of gendarmes responsible for internal security in Paris, was withdrawn from the Rue Mouffetard barracks, isolated amid a traditionally turbulent population.[9]

The climax of this tense week was the assembly of several thousand National Guards in the Champs Elysées during the night preceding the Prussian occupation, 28 February, apparently with the intention of resisting their entry. Prudence prevailed and the idea of armed resistance was abandoned on the advice of the provisional Commission of the National Guard Federation. Only a small crowd of sightseers and rowdies greeted the enemy next morning. Vinoy, supplementing his meagre forces with National Guards, had cordoned off the area, and most observers felt that Paris had shown a dignified restraint. Although incidents continued after the Prussians withdrew on 3 March, the worst seemed to have passed. Such was the opinion of those civilian members of the government present in Paris.[10]

Their guarded optimism was not shared by their military colleagues, who found them deplorably unconcerned. General d'Aurelle, Commander of the National Guard, stated that no serious discussion took place at the daily ministerial meetings, to his and Vinoy's impatience. The two generals, directly responsible for public order, but lacking the forces to maintain it, were pessimistic and cautious. On 3 March, Jules Favre, Foreign Minister and the senior Minister in Paris, wanted to oppose by force the National Guards' seizure of the Gobelins police post, but Vinoy refused to engage his troops. D'Aurelle, who arrived on 4 March, supported him, for both were conscious of shortcomings of their forces and so opposed military action against the dissident National Guard, whether in seizing its artillery or arresting its leaders. 'I was never in favour of taking the cannon', stated Vinoy. 'First of all, I had not the means.'[11] He received reinforcements, but the result was unsatisfactory, for he found them worn out and insubordinate, and the first review nearly turned into a mutiny.[12] In theory, large numbers of troops were available for service in Paris, to reinforce General Faron's division and the lukewarm 'good' National Guard, incapable even of guarding military installations. Units could be sent from Chanzy's Army of the Loire, and from Faidherbe's Army of the North. But there were practical problems. The railways were only beginning to resume normal operations. The Prussians were occupying a belt twenty-five miles wide round Paris, and their permission had to be obtained for the movement of troops through it. This was not always given readily.[13] In Paris the authorities were faced with huge administrative problems. At the armistice, the whole garrison had been brought inside the walls to be disarmed, and so before new troops could be brought in, the problem of feeding, lodging and finally disposing of these 7,504 officers and 243,165 men had to be solved. They bivouacked in the streets and parks, occupied wooden huts in the public squares and were billeted on the population. Public buildings had been turned into hospitals, for there were 40,000 sick and wounded. This vast crowd of disarmed soldiers, sullen after its defeat, was itself a threat to public order. It had formed dangerous contacts with the civil population – to the military mind, the root of all evil. As the railways were unable to evacuate them quickly enough, Vinoy organized three large columns which left on foot, for Orleans, Chartres and Evreux; many men, deliberately or not, missed the departure.[14]

By the second week in March the Army of Paris was in total chaos. Reinforcements from the provinces had begun to arrive, but often nothing was prepared for them. Five hundred men destined for the 120th *de ligne* found that there was no bedding, and that their barracks were still occupied by Mobiles. The 67th *de marche* was camping on wet ground in the Luxembourg Gardens, which encouraged officers and men to sleep elsewhere. The food supply seems to have been a problem: on 10 March rations were reduced. In the circumstances, there were many men sick: by 18 March the 110th *de ligne* had 492 men on the sick list, due mainly to exhaustion and having to camp without proper equipment, even bedding.[15] The effects on morale can easily be imagined, especially as the weather had turned cold. A report written at this time on army pay and rations referred to 'the malaise reigning in the ranks of the army, which revolutionary newspapers seek to exploit'.[16] *Le Soir* (12 March) reported 'shocking incidents' committed by drunken soldiers, and gave regimental numbers which were those of newly arrived troops, not only of the old garrison. The failings of the administration contrasted with the solicitude of the population: 'the women of Paris brought them soup and blankets in the huts where they were freezing'.[17]

There was a greater problem even than these. As the provincial armies were in such a poor state, it was necessary to pick out strong and well disciplined regiments for service in Paris. The Minister of War, General Le Flô, had undertaken this task. He intended to form three new divisions of infantry for Paris, totalling over 20,000 men. A cavalry division was to follow later. They were supposed to be the elite of the provincial armies. Le Flô was confident, telling Vinoy to maintain the organization of the divisions 'without changing anything', for he had grouped them 'after much thought and after gathering much information'.[18] This was an astonishing blunder, for all the wartime formations contained a high proportion of reservists and volunteers due for demobilization. When the regiments arrived finally in Paris they, like the existing garrison, had immediately to start sending these men home. On 15 March the 120th *de ligne* still had 647 men *libérables* out of its total of 2,200; the 119th had 803 out of 2,935. Some companies lost half their strength, a company of the 119th, for example, losing 70 men out of 153. When new drafts arrived to fill the gaps, they too included *libérables*. The effect was to destroy whatever cohesion had survived the end of the war. Those who were released were the older, more experienced men, who had provided many of the NCOs. The 119th had lost twenty-three sergeants and forty-two corporals by 15 March. Captain Patry found that a handful of wartime volunteers had formed the backbone of his company, of the 67th *de marche*, purely by force of example. They left, and were replaced by a draft of the 106th *de ligne* of the Army of Paris, whose discipline was deplorable.[19] The regiments were not reduced numerically: the damage was caused by lumping together contingents from various units, so that officers and NCOs did not know each other or their men.

The shortcomings of the officers aggravated the problem. After the elimination of the regular army at Sedan and Metz, the Government of National Defence had had to accept what was available. General Susbielle, for example, who was to command the operation at Montmartre on 18 March, was an elderly brigadier with an honourable but undistinguished record, promoted to command a division of the Army of Paris only in November 1870.[20] At regimental level, the shortage of officers had been made up by rapid promotion. In the 37th *de marche* only one officer held the same rank as before the war; two of the three battalion commanders were appointed in late January 1871, and all the second-lieutenants except one had been commissioned since the beginning of the year. There was not only the question of inexperience: the officer corps had been replaced wholesale. Fifty-one officers of the 74th regiment, for example, fought in the civil war. Of these, only three had passed through the military schools; ten others, promoted from the ranks, held pre-war commissions; of the remaining thirty-seven, eighteen were reservists promoted from the ranks during the war, ten had been serving in the ranks before the war, and ten had no pre-war military experience. In short, only a small proportion were career officers, and the largest category, the reservists, were probably for the most part eager to leave the army as soon as possible.[21]

These temporary officers had political sympathies and social contacts more diverse than those of the career officers, which, from the point of view of the government, made them far less trustworthy. Their professional abilities were also questionable. In some cases the hastily formed *régiments de marche* were officered by ageing non-combatants pressed into service – 'former NCOs, storemen or secretaries'[22] – supplemented by officer cadets. It would be unwise to accept entirely the dismissive judgment of jealous career officers on these their rivals for place, but it seems, none the less, likely that there were many who lacked the capacity or motivation to end the indiscipline and apathy that was crippling the Paris garrison. Such was Vinoy's impression, for on 16 March he sent a circular to all officers, complaining of general indiscipline, disorder and slovenliness, acts 'often committed in the presence of officers who, by their blameworthy indifference, leave them unpunished'. This was not merely a martinet's obsession with smartness but a complaint about the widespread spirit of *laisser-aller*: in the same circular he censures an officer who had permitted the crowd to invade a building he was guarding 'without taking any measures, and calmly watching the spectacle'. This was not an isolated example of slackness, for during the early evening of 17 March, when an officer was sent to warn the guard commander at the Napoleon barracks, behind the Hôtel de Ville, to be ready to march when orders came, he found no officers on duty and no guard commander.[23] As they were to show a few hours later, these were not the officers for a *coup de main*.

With the regular forces weak and unreliable, the loyalty of the National Guard was vital to any attempt to impose order. General d'Aurelle de Paladines's appointment as its Commander-in-Chief had been decided by Thiers himself, who intended it, in vain, as a conciliatory gesture. He believed that d'Aurelle would be popular because of his success at Coulmiers against the Prussians. In Paris, however, he was known as the man sacked by Gambetta, and in any case a large section of the National Guard wanted to elect its own commander. D'Aurelle, who had a notable capacity for leadership, began with an effort to win over his subordinates, calling daily meetings with groups of senior National Guard officers, mayors and sector commanders. The safety of the Republic was the principal topic. He pledged his own loyalty, being quoted as saying, 'The Republic is the only honest government that can get us out of the dead end we are in, and I am absolutely devoted to it.' He also gave assurances as to the future of the National Guard: it was not to be disarmed before a reorganization of the armed forces as a whole had been carried out. D'Aurelle and Roger, his chief of staff, were dubious about the success of these discussions, d'Aurelle concluding that most of the National Guard were 'favourable to insurrection', and Roger interpreting their demands, especially that for an elected Commander-in-Chief, as deliberate provocation: 'Those people obviously wanted a fight.' He wrote unofficially to Thiers on d'Aurelle's behalf, bypassing Ernest Picard, Minister of the Interior and their direct superior, to warn him of the unreliability of the force. The civilians in the government were still unconvinced, not realizing that the National Guard would not support them. 'They believed to the last moment that it would awaken when it realized the enormity of the peril', wrote Jules Simon, Minister of Public Instruction. This was not a totally absurd belief, for the majority of the National Guard had shown during the siege that it was not revolutionary, and there were signs that d'Aurelle's conciliatory efforts were having some effect. Dubail, mayor of the 10th *arrondissement*, who was present at one of the meetings, said that he even seemed to rally the sympathies of the Belleville battalions. According to Picard, d'Aurelle's own first impression was favourable, but after a few days he had lost faith in his vacillating battalion commanders: 'he found them cold'.[24]

The generals, then, had ample reason to insist on caution, and Thiers, from Bordeaux, supported them. On 4 March he wrote to approve Vinoy's refusal to attack the Gobelins, and expressed the belief that the National Guard would put an end to the disorders – as if not realizing that a large part of the National Guard was responsible for them. He warned, however, that reinforcements of troops could not arrive quickly. On the 6th he again urged temporization, hoping that the eventual arrival of reinforcements would overawe the dissidents 'who seem to be becoming tired and divided. Each day that passes is for you and against them. Let us not give battle.' He had expressed the same idea the previous day in a dispatch to Generals Suzanne and Vinoy: while the 'rowdies' were getting tired and falling out among themselves, the reinforcements would arrive, and then, with 40,000 men, 'we shall dominate the disorder almost without meeting opposition'. Vinoy and d'Aurelle were of the same opinion, thinking that 'the ringleaders, very well aware of the measures taken by us, will disarm of their own accord'.[25]

This confidence that the troubles would die down was widely shared by public opinion. The tense watchfulness existing between the military authorities and the 'reds', still occasionally seizing arms and ammunition, and guarding their cannon and their leaders in areas of the city where the police did not venture, seems not to have disturbed the public greatly, accustomed as they had been to such a state of affairs for several months. During the second week in March, however, there occurred a series of events which caused widespread anger against the National Assembly and the government. On 10 March, at its last session at Bordeaux, the Assembly voted to move not to Paris, which the Right would not consider, but to Versailles. The government had hoped that this compromise would mollify opinion in the capital, but it was taken, on the contrary, as a sign of calculated hostility towards the people of Paris and of an intention to tamper with the Republic at a safe distance from its most powerful defenders. The same day, the Assembly also voted a law to normalize the payment of bills of exchange, which had been suspended during the war. This threatened thousands of businessmen with bankruptcy, and again was felt to be a gratuitously hostile act against Paris, whose economy had been brought to a standstill by the siege. All observers felt that this measure turned thousands of men of order against the government, and explained the inactivity of the 'good' National Guard, on whom the government depended for support, at the beginning of the insurrection. It seems likely that these measures created other fears for the future: that the Assembly would be equally rigorous with regard to National Guard pay and the payment of arrears of rent, which affected far more people than the law on bills of exchange. Indeed, it may be that many people thought that all debts and rents had already been made payable. The day that this news reached Paris, 11 March, court-martial sentences on some of the rioters of 31 October were also published. Their comparative leniency was overshadowed by the (purely nominal) death sentences *in absentia* pronounced on the popular revolutionary leaders Blanqui and Flourens. To crown it all, the authorities in Paris announced that same day the suppression of six Left-wing newspapers, a measure that even the conservative press found excessive.

Nevertheless, negotiations for the return of the artillery seized by the National Guard at the time of the Prussian entry were only momentarily interrupted by the public outcry. These 300 or 400 cannon, most of which were parked at Montmartre, Belleville and the Place des Vosges, in the centre of the city, had taken on an importance for both sides as the symbol of the independent military power of the dissident National Guard. Even after 11 March it still seemed that negotiation was likely to produce a solution, and so Thiers's arrival from Bordeaux on 15 March caused no immediate change of policy, even though it lent greater significance to the daily government meetings. There was no lack of intermediaries in these negotiations. Clemenceau and

Vautrain, mayors of the 18th and 4th *arrondissements*, were urging their local National Guard commanders to hand over the guns, as were several other mayors.[26] Langlois and Schoelcher, who had a foot in each camp as Deputies for Paris and National Guard officers, as well as moderate or timid elements within the National Guard itself, were working both openly and secretly to reach a compromise.

Soon after the cannon had been taken, suggestions had been made for 'neutralizing' them: that they should be placed in parks guarded jointly by the army and National Guard, or by National Guard battalions in rotation under the direction of the official headquarters; or that the guns should be distributed among all the battalions that owned them, thus removing them from the control of the more turbulent battalions of Montmartre, Belleville and the Faubourg Saint Antoine, where most of the guns were parked. When nothing came of this, the government concentrated on negotiating a straightforward repossession of the guns, encouraged by the signs of apathy in the ranks of the National Guard. It was known that its commanders at Montmartre were having difficulties in finding enough men to guard the gun parks, and sightseers wandered round freely. On 11 March the 61st battalion from Montmartre, one of the most militant, offered publicly in the name of the National Guard of the *arrondissement* to return the guns to 'their true possessors, at their request'. Clemenceau sent copies of this proclamation to Picard, d'Aurelle and Ferry, mayor of Paris; d'Aurelle agreed to provide horses to remove the guns. The following day, 12 March, Vinoy sent two officers in civilian clothes to spy out the land, and next day the horses were sent as arranged. The situation, however, had changed. An angry crowd prevented movement of the guns. A staff officer present thought that the reason for the crowd's action was anger at the banning of the radical newspapers and the Assembly's law on bills; the Central Committee of the National Guard was in no way involved. The National Guards on duty claimed to be in good faith, but were powerless. The horse teams, without escort, were forced to withdraw. A second attempt – for it was said that there had been a misunderstanding – met with the same result. Similar but more secret negotiations were being carried out in the 4th *arrondissement* for the return of the guns parked in the Place des Vosges. Local National Guards, tradesmen who wanted an end to disorder, were said to have offered to hand them over. On 15 March emissaries were sent to the officer commanding the National Guard post at the Place des Vosges, who agreed to cooperate if given an order in writing.

The next day a small expedition was sent, this time with an escort for the gun-teams, but with no more success than at Montmartre: the local National Guards 'made the devil of a row' to stop it; 'all the population joined in; we were literally surrounded, overwhelmed'. The following day agitation continued in the district, with barricades being built, and the Central Committee ordered the guns, for greater safety, to the Rue Basfroi, its headquarters in the Faubourg Saint Antoine, and the *mairie* of the 20th *arrondissement* in the Place Puebla.[27]

After these two failures, there can have been few in government circles who remained hopeful of a negotiated settlement. The alternatives had been discussed inconclusively during the preceding weeks. D'Aurelle and Vinoy were only in favour of action that did not involve the army. Vinoy had argued that the pay of the National Guard should be stopped, assuming that the dissidents would then melt away. The two generals had also been pressing for the arrest by the police of the supposed ringleaders of the agitation. National Guard headquarters collected information on them, and prepared a list of twenty-nine men to be arrested. D'Aurelle gave it to the acting Prefect of Police, Choppin, on 11 March. The latter, however, was no more willing to take action than were the generals, and for the same reason, telling Vinoy: 'I cannot, I have not the means; have your troops arrest them.' To that Vinoy replied ' "No!" very definitely'.[28]

There were other objections both to making arrests and to stopping pay. In many cases the police knew nothing of those concerned, except their names taken from proclamations they had signed, and they were thought to change lodgings regularly. To try to make arrests secretly, by night, would be dangerous for the policemen involved; to do so openly, by day, and by mounting a large-scale military operation, would be a step that even the moderate press would denounce as provocative, and which risked raising a revolt. To stop National Guard pay would carry the same risk, as whole areas of the city depended on it, and would also harm the 'good' National Guard, on whose support the authorities were forced to rely. Finally, it would lay the government open to accusation, even in the moderate press (as had the earlier banning of the six newspapers), of plotting reaction.

No decision was taken, therefore, and no plan for military action was drawn up. The only activity on the part of the army was the gathering of basic intelligence by a few staff officers. A Colonel Varnet was obtaining information on the location of the disputed cannon and the defences guarding them, and making maps of the sites. Some

National Guard staff officers were made unofficially responsible for gauging public opinion and 'taking the pulse' of the dissidents. During the nights of 15 and 17 March they inspected the gun parks at the Place des Vosges and Montmartre, where possible chatting with the sentries. They found the dissident National Guard less than formidable; the sentries were lax and it was easier than before to enter the gun parks, where children played; the men seemed discouraged, and were scolded by their wives for spending their nights uselessly on guard. Such discouragement can only have been aggravated by the weather, as demoralizing for the National Guard as for the government's own troops. There was rain and then snow; and Montmartre is extremely exposed. The conclusion of the scouts was that 'a regiment of determined men could, in each of these districts, occupy the position and hold it against all attack'.[29]

This important intelligence was relayed to the government when it met at the Quai d'Orsay on 17 March, and it made an impression. 'We were assured that we should not meet serious resistance', wrote Favre, for the guns were 'only guarded by a few sentries . . .; a little vigour would be enough, we were told, to put an end to this intolerable play-acting.'[30] The situation had changed since the 15th, when everyone had been in favour of waiting. The attempts to negotiate the return of the cannon had failed resoundingly. The Assembly was due to meet in Versailles on the 20th, and it was taken for granted that unless it could be satisfied that the government was in control of Paris, it would itself take steps which, if its previous efforts were any guide, would stir up feeling again among the increasingly apathetic population.

Two incidents on 15 and 16 March may have helped the government make up its mind. At La Villette, two Prussian railway officials were being held hostage by the 147th battalion of the National Guard for the safety of one of their officers arrested by the Germans. General von Fabrice demanded their release, holding the French government responsible for their safety. The newly appointed acting Prefect of Police, General Valentin, planned to send two battalions, including one of the Garde Républicaine, to free the hostages by force if necessary. When their captors were informed of this by the local Commissaire of Police, they gave in and released them – an easy victory for that 'vigour' which Favre advocated and an apparent confirmation of the dissident National Guard's weakness. The same day a 'good' National Guard battalion, the 21st, had resisted a battalion of the Central Committee sent to disarm it and seize ammunition. Fighting was narrowly averted, and

1 The Fédérés and their cannon at Montmartre.

the 'red' 134th battalion retired – an encouragement to those who believed that the Central Committee of the National Guard Federation was bluffing, and that even if it did fight, the first shots would bring the 'good' National Guard in on the government side when they realized the danger of revolution, as had happened in October and January.[31]

The government met on 17 March, a few hours after the Central Committee had ordered the removal of the cannon from the Place des Vosges to the Place Puebla and Rue Basfroi, deep in the 'reds'' eastern stronghold. The gathering was larger than usual: Thiers, of course, was now present; the Minister of War, General Le Flô, arrived from Bordeaux during the meeting; the Prefect of Police, General Valentin, and his predecessor, Choppin, had been summoned; and Vinoy, d'Aurelle and Ferry were present as usual. Thiers asked for opinions of what should be done. Ferry, as ever, was confident and aggressive, and urged that the cannon should be taken by force, arguing that it would not be difficult to take Montmartre and the Buttes Chaumont by surprise during the night or early morning. Favre and Picard probably held similar opinions. Previous attempts to take back the guns had failed only because of the intervention of the crowd: by acting during the night this would be avoided. The troops would have time to establish themselves and measures could be taken to prevent crowds from forming and the 'red' National Guard from assembling. The negotiations that had been undertaken, though unsuccessful, wrote Simon, 'made us believe that we should not meet too stiff an opposition'. Vinoy and d'Aurelle were dubious: they knew the weak and unreliable state of the army and the 'good' National Guard, and Vinoy wanted to wait for more reinforcements. This time, however, Thiers was in favour of action. According to Simon, he too counted on weak resistance and the support of 'our' National Guard. If this failed, and if the Central Committee did not react violently, the government would continue as before, 'c'est à dire à peu près', and await events. Only if everything went wrong would they evacuate Paris – 'the plan that worked for Windischgraetz' in crushing revolt in 1848. It may be, as Thiers later claimed, that he did speak of this as a possibility, but the context here, and the other evidence, suggests that it was regarded as a remote one. Vinoy gave in: 'They insisted', he recalled, 'they said, it is absolutely necessary that these cannon should be removed before the Assembly arrives.' 'We have very few men', Thiers quotes him as answering. 'It is not impossible to take the positions. Give your orders, I am a soldier and will obey.'[32]

The military plan was decided by Thiers, Vinoy and d'Aurelle; the Minister of War, Le Flô, arrived late and took little part in the discussion, except to criticize the arrangement to leave the troops' packs behind. No one seems to have taken much notice.[33] D'Aurelle was to try to organize support from the 'good' National Guard, though without telling them what was planned.[34] Vinoy called a conference of his divisional and brigade commanders at his headquarters at the Louvre, to give them their orders. The cannon, parked in a dozen places in different parts of the city, could not all be taken at once, and so the attack was directed at the principal gun parks.

The plan aimed at occupying the city militarily, not merely removing the cannon as quickly as possible. There were several hundred of these, requiring about 2,000 horses to move them. Although General Susbielle was later to blame the lateness of the horses for the failure of the operation, it is clear that much time would have been needed – one observer suggested two days.[35] Besides, the operation had another object: Vinoy had long been urging the arrest of the 'red' leaders, and this deployment of force would provide an opportunity. No doubt it was thought that resistance would be hampered by their elimination. Choppin, assisting the Prefect of Police, spent the night making lists of those to be arrested, including all the members of the Central Committee of the National Guard and 'the most dangerous agitators'. The police were to operate behind each army column. Special attention was to be paid to the headquarters of the International in the Rue de la Corderie. Picard, for his part, was trying to organize an expedition to capture a 'committee of Fédérés' said to be meeting that night in the 14th *arrondissement*.[36]

The military plan was necessarily ambitious, for it had to provide for the occupation and control of large areas of the city in order to safeguard the army's communications and prevent the hostile part of the population and National Guard from assembling for a counter-attack. The army commanders were ordered to prevent all armed gatherings, and stop anyone in arms going towards Ménilmontant, Belleville, La Villette, La Chapelle, Clignancourt, Les Batignolles or Montmartre – the working-class *faubourgs* where the removal of the guns would be taking place.[37] With this intention, General de Maud'huy's division would occupy the Bastille and the Cité, to control the crossings from the turbulent Left Bank *arrondissements*, the 5th and 13th, and smaller units were to hold other strategic points.[38] The operation against the Montmartre gun parks was to be carried out by General Susbielle's division, of only about 4,000 men,[39] and against those in the eastern districts (La Villette, Belleville and Ménilmontant) by General Faron, with about 6,000.[40] The large

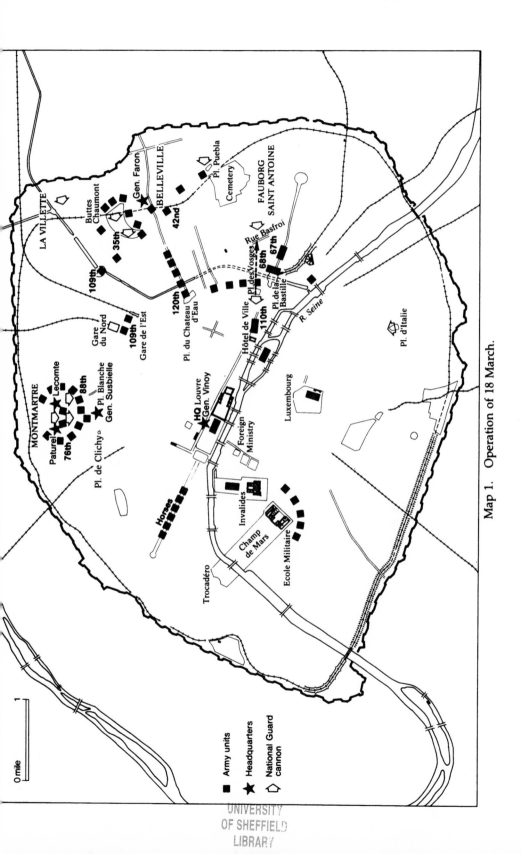

Map 1. Operation of 18 March.

MONTMARTRE

LA VILLETTE

Buttes Chaumont

Gen. Faron

BELLEVILLE

42nd

Pl. Puebla

Cemetery

FAUBORG
SAINT ANTOINE

Rue Basfroi

67th

68th

Pl. de la
Bastille

R. Seine

Pl. d'Italie

35th

109th

109th

Gare
du Nord

Gare de l'Est

120th

Pl. du Chateau
d'Eau

Pl. des Vosges

Hôtel de Ville

110th

Pl. Blanche

Gen. Susbielle

88th

Lecomte

Paturel

76th

Pl. de Clichy

HQ Louvre

Gen. Vinoy

Foreign
Ministry

Luxembourg

Horses

Invalides

Trocadéro

Champ
de Mars

Ecole Militaire

0 mile   1

Army units

Headquarters

National Guard
cannon

number of horses needed would stay in the rear until the infantry was firmly in control

The plan flouted the basic doctrine of urban military operations: that forces should not be spread out, with the danger of their being cut off and overwhelmed. This had been reiterated in the plans formulated over the years for dealing with disorders. General Roguet had written in 1830: 'To disperse . . . the troops by platoons in the open spaces and streets . . . is to gamble with the life and strength of the soldier, and to compromise military honour and the safety of the state itself.' Rather, vital points should be held in force, and afterwards, if necessary, insurgent strongpoints should be attacked, again in force. Strong reserves, secure communications and a solid base were essential.[41] The plan made by Thiers and Vinoy aimed to hold certain strategic points in the city, but only with small forces. The attacks on dispersed insurgent positions – Montmartre, Buttes Chaumont, Place Puebla – were to be simultaneous, and again with small forces. There were practically no reserves; communications were not secure; there was no base to fall back on.

They were willing to take a grave risk, presumably because they had been told that little or no resistance need be expected, and if things went wrong they took for granted that the 'good' National Guard would turn out as it had done on previous occasions. The plan presumed that thin cordons of troops would be able to prevent crowds or National Guard battalions from forming up to interfere with the main operations. The time expected to be taken seems to have been left vague, with little attention given to the possibility of delay or confusion arising from hasty planning. The authorities must have supposed that the 'reds' would react very slowly, if at all. The first step was to cripple the opposition to the government, apparently already in decline, by seizing its principal leaders and armament. Whatever remained could be dealt with at leisure.

General Susbielle did not believe that his men were in any condition to fight. His regiments from the Army of the Loire, mostly young and inexperienced troops, had been brought up to strength only two days earlier, after the departure of the *libérables*, by men from the disarmed Paris garrison. Many, especially those from the 136th regiment, had been billeted in Belleville, in contact with the population of the working-class districts, and were not in the mood for 'a serious struggle'. Susbielle had himself seen this, having passed several hours among the troops on 16 March, and hearing the opinions of the unit commanders. He went to report his conclusions verbally to Vinoy, but was unable to see him; his written report arrived too late.[42] There was little Vinoy could have done in any case. He was well aware of the state of the army, but no other troops were available except Daudel's brigade in the forts. There was no time to bring these in, and anyway to have done so would have warned the National Guard that action was imminent. The only precaution he could take was to give the police and gendarmerie the most active role in the operation; the infantry were merely to support.[43]

Apart from a little spying, the army had made no preparations for the action it was to perform. On the contrary, on 13 March Vinoy decided to send the Marines back to their ports, as their presence in Paris was considered unnecessary, and it was planned to send 1,600 unfit or untrained men back to their depots in the provinces on the very afternoon of 18 March.[44] No attempt had been made to organize horse transport for the removal of the guns: not only had the Remount Bureau no idea of how many horses were available, but the main preoccupation of the Ministry had been to send the mares out to foal with farmers and to give back 500 horses requisitioned from the Bus Company, both to save money and because the artillery had insufficient men to take care of them.[45]

During the early hours of 18 March, the troops stood to arms without noise. Susbielle's division assembled at the Place de Clichy between 4 and 5 o'clock, and the columns were sent forward with squads of policemen and Gardes Républicains in the lead. Paturel's column was to take the cannon parked at the Moulin de la Galette, at the top of the hill of Montmartre, where they arrived without incident from the northern side. The 17th battalion of *chasseurs* were left to occupy the windmill and park. Three companies of the 76th *de marche* and some policemen were sent to secure thirteen cannon in a nearby street. The rest of the regiment was strung out in a thin cordon round the hill, with orders to prevent all National Guards from approaching and to disarm all those leaving.[46] Lecomte's brigade, which was to take the other main gun park at the Château Rouge dance hall, to the east of the hill, was led by two columns, each of about 250 men. One, under Commandant Poussargues, commander of the 18th battalion of *chasseurs*, was to occupy the Tour Solférino, a small tower near the summit. The other, consisting of twenty policemen, a company of the Garde Républicaine, a company of *chasseurs*, and one of the 88th *de marche*, under a police officer, Commandant Vassal, was to seize the church of Saint Pierre, to prevent the tocsin from being rung, and the cannon at the Château Rouge. The remaining *chasseurs* were to occupy the top of the hill, and the rest of the 88th (the 2nd and 3rd battalions) were to form a cordon of small detachments on its eastern and southern sides.[47]

Vassal's men arrived just before dawn, taking the sentries by surprise. Shots were exchanged. The main body of National Guards at first mistook the police for their own men, the uniforms being similar, and shouted to Vassal to beat the *générale* (call to arms). Realizing their mistake, they opened fire, wounding a *chasseur*. A skirmish followed, 120 National Guards being surrounded in their headquarters, a house in the Rue des Rosiers, at the top of the hill, where they soon surrendered. By 5.45 a.m. the summit was firmly in the hands of the government forces. For several minutes shooting continued from the bottom of the hill, but without effect. The operation was quickly under way: the sappers began filling in the trenches surrounding the gun park, and the accompanying artillery officer counted the guns and went to fetch the horses waiting in the Champs Elysées and Place de la Concorde. The gendarmes searched the house in the Rue des Rosiers, finding some interesting documents. A number of 'important leaders of the Federation' were arrested. From the bottom of the hill, however, came the disquieting report of men of the 88th drinking in a bar with National Guards.[48]

On Paturel's side of the hill, two convoys of guns left without incident. A third convoy, of twelve guns from the Moulin de la Galette, was stopped as it descended the Rue Lepic by a crowd which 'intimidated' its escort of three companies of *chasseurs*. A company of the Garde Républicaine, under a Captain Kluber, was sent to clear a passage. Under 'a hail of stones and bottles' they pushed back the crowd, which was trying to cut the harnesses of the gun-teams, and escorted the convoy through, dragging by hand one gun which had been cut loose. They reached the Ecole Militaire without firing a shot.[49] This incident, soon after 9 o'clock, was the army's last success. Further up the hill a mass of National Guards had appeared, moving towards the Moulin de la Galette. A company of the 76th *de marche* was in their path, but its officers had difficulty in getting the men into line. Another company was sent, but it was equally half-hearted. A company of the 17th *chasseurs* was brought. It 'formed up very promptly', and was ordered to load, fix bayonets, and 'push back all that was before it'. There followed a kind of military work-to-rule: the *chasseurs* did as they were told, but with 'deplorable lack of intelligence', pushing their way

44

right through the crowd of National Guards, who had their rifle butts raised and were calling the soldiers 'brothers', but allowing it to flow back on either side behind them. An officer ran round to stop them, but they had already gone several hundred yards down the hill. Paturel was surrounded by National Guards, received a blow in the face from a rifle butt, and had to be rescued by his officers. Meanwhile, the rest of the *chasseurs* and the battalion of the 76th had come down the hill without orders, leaving it completely undefended. The hostile crowd was growing. Paturel gave up, and allowed the troops to continue their march back to camp. The 2nd battalion of the 76th, spread out in small detachments, was swamped by the crowd. Its commanding officer was captured, but most of the men made their way back to barracks. Paturel's brigade was ordered to the Champ de Mars, and from there to Versailles. On arrival, the 76th had 150 men missing, about one tenth of its strength.[50]

On the other side of the hill, General Lecomte was in an even worse predicament. As early as 8 o'clock, groups of National Guards and civilians started to force the infantry cordon and make their way up the hill, and it was soon clear, as Lecomte himself realized, that the 88th *de marche* would not stop them. The men were raw, and many were new to the regiment, some being 'fairly bad elements', especially those from the 136th, which had been billeted at Belleville, and whose unreliability Susbielle had earlier noted.[51] It was not only the men who were reluctant, however. The officers and NCOs commanding the detachments at the bottom of the hill were more than hesitant. When the National Guards reached one such squad in the Boulevard Ornano, 'the Lieutenant . . . cleared off and told us, do as you like'; only a corporal was left in charge, the rifles were empty, and the men made no resistance. Similarly, a little further on: 'We were never ordered to fire . . . Our second-lieutenant surrendered his sword, we were a dozen men.' The senior officers made every effort to be conciliatory, reluctant no doubt, to start a civil war, especially in the face of overwhelming odds. A battalion commander of the 88th *de marche* had his men put their ramrods in their rifle barrels to show that they were not loaded. Another, seeing several hundred National Guards approaching, put his *képi* on the end of his sword and waved it in the air, shouting 'Vive la République!' The colonel arrived and tried to parley with the National Guard, saying that he was willing to surrender the rifles if the men were allowed to leave; he was dragged away, calling vainly to his soldiers for assistance.[52]

The same fate befell Lecomte. When the crowd began to climb the hill, he shouted to them to keep their distance, and ordered the bugler to sound the *garde à vous* as a warning. The bluff did not work, and so the battalion of the 88th with Lecomte was ordered to load: many of the men only pretended to obey, throwing away their cartridges. A short distance away on the southern slopes of the hill, Commandant Poussargues, of the 18th battalion of *chasseurs*, made the three *sommations* (the legal summons to the crowd to disperse). He then called up to Lecomte for orders. 'He said nothing, but made a sign which meant that we should not fire.' A *chasseur* officer went up to him to ask for definite orders: he replied, 'Fix bayonets.' Poussargues, impatient, could only order his men to load: 'I could not take it upon myself to order them to fire.' Lecomte, according to his orderly officer, Lieutenant Toussaint, refused to give the order, knowing that the men would refuse to fire at point-blank range on the crowd, which included many women and children; another officer quoted Lecomte as saying 'No, do not fire, there are too many women and children.' Giving Toussaint his revolver, he sent him to ask Susbielle for help from the reserve battalion of the 88th, down the hill at the Place Blanche.[53]

Toussaint forced his way down the Rue Lepic using sword and pistol, arriving at Susbielle's position just as the only serious fighting of the day was taking place. Susbielle had ordered his small escort of *chasseurs à cheval* and mounted gendarmes to push back the crowd which was coming through the cordon of infantry. Hesitantly, they tried to do so, but without effect. Then they charged, and were met by a volley of rifle fire which scattered them: the *chasseurs'* commander, Commandant de Saint-James, was killed, a gendarmerie officer was shot in the leg, and five of his men were slightly wounded. Three gunners caught in the line of fire were killed, and three wounded. Toussaint's horse was killed under him, as were the four horses of a *mitrailleuse*, which had to be abandoned.[54]

Susbielle, with his officers and escort, tried again twice to clear the square, then retired, covered by a detachment of gendarmes. Most of the battalion of the 88th, which had raised *la crosse en l'air*, eventually followed. Lecomte was left isolated. The whole of the top of the hill was retaken by the crowd. The troops fraternized, and some of the officers were arrested, including Commandant Poussargues, Commandant Vassal and Lecomte himself, when he rode forward to parley with the crowd. Most of the officers and men returned to camp: the 1st battalion of the 88th was marched back by its commanding officer, still with its rifles. The 3rd battalion, however, which had formed the cordon along the Boulevard Ornano, to the east of the hill, had been completely dispersed.[55] Later that day, Lecomte was shot by the insurgents.

In the eastern districts of the city, General Faron's men had behaved in the same way, although they were more seasoned troops and commanded by far more experienced officers. A small force, nine companies of the 109th *de ligne* and a battery of artillery, had been sent to La Villette. The commander, Colonel Lespiau, was to meet a squad of policemen, 'who were to inform me of the location of a hall known as the Marseillaise where it was supposed that there ought to be some cannon'. After the troops had waited three and a half hours, a Commissaire of Police finally arrived, alone, at 8.30 a.m. By this time a crowd had gathered. The troops were ordered to move them back, but failed to show 'the least mark of energy'. They were ordered to fix bayonets. 'It could be said that not a single soldier obeyed; not that they refused openly, but those who marched did so with such nonchalance and embarassment that I realized how little reliance should be placed on my troops.' By this time they had heard the news from Montmartre, and Lespiau negotiated his withdrawal with the local National Guard, abandoning his guns to the crowd: 'better to save something than to risk losing everything'. The regiment returned to the Napoleon barracks, behind the Hôtel de Ville. That evening, a number of National Guards tried to get inside, and began to break down the door. The soldiers were unwilling to resist, even talking to their besiegers through the windows. Finally, the officers ordered them to open fire, but again they showed 'weakness', and the officers could only interrupt the attempts to fraternize by firing a few shots themselves, thus provoking an exchange of fire which caused casualties among their own men and scattered the National Guards.[56]

Faron's main attempt had been made against the gun parks at the Place Puebla, where guns from the Place des Vosges had been taken, and the Buttes Chaumont, a public park north of Belleville. Four companies of the 42nd *de ligne*, with their colonel, occupied the Place Puebla, defended by only fifty National Guards, and took possession of the sixteen cannon and seven howitzers. The horses took over an hour to arrive, and then were without the necessary towing equipment for the howitzers, although warned of the need. An escort for the convoy was taken from two companies guarding the line of communications with Faron at Belleville, about a mile away. This so weakened them in numbers that they were easily disarmed by the crowd at about 11 o'clock. The colonel himself was seized and, 'le couteau à la gorge', forced to send an order to the troops in the Place Puebla to lay down their arms. Three companies were allowed to march away, after negotiation, and the officers were escorted from the area and released. The 1st battalion, with Faron at Belleville church, was disarmed by the National Guard. Their colonel was convinced that 'the men would not have fired; they offered not the slightest resistance to surrendering their rifles and left arm in arm, fraternizing and singing with the National Guards'.[57] Further north, near the Buttes Chaumont, the same had happened to the 35th *de ligne*. There was no trouble until about 11 o'clock, and eighteen guns were dispatched to the Ecole Militaire with only twenty gendarmes as escort. But the 3rd battalion in the Rue d'Allemagne was faced by a large crowd; its commander ordered a withdrawal, but he was seized, and the battalion was overwhelmed by numbers and disarmed. Only a sergeant and 150 men remained to rejoin the regiment. Faron withdrew his remaining troops outside the fortifications and marched away south. Commissaire of Police Macé, in charge of the arrest of 'political people' at Belleville, threw away his arrest warrants and managed to talk his way out of trouble.[58]

During the early hours of the morning, army headquarters had been optimistic. The first reports indicated that the operation was proceeding as planned. The government expected no serious resistance; the military officers, calm and unworried, were sure that everything was over.[59] Bad news began to arrive in mid-morning. At 10.20, 'effervescence' in the 11th *arrondissement* was reported, and at 10.35, Ferry cabled that the regiment occupying the Place de la Bastille did not seem 'well disposed' and was fraternizing too much. Almost simultaneously, the Prefect of Police General Valentin reported 'very bad news from Montmartre'. Soon the details were known. Susbielle arrived at the Louvre headquarters at about noon, followed by Faron and a succession of officers all looking very depressed.[60] Colonel Lespiau returned to the Hôtel de Ville with the remnants of the 109th, so ashamed that he talked of shooting himself. The colonel of the 120th *de ligne*, most of which had been disarmed at the Prince Eugène barracks, wrote officially that he and his officers no longer wished to command 'such scum'. The colonel of the 35th was 'too tired and ill' even to write his report.[61] It is hard to imagine a more humiliating and frightening experience for army officers than that of 18 March. If the Fédérés had seen the despair on their faces, thought one, they would have realized 'the hatred they were accumulating'.[62] The deaths of General Lecomte and the former Commander-in-Chief of the National Guard, Clément Thomas, shot by a Montmartre mob that included soldiers, added to the feeling of outrage which found expression in the vengeance meted out to suspected deserters, and finally to many hundreds of inhabitants of Montmartre. Years later, the memory persisted, a reminder of the dangers of involving the army in politics.

These feelings of shock and anger were not shared by all the junior officers, however. The memoirs of Captain Patry, an experienced regular officer,[63] give a valuable insight into their attitude. His regiment, the 67th *de marche*, had been sent to the Place de la Bastille, where it arrived soon after dawn. A crowd began to collect, asking the soldiers what they were doing, and talking of a *coup d'état*. 'What, indeed, were we going to do?' thought Patry; 'I began to feel the business . . . distasteful.' Knowing Thiers's reputation as an Orleanist, he wondered if they were indeed engaged in a 'criminal' monarchist coup, and was disgusted by the thought that he might be obliged to fire on his fellow countrymen to bring back 'a fallen regime, whichever it might be'. Later, he and his company were sent forward to the Rue de Charonne with orders to prevent crowds from forming, but without the use of rifles or bayonets. This was impossible, and soon they were completely surrounded by a friendly and talkative crowd. He reassured them that he did not support the return of 'some Badinguet or other',[64] and was taken into a café and bought a drink. After persuading a National Guard officer to take his men elsewhere so as to avoid the risk of unpleasantness, he returned with his company to the Bastille at about 11 o'clock. There the crowd was less friendly and they had to force a passage at bayonet point. Amazingly, the officers were then allowed by their superiors to go to nearby restaurants, and the men sent in groups under their NCOs to buy food. Patry spent an hour over lunch, and returned to find that the regiment had left. He finally rejoined it at the Champ de Mars at 5 o'clock. At nightfall they returned to the Luxembourg, and the officers were allowed, as usual, to sleep out. His conclusion on the day's events was that the cannon were only a pretext, for they were doing no harm to anybody, though a pretext for what he did not know.[65] Dr Flamarion, of the same regiment, noted, 'We are in the greatest confusion as to what is happening . . . there is talk of cannon . . . Others whisper of an abortive *coup d'état* . . . the ordinary soldiers understand nothing at all.'[66] Patry's account of the day's events as seen by an officer of the army is unique. His behaviour, however, seems to have been typical, and it is reasonable to assume that his reactions – those of a confused junior officer, little involved in politics, well meaning and quite ignorant of the significance of the happenings round him – were typical too.

The sudden withdrawal to the Left Bank, which had caused Patry to lose his regiment, had been ordered by Vinoy when it became clear that the troops were fraternizing with the crowd.[67] At about midday, General Le Flô went to the Quai d'Orsay, where the government was meeting, and explained that the situation was grave and rapidly worsening. Thiers mentioned the possibility of evacuating the city, but no definite order was given. Thiers himself left for Versailles in a panic at about 4 p.m., after the noisy arrival of a National Guard battalion outside aroused fears that the building would be invaded. After his departure, his authority was greatly weakened, and the old division within the government reappeared, with the soldiers again pessimistic, and the civilians unconvinced that all was lost. 'It was greatly to be feared that if we spent another twelve hours in Paris, we should not be able to bring out a single regiment', stated Le Flô. 'This opinion prevailed among the military. It did not prevail among the other members of the government.'[68]

The Ministers met that evening in secret. All except Le Flô were against evacuation, arguing that some foothold at least, such as the Ecole Militaire or the Trocadéro, should be retained. This accorded with accepted military thinking. General Roguet had written in 1839, 'A great capital must not be entirely abandoned by the government . . . a retrograde movement gives 50,000 auxiliaries to the rebels and can bring the greatest of disasters.' It is true that Roguet had mentioned as the least desirable of choices in case of grave disorder that of withdrawing from the city to a neighbouring base, in order to return later, and that General Laveaucoupet, when *chef de cabinet* to the Minister, had noted in the margin 'Versailles?' But it would be wrong to interpret this, as certain historians have done, as evidence that the idea of withdrawing to Versailles in case of troubles in Paris was accepted. Roguet was thinking of a fortified town (which Versailles was not), and besides concluded that it would not be practicable in case of insurrection in a fortified city (which the Paris of 1871 was). It would in any case be imprudent to assume that Roguet's ideas had been universally adopted. Laveaucoupet, for example, showed by his notes that he was sceptical, and concluded, with dramatic irony, 'Never would a riot be capable of defending the forts and ramparts [of Paris]; that would be a revolution.'[69]

It was therefore in accordance with common sense as well as military orthodoxy that the remaining civilian Ministers opposed withdrawal. They stated formally that they would not evacuate Paris, but would remain whatever happened. Le Flô, who, like Vinoy, seems to have been appalled by the disintegration of his forces, replied, 'Do as you like. It is my duty to save the army, and I will save it at any price.' He had already given Vinoy, at his request, a written order to evacuate at 6 p.m. The opposition within the government caused a delay, however, and late that night Favre, Picard, Simon, Pothuau and Le Flô went to see Vinoy at the Ecole Militaire, where there was 'another scene', but by then the two generals were determined to wait no longer and they insisted that complete evacuation of the city by the army should begin at 2 a.m.[70]

Evacuation, it has been said, was unnecessary and provocative. It is indeed arguable, with the benefit of hindsight, that the army and the government were under no immediate threat from the forces of the Central Committee of the National Guard, whose power and aggressiveness they exaggerated. Quite possibly they could have retained possession of the south-western third of the city, where the population was not hostile, though whether this would have made compromise easier and civil war avoidable is another matter. Nevertheless, their decision to withdraw to Versailles is explicable on grounds of simple prudence, to prevent the possible disintegration of the army.

There is, then, no evidence that the government foresaw the outcome of the 18 March operation and anticipated withdrawing to Versailles. No serious resistance was expected on 18 March: it was simply a matter of accelerating a result that Thiers had thought 'patience and ridicule' would be sufficient to obtain.[71] Probably the authorities were prepared for another 22 January, with a whiff of grapeshot leading to the arrest of 'red' leaders and the disarmament of the dissident National Guard. Had a general conflict been intended, the obvious course would have been to wait and increase the strength of the army as Vinoy, a harsh veteran of the 1851 *coup d'état*, had advised. The risky decision to seize the cannon on 18 March, and Vinoy's acquiescence in it on behalf of the army,[72] is less evidence of a desire to provoke civil conflict than of a desperate attempt to avert it.

The events of 18 March justified the pessimism of the army commanders. The failure of the operation had been due not merely to minor faults in planning or execution. Of course, it did not help that the police did not arrive for hours at La Villette, keeping the 109th *de ligne* helpless while the crowds gathered, or that the horses were slow in coming to remove the guns and sometimes lacked the proper towing equipment. But even if such hitches had not occurred, it is hard to see how the major operations at Montmartre and Belleville could have been completed before the popular reaction developed. The real reasons for failure were that the number of troops available was insufficient, they were reluctant to act, and the reaction of the population was unexpectedly hostile: inactivity on the part of those who would normally have supported order (weakened numerically by the departure of so many after the Prussian siege, and angry at the measures taken by the National Assembly), and militancy in the working-class *faubourgs*. In these circumstances, the army could only have succeeded in its task by taking the most vigorous, and where necessary ruthless, action, as prescribed in existing orders:

Never must troops be uncertain against a riot . . . [They] must never allow themselves to be approached by a column of rioters, by women and children; hesitation by infantry in opening fire can compromise it and cause it to be disarmed. At 200 paces the rioters must be warned to stop; if they disobey, once the *sommations* have been made . . . fire must be opened immediately. Women and children . . . are the vanguard of the enemy and must be treated as such.[73]

Vinoy and his senior officers could hardly have been surprised when no such action was taken. The hesitancy was universal, affecting officers and men, veterans of the 35th and 42nd, recruits of the 76th and 88th, units newly arrived from the provinces and those that had spent the war in Paris. That it was in part a failure of will is shown by the contrasting behaviour of the gendarmerie, disciplined and without ties with the poorer classes: small detachments were able to force their way through the crowds without great difficulty. Similarly, a tough commander such as Poussargues was able to keep his men relatively well in hand, whereas the officers of the 88th, reported Vinoy, 'were incapable of exercising proper influence over their men'. He noted that few junior officers had shown energy.[74] The troops' attitude was one of reluctance to take part in a dubious operation rather than active sympathy for the cause of the National Guard, probably as little understood as that of the government. The number of those who wilfully deserted their regiments is small: most straggled into Versailles before long and settled into a sullen neutrality, unwilling to fight for or against Paris.[75]

The reaction of the troops in fraternizing with the National Guard set the course of events from 18 March onwards. It frightened the government into evacuating the city; it thus placed the Central Committee in power, with all the immense resources of the fortress of Paris, the reduction of which required a long siege; it made manifest the impotence of the government, at least for the time being; and it encouraged a lasting over-confidence on the part of the insurgents, who were convinced that a conscript army would never stand against them. This was too simple for two reasons. First, it overlooked the material, as opposed to moral, reasons for the defeat: the troops had been too few, and had been asked to perform a difficult and daunting task. Used prudently, and in greater number, they could suffice. Second, it assumed that the troops had sided with the National Guards, whereas they had merely opted out, and were therefore easier to push back into line. The government and, as time would show, the insurgents, would have done well to act with the prudence enjoined by General Roguet, whose words could stand as an epitaph to the operation of 18 March:

There is danger for the government in counting too much on the service the army can render. It will act with confidence and vigour if the National Guard is on its side, otherwise its effectiveness should be little counted on . . . In this sort of war, he who begins the struggle is almost always in the wrong and faces defeat; he who defends himself, and can cause himself to be attacked, succeeds.[76]

4

vvvvvvvvvvvvvvvvvvvvvvvvvvvvvvvvvvvvvvvvvvvvvvvvvvvvvvvvvvvvvvvvvvvvvvvvvvvvvvv

Interlude

The next fortnight, Thiers said later, was the worst time of his life.[1] The government had completely lost control of events. Politically it was trapped between the conservative majority in the Assembly, which met for the first time in Versailles on 20 March, and republican opinion in Paris and the provincial cities. The former set its face against all concessions to 'the mob'. The latter, suspicious that Thiers was hatching a royalist *coup d'état*, seemed prepared to unite in sympathy with the Paris National Guard.[2] Insurrection broke out in Lyons on 22 March, in Marseilles on the 23rd, in Narbonne on the 24th, in Saint Etienne on the 25th and in Le Creusot on the 26th.[3] There was an obvious danger that the Paris insurgents would march on Versailles, in which case, as Thiers later admitted, he 'would not have wanted to answer for the solidity of the army'.[4]

This was no exaggeration. The state of the army was such that it could hardly be placed even in defensive positions, for to spread out large numbers of men in small outposts near Paris would be to invite massive desertions. Those considered the best troops, Daudel's brigade (113th and 114th *de ligne*), whose commander had been ready to march into Paris on 18 March to support Vinoy, had been withdrawn to Versailles itself on Thiers's express orders to protect the government and the Assembly. This had left the five southern forts and the great western fortress of Mont Valérien almost undefended, though the latter was reoccupied at Vinoy's insistence on the morning of the 20th by the 119th *de ligne*.[5]

Apart from this, the most that could be done was to send the more dependable troops to watch the main roads to Versailles in case of a sortie from Paris, which police reports said was being planned for 20 or 21 March. The river crossings at Sèvres and Saint-Cloud, the shortest routes to Versailles, were guarded by the government's only dependable force, the gendarmerie, well placed there to prevent deserters from reaching Paris. They were supported a safe four miles in the rear at Viroflay by General de la Mariouse's brigade, the 35th and 42nd *de ligne*, the only surviving infantry regiments of the Imperial Army. Further south, General Derroja's brigade, the 109th and 110th *de ligne*, was encamped near Vélizy, watching the southern route from Paris. As an extra precaution, repair work was stopped on the Seine bridges blown up during the war. A small cavalry force, General de Galliffet's brigade, 9th and 12th *chasseurs à cheval*, patrolled no-man's-land.[6]

These forces were insufficient to resist a large-scale attack, had the Fédérés (as adherents to the Fédération Républicaine de la Garde Nationale came to be called) been capable of mounting one. At Mont Valérien, a key position which had been disarmed at the armistice, the garrison was engaged in placing a few howitzers on the ramparts to defend the fort itself against infantry attack. The gendarmes at Sèvres, who had been on duty since 18 March, were so exhausted that their colonel asked, in vain, for the regiment to be relieved. The units under de la Mariouse and Derroja were under strength: the 109th was 550 and the 110th 460 men short of full establishment. Moreover, like the rest of the army, they were far from reliable. A soldier of the 110th assured police officers that in the event of hostilities the men would kill their officers and join with the National Guard, because 'l'on avait été trahi'. The outposts were in close contact with the population and exposed to its influence.[7]

The government therefore had no choice but to try to maintain peace. This is shown clearly by the restraint Thiers placed on those in Versailles and Paris who wanted to renew the offensive abandoned on 18 March. Galliffet was one: he urged Thiers to permit a surprise cavalry attack on the Porte Maillot and Trocadéro. Thiers told him he was mad.[8] Most of the generals would have agreed, being 'not very confident in the dispositions of their men'.[9] MacMahon saw at a glance that the army was useless,[10] as did others in Versailles. 'Nothing more wretched than the sight of the regiments crammed . . . into the avenues [of Versailles] . . . the men badly dressed, badly behaved, nearly always drunk and saying the most dreadful things', recalled a monarchist deputy.[11] This did not deter the Right from adopting an aggressive attitude, however. They caused a scene in the Assembly on 20 March when a delegation of the mayors of Paris arrived as mediators, and fear that they would sabotage all attempts at negotiation, perhaps by trying to overthrow the government and nominate an Orleanist prince to head a new one, caused Thiers to cut short the night session of 24 March, warning the Right that 'a careless word can shed torrents of blood'.[12]

Similarly, he restrained the pro-government forces that had begun to assemble inside the capital. These, composed of several thousand National Guards, Mobiles and isolated regulars under the command of Admiral Saisset, a popular hero of the siege, were occupying the Gare Saint Lazare, the Bourse, the Opera and the *mairies* of the 1st and 2nd *arrondissements*. Some of the more ardent elements were planning, and even carrying out, offensive action against the Fédérés, and a police report on 24 March warned Versailles that serious fighting was expected soon.[13] Saisset asked the government to send arms, ammunition, tools and sandbags by rail to the Gare Saint Lazare. Nothing was sent. Le Flô was asked for artillery. He refused. Thiers was asked for 5,000 troops to support the National Guard 'of order', as the loyalists were now being called. 'Neither 5,000 nor 500 nor 5', he replied. 'I need the few troops I have at my disposal, and I am not quite sure of them.'[14] Saisset himself went to see Thiers, and on his return to Paris ordered his men to abstain from all offensive action. On 25 March, the day the mayors of Paris and the Central Committee of the National Guard signed an agreement to hold municipal elections, Saisset disbanded his forces and left for Versailles. On the same day, Thiers, according to Galliffet, countermanded an order to clear a Fédéré post threatening communications with the Gare Saint Lazare.[15] Some pro-government National Guards continued for a few days more to hold the gates on the western side of Paris, until, receiving no encouragement from Versailles, they drifted away. There could hardly be clearer indication of the government's desire to avoid hostilities. Otherwise, encouragement of its Fifth Column would have been an elementary stratagem.

It had little choice in the matter. There was widespread fear in Versailles of the consequences of a trial of strength, and when the government met on 25 March it was reported (*Le Soir*, 26 March) that only one Minister advocated the use of force. Some deputies even wanted the Assembly to retire immediately to Tours or Bourdeaux, out of reach of the insurgents, for if the army failed again and the existence of the Assembly were endangered, 'France would be finished'.[16] The government hoped to avert that danger. Thiers told Lord Lyons that the army was being built up and would, in a few weeks, be a considerable force before which 'Jules Favre thinks the insurgents . . . will cave in'. Lyons wrote to Lord Granville on 30 March: 'The great hope appears to be that the members of the Commune will quarrel among themselves, and that their social measures may be so thoroughly socialist as to rouse resistance among the Parisians.'[17]

The failure of the mayors and deputies of Paris to negotiate a settlement, and the result of the semi-legal elections in Paris on 26 March which produced a Commune that was evidently not prepared to compromise, changed nothing of the government's immediate plans, though clearly armed conflict was more than ever a danger, and fears were widely expressed that the Fédérés would launch an attack on Versailles. Thiers told Mayor Tirard, one of the chief negotiators, that the main thing for the moment was to prevent bloodshed in the hope that the government would in time be able to assemble forces capable of 'liberating' Paris.[18] That time was not yet, for the army remained much weaker and more unreliable than historians have usually believed.[19] The rest of this chapter will be devoted to examining its condition.

The state of the army during its retreat from Paris and on its arrival in Versailles was 'truly deplorable': the soldiers scuffled with policemen and gendarmes and ignored orders. The officers dared not take strong measures.[20] The authorities, though necessarily conscious of the seriousness of the problem, at first underestimated its extent and mistook its causes. They assumed that the troops' reluctance to oppose the Fédérés was due to contacts made before 18 March with the Parisians, to organized propaganda and sedition, and to the presence of Parisians within their ranks. This was not the complete explanation, and so the steps taken at first to remedy the condition of the army were inadequate. As was recommended by senior officers of Faron's division, Parisians and men who sympathized with Paris (thought to be a small and identifiable minority) were to be weeded out. At once, the 23rd battalion of *chasseurs*, concerned in the Bastille demonstrations of early March, and the 88th *de marche*, blamed for the events at Montmartre on the 18th, were ordered to North Africa. Other regiments prepared lists of men considered unreliable, who were to be sent to the regimental depots in the provinces. The lists were long: the 42nd *de ligne* had 105 NCOs and men 'nearly all Parisians, bad elements, capable of having the most undesirable influence', who were to be disarmed and returned to the depot; the 109th ordered 100 NCOs and men to leave at once, and by early April had sent away 800 'bad spirited' men – about half its total strength; the 110th sent away 265.[21] Every unit did the same, including the artillery and cavalry. The number of men involved was evidently large: I have found no total, but it must have reached several thousand. The commander at Evreux reported having received 6,000 disarmed men since 14 March,[22] though these may not all have been sent away for unreliability. Many of those who were thus disposed of were simply bad soldiers of whom commanding officers took the chance of ridding themselves, rather than partisans of the Commune. This may be taken as a sign of the tendency of officers to regard the disaffection that showed itself on 18 March as being a military rather than a political problem, on the same level as drunkenness or slovenly dress and probably associated with such unsoldierly vices. One gun battery, for example, sent away fifteen men 'who cannot be counted upon', including two drunken NCOs and, among the men, two 'rowdies', a 'barrack-room lawyer' (*raisonneur*), two drunkards, three 'bad types', but only two Parisians and one man having 'contacts with the rioters'.[23] This rough and ready purge no doubt eliminated a number who would have been unreliable in any difficult situation, but its limitations in dealing with widespread reluctance to engage in civil war are evident.

The extent of such reluctance is difficult to gauge. Those who felt it, except in a very small number of cases, were obviously careful to conceal it. Officers in their turn might feel it wise to minimize the extent of disaffection among their subordinates. There must have been many like the corporal who had handed his rifle over to the National Guards 'with great pleasure' and gone home to his family in Paris, but who, on finally rejoining his regiment in Versailles was able to arrange matters with a friendly sergeant-major so as not to lose his stripes.[24] Nevertheless, much evidence exists concerning the state of the Army of Paris, for most of the Paris police had been withdrawn to Versailles, where one of their main tasks was to keep watch on the troops. From the beginning, their reports were disquieting (though sometimes exaggerated), mentioning desertions, seditious meetings of soldiers nightly, and even talk of shooting General Ducrot.[25]

Sometimes the troops made their attitude unmistakable: 400 men of the 46th *de marche* entering Versailles on 29 March met three policemen and jeered at them as 'mouchards, casse-têtes, assassins', producing a bad effect on the population which was 'hardly confident in the morale of certain regiments',[26] Generally, however, the police had to rely on their usual methods of listening to conversations and chatting with the troops. Inevitably, their reports were incomplete, subjective and sometimes contradictory. Some officers pressed their own points of view, for example the head of the 5th *brigade de recherches*, who wanted stern action against the Fédérés and was therefore invariably optimistic about the troops' morale. Sometimes reports were contradictory: one on 29 March found the spirit of the troops at Satory camp 'good'; another the same day found it 'detestable'.[27] Young soldiers brought from the provinces, it was reported, 'miss their homes and ask why the government does not give the insurgents what they want'; but another informant found them 'serious, polite', although he noted that many sympathized with Paris 'because they have not had the situation explained to them, and they all march like brutes, and no one takes any interest in them'.[28]

There were difficulties in obtaining definite information on the spirit of the troops, it was reported. The regiments were newly formed from disparate detachments, so that officers and men did not know each other. Also, the troops, realizing that they were being watched, became circumspect.[29] But on the whole, the evidence gives an impression well summed up by a senior police officer as a sullen resentfulness, liable to flare up at any cause:

The slightest annoyance in the course of their duties causes an outcry which takes the form of a promise to join hands with the National Guard. On the other hand, the soldiers are displeased with sleeping on the ground, which they blame on the insurgents. They would fire on them, they say, to get the business over with, but only if they are well led, and not spread out, as was done at Montmartre.[30]

Police reports of disaffection were confirmed by commanding officers. Colonel Lespiau wrote on 22 March of the 'bad spirit that reigns' in the 109th, caused by the demobilization of many men, and their replacement by 600 others from four different regiments. Moreover, many of his men were 'Parisians or . . . workers' called up at the beginning of the Prussian siege. 'Some soldiers declare openly that they will not fire on their "brothers from Paris" ', and that morning alone, twenty men had deserted from the second battalion at the outposts, four taking their rifles.[31] 'Parisians and workers', including workers from provincial towns, formed an important section of the army for they provided, no doubt because of their superior literacy, a high proportion of N C Os. Colonel Roblastre had misgivings about the 110th, which included 500 recruits of the Class of 1870, from the Department of the Seine, who had 'nothing soldierly about them except the uniform', and showed 'a detestable spirit of opposition'. They took their ideas from *La Marseillaise, Le Cri du Peuple, Le Rappel* and other such papers, which they read aloud to their comrades, and 'shamelessly' expressed their intention of 'not using their arms if called upon to fight the insurrection'.[32]

The problem still seemed, therefore, to be on the one hand that of a certain number of individuals – Parisians and workers – who sympathized actively with the Commune, and who would have to be sent away from the army, and on the other, that of a mass of inexperienced and demoralized men, having no reason to sympathize with the Commune, who simply needed to be licked into shape using normal military methods. The authorities still assumed, as they had done before 18 March, and in spite of the events of that day, that troops brought in from the provinces would not be unwilling to fight against Paris, and that the problem could therefore be solved by bringing in large numbers of reinforcements. They were soon disabused of this notion, as reports of 'bad spirit' arrived even while the troops were *en route*: it was noted that soldiers of the 72nd and 91st 'said very openly, without being contradicted by their comrades, that they would not fire on the people'; from Nevers the police reported the passage of 3,000 soldiers, of whom many were said to be ready to 'make common cause with the insurgents'.[33] Once at Versailles, the new troops were watched closely by the police, who reported that the 39th and 41st *de marche* were 'a jumble of twenty regiments, they seem very tired and have not the slightest desire to fire on their brothers from Paris'. Similar reports were made concerning the 1st, 10th and 20th battalions of *chasseurs*, and the 48th, 72nd, 90th and 91st *de marche*.[34] In short, the loyalty of most of the newly arrived units was considered doubtful.

To remedy this state of affairs, the resolute cooperation of the officers was essential. But, as on 18 March, it could not be taken for granted. Most officers were from Gambetta's armies, recently promoted and often inexperienced. In an obscure political situation, when the army knew little of the government's intentions and as little about the Central Committee, many must at first have believed the dispute to be between a patriotic movement wishing to continue the war and a shameful government of 'peace at any price'. It was widely believed, including by some in authority, that Gambetta would participate in such a movement, if indeed he were not its secret inspiration.[35] The Gambettist General Cremer, a former Metz *perceur*, who had commanded an army corps in the Army of the East, was reported to have accepted a command from the Central Committee, and Garibaldi was invited to take command of the National Guard of the Seine. The Versailles government, on the other hand, included, and was identified with, men loathed for their failures during the siege. In the opinion of officers of the 64th *de marche*, 'The government are all swine . . . Trochu was out riding today on a fine Arab horse; he receives his *rente*; he is the cause of the situation we are in; he conducted the siege very badly; it will not be long before he is shot, and Jules Favre deserves the same.'[36] And these men, it seemed, having lost the foreign war, were undertaking a civil war for political advantage. 'Paris is completely calm', said an officer of the 8th. 'There is nothing at all wrong. It is here that there is a bunch of cowards; they want a revolution so as to bring us back a prince.'[37] Captain Patry of the 67th *de marche* agreed in judging the situation 'from the political point of view clumsy and even dishonest . . . With a few minor concessions it would have been easy to bring the insurrection to an end . . . Nothing of that escaped us, and for all these reasons the campaign was deeply repugnant to me.'[38]

Such repugnance led some officers to avoid service. Patry asked to be posted to Africa.[39] Others asked to resign, such as Captain Bocher and Lieutenant Guérin, of the 42nd *de ligne*, who did so on 21 March, stating that they were not prepared to lead their men against the insurrection, though they were finally persuaded to reconsider by their colonel.[40] Three officers of the 26th *de ligne*, newly formed at Cherbourg from returned prisoners of war, asked to be placed on half pay.[41] A larger number reported sick: four captains of the 113th *de ligne* were allowed to go on 'convalescent leave' on 19 March;[42] a Captain Quenille of the 46th *de marche* feigned illness, and was sent to prison and later allowed to resign;[43] Second-Lieutenant Arnaud, 30th battalion *chasseurs*, resigned when ordered to leave hospital as fit for service;[44] Second-Lieutenant Serres, 109th *de ligne*, went off duty claiming to be sick on the evening of 18 March, and stayed in Paris.[45] A number simply absented themselves. Captain Guillard, 110th *de ligne*, was sentenced to sixty days prison for having stayed away from the regiment for four days.[46]

The numbers here are small, and the number of those who went so far as to desert or join the Commune is infinitesimal. But they were only the visible sign of a larger malaise, deliberately concealed. Senior officers, intent on protecting the reputation of the regiment (and their own), urged their subordinates not to act hastily. Guérin and Bocher, of the 42nd, finally agreed to stay with the regiment, after arrest and threats of court martial, and their rebelliousness was overlooked after they had fought at Meudon on 3 April, when the Fédérés marched on

Versailles.[47] Patry, who had remained for several days in Paris, was persuaded by friends to rejoin the regiment as his absence was having a bad effect; but neither this unauthorized stay in Paris nor his request for a posting to avoid the civil war left any trace in his records or slowed his subsequent rapid promotion.[48] Colonel Boulanger, 114th *de ligne*, tried to persuade an officer with 'very advanced opinions', Captain Bourgogne, to stay with the regiment and keep silent, though in this case the attempt was in vain: Bourgogne left for Paris on 22 March saying (it was alleged), 'Only this Committee [of the National Guard] is capable of saving France; it will make the heads roll of the generals and lawyers [who have] betrayed the people.'[49] Usually, commanding officers denied reports that their regiments, and especially their officers, were unreliable. The colonel of the 64th denied that his officers could have made the seditious statements overheard, as they all had 'the best possible spirit'. Colonel Roblastre, 110th *de ligne*, reported that all his officers were satisfactory. Colonel Lespiau, 109th *de ligne*, was the exception: he wanted a purge of his officers, getting rid of five who were 'without energy, without authority over their men, and whose attitude I have already had the occasion to deplore'; he had one, Lieutenant Serres, declared a deserter when he remained in Paris claiming to be sick. Colonel Pottier, in contrast, allowed five captains of the 113th to go on sick leave on 19 March – a coincidence, perhaps, but a strange one.[50] The government, too, had an interest in concealing the extent of disaffection, so as not to invite attack from Paris, and to reassure the provinces that the government was in command of the situation, hence Thiers's famous dispatch announcing the organization of 'one of the finest armies that France has ever had'.[51]

These few individual cases, supported by the secondary evidence of reports and memoirs, indicate that the National Defence officers – with so many ex-rankers, semi-civilians and republicans among them, all of whom stood to lose from the reaction in the army that would accompany reaction in the state – were reluctant to become involved in civil war. The military authorities, generally of the old army, held them all in suspicion. As always, personalities burst through categories: for example, Colonel Lespiau, enthusiastic for a fight to the finish during the siege, and consequently understanding towards the 31 October rioters,[52] turned stern anti-Communard (a process in which the disgrace of 18 March must have played a part); or on the other hand, the exemplary Colonel Piquemal, imperial courtier and chief of staff of

Vergé's Division, told Du Barail that he was not sure which side was in the right.[53] But in general, the categories hold good, if only because there was and is no other indication of the attitudes and loyalties of the mass, either for the Versailles authorities or for the historian. The authorities therefore tried to solve the problem of unreliability among the officers by replacing where possible those of wartime creation by regulars returning from captivity in Germany. Nevertheless, large numbers of the former remained in most of the Versailles regiments, and in the end remained loyal to the government. The changed situation provides much of the explanation for their more or less grudging fidelity. It was soon clear that the Thiers government had survived the fiasco of 18 March and that a negotiated settlement with Paris was unlikely after the Commune elections on 26 March. The results of these also made it clear that the Parisian movement was more than a purely patriotic upsurge, and that it was not led by the kind of men to whom a moderate republican officer might be expected to rally. Those who went to Paris to see for themselves were not impressed. Captain Bourgogne soon returned, 'protesting energetically not only against all complicity with the insurgents but also against all suspicion of adherence to their beliefs, if one can say that they have any beliefs'.[54] General Cremer, escorted by a cheering crowd to the Hôtel de Ville, may have been persuaded by what he saw there to leave for Versailles. The Fédérés' hostility towards the army discouraged sympathy: their fraternal appeals were aimed at soldiers as individuals, for they were the declared enemies of the army as an institution and of its officers, as was shown by the arrest and rough treatment of Generals Chanzy and Langourian, in spite of their fine war records. For the professional soldier the army was, on the contrary, something to hold on to in a confused political situation in which all else in the nation seemed in danger of collapse: 'How to find oneself amid the chaos? . . . I was eager to find the depot of my regiment and get back into uniform.'[55] Thiers appealed to this feeling when speaking to the officers of the 67th *de marche*, saying that 'everything was rotten in France, and only the army remained clean and honourable'.[56]

There were also personal considerations. In one way, to remain neutral would have been easy; as General Lacretelle informed a friend whom he was advising not to seek service with the Army of Versailles, not only was civil war 'nauseating', but there was 'a superabundance of officers who cannot be used'.[57] But to heed such sage advice would probably mean the end of a career, and there was therefore a scramble for employment by officers of all ranks trying to prove that they would merit special consideration when the reduced peacetime army was re-established.

The dilemma of officers unconvinced of the rightness of the Versailles cause was brief: after the first few days of the insurrection the choice was practically made for them. Those arriving from Germany or Switzerland were obliged to report to the Minister of War on their return; General Cremer narrowly avoided a court martial for his delay in doing so. There were some, particularly those who had ties with Paris, who had motives for informing themselves more thoroughly of events from the point of view of the capital, but entry into the fortified city was becoming difficult, and it was far from certain that the reception there would be cordial. The rest, who derived their only knowledge of events from the Versailles press, could hardly help but be in the Versaillais camp, especially when the Parisian movement began to appear extremist, with the continuing departure of middle-class refugees, the shooting of demonstrators by Fédéré pickets in the Rue de la Paix on 22 March, the failure of the mayors to arrange a compromise, the departure from the city of most of its Deputies, and the election results which showed that the Commune had limited support.

Much attention has been paid here to officers who had (or who, by reason of their background, were assumed to have had) doubts; for even a limited degree of dissent could paralyse the army. But there were many, perhaps a majority (certainly in the higher ranks), who had no such scruples. They were placed by their origins, positions or beliefs firmly on the side of 'order' against 'disorder', hierarchy against democracy, nation against faction. 'In the face of this abominable insurrection, taking place under the gaze of the enemy, my duty seemed clear; I hastened to leave that city fallen prey to the mob, to all those *déclassés* without courage or patriotism who seek by every means to satisfy their appetites, to give free rein to their lust for pleasure and power.'[58] The subsequent actions of men who saw the conflict in such terms need no explanation. For many on both sides, 1871 was no more than the renewal of a perennial struggle in which their loyalties were pledged in advance. In the case of Colonel Rossel, outraged patriotism combined with an extraordinary belief in his own destiny outweighed class prejudice and caste loyalty, but he was the only regular officer who chose the side of the Commune openly and unequivocally. The rest remained, with more or less enthusiasm, on the side of its enemies.

Interlude

It was enthusiasm that the authorities needed, and they took steps to obtain it. Officers were called together and harangued by their superiors: General Montaudon made a 'warm appeal' to his subordinates' patriotism and sense of duty after being informed by Vinoy that two of his regiments had made pro-Commune demonstrations on their way to Versailles. He investigated the 'aptitude, zeal and willingness' of each, since many had been promoted during the war 'without any hierarchy and merely by the caprice of civilians commanding armies'. Similarly, General de la Mariouse addressed the senior officers of his brigade 'to urge them to make the officers understand . . . how important it was that the attitude of the troops should be unhesitating and of the utmost energy'. Thiers too was active, visiting the regiments and promising the officers that promotion won during the war would be confirmed for those who formed part of the Versailles army.[59] The fate of those who failed to measure up to these demands was also made clear: wherever a pretext could be found they were removed from the active list, and in flagrant cases court-martialled.

Thus stimulated, a number of officers tried actively to win over their men. Such a change seems to have been much needed, for it was not the custom for French officers, particularly senior ones, to look after the details of the men's daily lives, and complaints from the troops on this score were frequently reported; perhaps young recruits were more demanding than old soldiers would have been. According to the Marines at Satory, the officers were 'always at the café or . . . with whores, they abandon us, do not try to get to know us and do not seem friendly'. The bad food was their fault too: 'we are robbed, and we think that the officers live at our expense'. A police officer agreed that 'the officers in general do not take an interest in their men, who are young and inexperienced, and quite ready to do the right thing if . . . the officers would busy themselves less with their pleasures and explain to the men what position France is in'. To remedy this state of affairs, the officers at Trianon camp were reported to be making sure personally that the men had everything they needed. The colonel of the 67th was observed visiting his soldiers asking if they had been paid, if they were happy, and if they liked the food. The colonel of the 113th gave 100 francs to buy wine for his men. This sudden solicitude must have caused some cynical amusement among the old soldiers: 'ils ne se donnent pas dans cette marchandise-là'.[60]

To improve the physical conditions of the troops was an elementary first step for the authorities, especially as the police reports emphasized it as a cause of discontent. At Satory, the men were complaining about the food, and a company of the 91st *de marche*, recently arrived, claimed to have eaten only once in two days; the men were reported to be very sullen.[61] The government had to show that it cared more about the troops than did the Fédérés. A propaganda point was scored when army stragglers arrived destitute from Paris, and complained of the difficulties they had met with from the Fédérés, for no provision had been made for them by the Paris authorities after the first few days.[62] Consequently, Thiers took a personal interest in the food supply, but nevertheless there is no sign of extraordinary generosity on the part of the government. From 19 March, the troops were given a daily wine ration – only 25 centilitres, the normal campaign allowance – and a supplement to their pay of 25 centimes, raised the following day to 50. This was merely a temporary measure to compensate for the higher price of food due to the influx of troops and refugees into Versailles, and from 4 April the money was replaced by a daily meat ration of 300 grams (as compared with 500 in the British and 625 in the United States army at that time). In short, if steps were taken to remedy the worst supply problems, nothing unusual was done to bribe or pamper the troops, for under the French system they received little of their nominal pay, most of which was deducted for food.[63]

In general, conditions remained far from ideal. On 1 April, the 110th still had 390 men sick out of a total strength of about 1,500, thought to be due to camping in the cold and wet – for they were short of sleeping straw – and to the poor quality brandy ration, used for sterilizing drinking water. On 8 April, police reported that bad hospital conditions were affecting morale, and as late as 7 May a general complained in strong terms that the sick were still without clothes or bedding.[64]

While beginning to remedy the most obvious grievances, the authorities took steps to re-establish discipline by the orthodox military methods. The troops were not to be left idle: there was to be drill twice a day which all the officers were to attend. The latter were strictly forbidden to sleep out of camp, so that they could supervise and set an example to the men.[65] Orders were given to isolate the troops. As it was assumed that the troops in general, particularly those from the provinces, would have no predisposition to sympathize with the Fédérés, the intention was simply to prevent them from coming into contact with agitators whom the Commune was expected to send. A General Order (22 March) warned of 'agents' distributing 'unhealthy newspapers' and luring soldiers into wineshops 'where they were urged to revolt and not to fire on the people'.[66] It was feared that disbanded soldiers of the Army of Paris were arriving in Versailles to mix with their former comrades and spread propaganda: their arrest was ordered. Vinoy warned Faron on 31 March that his outposts were so easy to pass that soldiers were able to go and meet agitators in the surrounding villages. Even the women selling liquor inside Satory camp were thought to try to influence the soldiers so that they would refuse to fight.[67] The authorities overestimated the capacity of the Commune to organize sedition. The police do not seem ever to have caught any agitators, or found any inflammatory literature other than a song being sung in a café by some sailors, who had obtained it from a line soldier: it dealt at length with the perfidy of the generals, and was called 'Paris libre, ou, le Peuple et l'Armée'.[68] That pro-Commune propaganda was negligible was fortunate for the authorities, for their counter measures were of limited effectiveness.

It was impossible to confine the troops to their camps or barracks – some, in any case, were camping in Versailles itself – and many officers seem to have continued to lodge in town away from their men. When off duty, the soldiers mingled with civilians in bars and restaurants, and there was little the authorities could do to prevent it.[69] Soldiers at the outposts frequented the suburban villages, where it was feared they would obtain Paris newspapers, and even in the camps there were many outsiders, especially sellers of drink. It proved impossible to keep camp followers away, whether at Versailles or the outposts, in spite of repeated orders. Efforts were made: six women selling drink at Satory camp were ordered out of Versailles (those from Paris being sent back there); the same was done at the outposts, but they continued to linger nearby 'quarrelling and causing scandal'. Efforts to apply Vinoy's orders strictly could provoke disorder. On one occasion, a crowd of soldiers prevented the police from arresting two women seen leaving a soldier's tent.[70]

The authorities feared these civilian contacts not only as causes of drunkenness and disease, but also because it was reported that most drink stalls at Satory camp were meeting places for soldiers who liked to talk politics. 'Vendors and soldiers hold very animated conversations there and immediately go silent at the approach of an unknown civilian or an officer.'[71] Nevertheless, the attempt to exclude camp followers seems to have been dropped. Sellers of drink had merely to obtain a permit from the provost-marshal. Thiers later declared that he had ordered sentries to fire on unauthorized persons who approached the camps, but it seems that no such order was in fact given, let alone obeyed.[72]

Newspapers were another preoccupation of the authorities. At first, Vinoy gave orders that their sale should be absolutely forbidden in the camps and barracks. The police took steps to prevent the circulation of all Paris papers in Versailles; even those belonging to private citizens arriving from Paris were confiscated at the railway stations. A certain traffic went on in the suburbs as enterprising sellers tried to profit from the demand. Those caught merely had their stocks confiscated.[73] It would seem on the whole that the police were successful in preventing the distribution of pro-Commune papers: there were very few reports indeed of the troops reading them. The importance of this, when most of the newly arrived officers and men knew little or nothing about the causes of the conflict, can hardly be exaggerated. For the moment, there was no attempt at counter propaganda: soldiers were not supposed to think.

Having done what was possible to remove the men from subversive influences, Vinoy took measures of what he called 'necessary severity'.[74] The events in Paris culminating in the failure of 18 March had shown the extent to which discipline had collapsed. The disorganization of units due to demobilization, added to the demoralization caused by defeat, had meant that little was left of the mutual acquaintance and respect between officers and men upon which, ideally, discipline is based; more to the point in these circumstances, the fear of detection and punishment for acts of indiscipline was slight. To alter this, two men of the 110th were ordered on 24 March to appear before a *Conseil de Guerre* (the highest military tribunal), accused of having said that they would refuse to fight against the National Guard. On the 26th, *Conseils de Discipline* (regimental tribunals) were ordered to be re-established, and close enquiries made into the activities of men arriving late from Paris. Vinoy himself retained the final word in deciding punishments. On the 27th, the military police (*prévôté*) was organized, and the same day two men of the 109th were sentenced to thirty days' cells for being absent for two days, and another two men received sixty days – the maximum administrative punishment – for a four day absence. The 88th and 120th, because 'Some officers and most NCOs and men . . . betrayed their duties', were disbanded, the officers placed on half pay, and the other ranks sent to North Africa. The decree was to be read three times to the troops on parade.[75]

It is as difficult to gauge the effect of these far from radical measures as it is to judge the extent of the disaffection that provoked them. The historian, like Thiers and Vinoy, is aware only that it existed and could not be ignored. That the authorities took the problem seriously is clear: the Minister of War was frequently informed even of trivial matters, and rapid action taken at the highest levels. For example, the report that soldiers were discussing politics at camp drink stalls on 5 April was passed on to Vinoy on the 6th, and action was taken by the gendarmes the same day.[76] In deciding whether or not the fears of the authorities were justified, the historian has few advantages over them, other than that of hindsight: and this shows how important the problem of morale remained throughout the civil war. The later writings of some of the officers give additional information concerning their state of mind and that of their colleagues. No such advantage exists when considering the rank and file: memoirs written by ordinary soldiers of the Versailles army are conspicuous by their absence. This may be significant, for in a conscript army, many men are literate, as is shown by the number of books they wrote dealing with the war against the Prussians. Perhaps the rank and file found the experience of the war against the Commune so inglorious that they were reluctant to record their participation.

The impression given by the evidence as a whole is that 'the spirit of the troops in general is . . . very lukewarm'.[77] If there was resentment against the government for provoking the conflict, there were few signs of enthusiasm for the Parisian cause, about which the newly arrived soldiers from the provinces knew little. Their most frequently reported grievances were not political, but rather against their officers, the food, living conditions, and the police and gendarmes – common enemy of the ordinary people of Paris and of the soldiers from the provinces. Otherwise, the men's opinions wavered: the young recruits 'do not know and do not understand what they are saying (the war is finished so why are we fighting) . . . They agree with and approve whoever is the last to speak to them; they are completely ignorant of what they have to do.'[78]

The army was in no condition to take the offensive. The officers, it was reported, would be unable to control the men if they found themselves in the same circumstances as a few days previously – that is to say, as on 18 March.[79] Even if they did not fraternize or desert, there were forms of passive resistance less easy to detect. 'If they make me march against the Parisians, I shall march', said a *chasseur* of the 17th battalion, 'but in no case will I fire on them, and every other member of the army must do the same.' On the other hand, if the Parisians attacked, many soldiers were reported to say that 'they would defend themselves . . . but they would not march on Paris'.[80] Unfortunately for Paris, the Fédérés attacked on 3 April, and the small number of Versailles troops engaged did indeed 'defend themselves'. Inevitably, as time went on and the fighting increased in intensity, this minimum and grudging commitment to Versailles grew. The ties between the troops and the people of Paris became more tenuous: the men had little idea of what was happening in the city, except from Versailles sources, and the attitude of the Communards towards them became at best ambiguous, and often greatly hostile. There was no longer the immense pressure to disobey and break away from the army, as there had been on 18 March, when the alternative to surrender was to fire at point-blank range on a friendly crowd and risk battle with overwhelming numbers of Fédérés. Then, the soldiers had merely to take the line of least resistance in order to find themselves on the side of Paris; once in Versailles, it required an ever increasing effort to do so, as chaos in the army gave way to a degree of order, and desertion and disobedience entailed serious risks. It became the policy of the Versaillais to ensure that the army was never again exposed to a test such as that of 18 March. A rapid assault on Paris, as advocated by some Right-wing Deputies, was therefore out of the question.

5

Civil war

In the light of what has been said concerning the weakness and unreliability of the army and the caution this imposed on the government, the question of how an acute political crisis turned into a full-scale civil war takes on a special significance. If, as has generally been supposed, the fighting started because the Versaillais decided that the time was ripe to attack Paris, then the argument of the last chapter is clearly fallacious. For if the government felt strong enough to begin an offensive deliberately on 2 April, it cannot be assumed that it knew the army to be weak and had therefore attempted to reach a compromise, or even that a violent conflict with the 'reds' had not been all along an object of its calculations. Secondly, there is the question of how the army came to fight at all, given its reluctance on 18 March and afterwards. Had the problem of discipline been solved? Had it been exaggerated? A detailed examination of how hostilities actually began is therefore necessary.

The activity of the army during the last week of March was limited to watching the approaches to Versailles and carrying out cautious patrols, as reports from Paris became more ominous. In the early hours of 27 March, a battalion of the 109th *de ligne* and a squadron of cavalry, commanded by General de Galliffet, were sent to reconnoitre to the south of Paris, through Petit Bicêtre, Châtillon and Sceaux; another battalion patrolled from Satory camp along the valley of the Bièvre. Galliffet had received instructions, he claimed, to take the Châtillon redoubt by surprise. Although the redoubt – a large earthwork on high ground covering the southern road to Versailles – was found to be unoccupied, and Galliffet was able to enter with a few horsemen, an order came from Thiers to return to Versailles. The exercise had been a defensive one: Thiers was nervous about the possibility of a night attack by the Fédérés, in spite of the generals' scepticism, and on the 26th information had arrived that the Fédérés were planning a sortie to

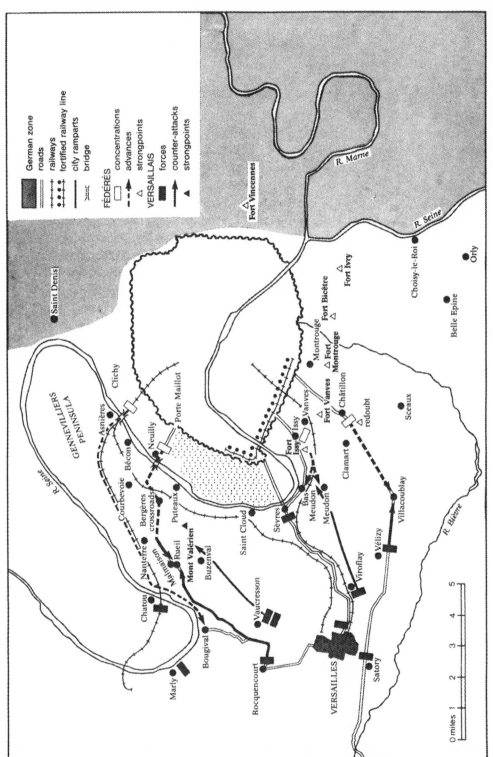

Map 2. The sortie of 3 April.

the south.[1] The following day Galliffet was transferred to Saint Germain-en-Laye to patrol the Gennevilliers peninsula, in a loop of the Seine to the north of Versailles. Perhaps this assignment was connected with a report that the Fédérés of northern Paris planned to march on Versailles 'to chase away or dissolve the Assembly'.[2] For the moment, however, all remained calm, except for an occasional exchange of shots at Sèvres, apparently too trivial to be reported officially.

The Fédérés too were carrying out patrols. On the 29th, 150 men from Fort Issy (which, with the other Left Bank forts, had been occupied two days after the army withdrew) marched along the railway line towards Meudon and arrested a civilian (later released) suspected of being a policeman. The following day, fifty men appeared at Clamart, urging the inhabitants to hold immediate elections.[3] This was harmless enough (though considered sufficiently important for Thiers to be informed), but the government had begun to receive more disquieting reports from sources in Paris. A rumour that Thiers was to be replaced by an Orleanist prince, the Duc d'Aumale, which had helped to decide the mayors of Paris to sign an agreement with the Central Committee to hold the Commune elections on 26 April, was circulating in Paris. Aumale was said to be already at Versailles, and about to be named Regent. Fédéré battalions, the report stated, were to march on Versailles to prevent this.[4] On 30 March, more information arrived: a Fédéré NCO had said that 150,000 National Guards were ready to march on Versailles that night or the next; fifty *bataillons de marche* (the active service units of the National Guard) were said to be ready to move, and 100 horses had been requisitioned to pull artillery; Fédérés posted near the Hôtel de Ville had been overheard discussing a march on Versailles.[5]

This information, however exaggerated, was not baseless. In Paris the popular newspapers were demanding a sortie, and talking of the journey to Versailles 'as if it were a promenade'; and at a public meeting at the Salle de la Marseillaise, at La Villette, there was much talk of marching on Versailles.[6] The Fédérés, stirred into action by the National Guard of Order, interrupted rail traffic, and the rumour spread that the city gates were to be closed, which caused traffic jams of those eager to leave while there was still time.[7] There was much marching and counter marching by National Guard battalions, and the new Fédéré generals proclaimed that 'we must act and severely punish the enemies of the Republic'.[8] Echoes of this naturally reached Versailles.

On Friday 31st, the warnings continued: men of the National Guard were heard saying that fourteen new battalions would be ready by Saturday or Sunday, and that 40,000 or 50,000 men would march on Versailles. 'There is much talk of a sortie', reported the police on 31 March. 'It is certain that they are organizing combat companies and requisitioning horses for the artillery . . . There was a rumour [in the 11th *arrondissement*] that next Sunday [1 April] 200,000 very determined National Guards would attack Versailles.'[9] These rumours must have been circulating widely in Versailles, for on the same day appeared a press report that the National Guards were organizing gun batteries, *bataillons de marche* and scouts, ordering stocks of explosives and preventing horses from leaving the city: 'What can their intentions be? To take the offensive, without any doubt.'[10] Warnings of Fédéré movements were arriving too from more direct sources. The commander of the hilltop fortress of Mont Valérien, Colonel Lochner, telegraphed to Vinoy that same morning that the gates of Paris were closed and no one allowed to enter, that detachments of Fédérés had crossed the river to the Courbevoie crossroads, and that the call to arms had been beaten in the neighbouring villages.[11] Earlier that morning, Galliffet had arrived on the spot with two squadrons of cavalry, surrounded and disarmed the Fédérés at the Courbevoie crossroads, and advanced as far as the Neuilly bridge. This was occupied by National Guards who informed him of their intention to be 'masters in their own house'. There was no fighting: 'I had forbidden my men to use their weapons.' In his report Galliffet urged the occupation of Courbevoie and the Neuilly bridge. This would prevent the Fédérés from moving their forces to the Versailles side of the Seine. Returning to the crossroads, he released the 200 Fédérés held by his men, and gave them back their rifles. He then withdrew, and the National Guard promptly reinforced their outpost at Courbevoie.[12] Colonel Lochner complained that Galliffet's patrols had no useful results. On the contrary, they were provoking a reaction from the Fédérés, who had begun to send patrols into the villages between the fortress and Paris. Trains had been stopped, the village of Puteaux had been occupied, many workers had left the factories, and a fatigue party from the fort had been cut off.[13]

Vinoy had more important concerns. Just before 9 p.m. he telegraphed to the fort, 'It is believed that the insurgents wish to attempt an attack on Versailles. Keep attentive watch, and if a force passes near you, moving on our positions, fire on it with cannon.'[14] At midnight, General Valentin, Prefect of Police, warned that a trustworthy person had heard a Fédéré officer order his men to be ready to leave for Versailles that night. The informant had brought the message late that evening, passing by way of Courbevoie, and saw on the way 'a fairly large number' of National Guards, including 'several thousand' at Puteaux.[15] No attack materialized during the night, though the Fédérés seemed to be continuing to increase their forces. During the early hours of 1 April, the Ministry of War passed on two more police reports to General Vinoy, one saying that there were already 12,000 Fédérés between Asnières (the site of the second intact bridge over the Seine) and Courbevoie, with more expected; the other giving details of Fédéré positions in the area – the 132nd battalion had dislodged the local National Guard from Asnières station and was checking the trains from Paris (and drinking 'on credit' in the neighbourhood), and there were also four or five battalions at Courbevoie with outposts at the crossroads and along the Nanterre road.[16]

By 6 a.m. Mont Valérien could see what was happening. A company of National Guards had arrived at the Bergères crossroads halfway between Courbevoie and the fort. It began to advance slowly towards Nanterre, a mile and a half to the west. Lochner telegraphed to Vinoy that these preparations seemed to indicate that the Fédérés intended to occupy the Gennevilliers peninsula.[17] This was most important because it would enable the Fédérés to build up their forces on the Versailles side of the Seine, using the two intact bridges, and then to advance through open country on Versailles itself; it would also enable them to cut off and neutralize Mont Valérien. Early that afternoon, Galliffet estimated the Fédérés' strength as 800 at Neuilly, 500 at Courbevoie and 200–300 at Nanterre – far more men than he himself had: 'I await your orders, but to act need infantry.' Apparently none was sent, for soon afterwards his outpost at La Malmaison informed him that the Fédérés appeared to be advancing on Rueil, south of Nanterre, forcing Galliffet's men to retire. He warned Vinoy that he expected Rueil to be occupied by the Fédérés before evening.[18] This would have placed them between Mont Valérien and Versailles.

Throughout the afternoon of 1 April, the Fédérés continued to advance. At 5.50, Lochner transmitted information from the mayor of Nanterre that his commune was being invaded and the population alarmed. In the evening, Galliffet made a cavalry demonstration, which caused the Fédérés to evacuate Nanterre, but he remained worried, for their forces were still growing. He left two squadrons at La Malmaison, deciding to spend the night there in case of emergency.[19]

Vinoy was not unduly alarmed. He asked General Faron to exercise the greatest vigilance; 'although no attack is reliably reported, we must be ready for any eventuality'.[20] The Parisian authorities' view of the situation was remarkably similar: 'Rumours of attack circulating; so make sure of . . . the battalions guarding the gates; however, in our view attack improbable tonight.'[21]

The immediate cause of this mutual apprehension may well have been Galliffet's activities round Courbevoie and Neuilly, which, as Lochner noticed, had provoked counter measures on the part of the Fédérés, which in turn had been reported to Versailles. It seems evident that neither side was preparing to attack the other at that moment. But if Galliffet, among the Versaillais, was reckless enough to risk precipitating a conflict, he had his counterparts in Paris. That same day, Rossel (who had been appointed commander of the 17th National Guard Legion) was discussing in a letter to the Fédéré General Bergeret, who had asked for his advice, the preparations that would be necessary for an attack on Mont Valérien – an operation which was 'as serious with regard to the number of troops it requires as a march on Versailles'. It could be done, thought Rossel, with 30,000 men. Already that day he had sent a force to secure the crossroads at Courbevoie.[22]

Vinoy, though sceptical, took sensible precautions. In case of attack, the army would cover Versailles on three sides: Grenier's division was to take up a position at Rocquencourt, a mile and a half north-east of the Château of Versailles; Bruat's division was to place a brigade on Grenier's left, and keep the other back in Versailles; Montaudon's division was to move up on Bruat's right, on the Vaucresson road; Faron was to continue to guard the approaches from Sèvres, with de la Mariouse and the gendarmes at Meudon and the river crossing, and Derroja further south; Susbielle was to defend the approaches to Satory, south of Versailles, with Maud'huy in reserve in the camp itself; and Pellé, Vergé and Du Barail (cavalry) were to remain in reserve. The Garde Républicaine and the police were to form up in the centre of Versailles to protect the Assembly and Thiers's residence.[23] Nothing could be more prudent and less aggressive: the bulk of the army, now about 55,000 men, was to be held within a couple of miles of Versailles.

Thiers was not satisfied, however. He believed reports that an attack was imminent, and only the day before he had told the American Minister, Washburne, that the troops 'cannot be depended upon'.[24] He could have had little taste for waiting in Versailles to be attacked, with such unreliable defenders. Perhaps he preferred to find out more about the Fédérés' intentions, halt their incursions, and meet their attack, if it came, as far away from Versailles as possible. If the worst happened, at least he and the Assembly would have the chance to escape: there was already discussion of its leaving for Tours, Bordeaux or Rambouillet.[25] At 11 p.m. on 1 April he called a council of war. It was decided that a reconnaissance in force would be made next morning. A column of infantry, with some of Galliffet's calvalry, was to advance towards Courbevoie and Neuilly, where the main threat seemed to be coming from. They were not to move, however, until General Du Barail in person had reconnoitred to the south of Paris at daybreak, to make sure that no attack was being mounted from that side. It was finally decided that Vinoy would direct the main operation in person, after the general originally chosen had refused the task, on the grounds that the troops were so unreliable that he would not be responsible for the outcome.[26] The army, moreover, was unprepared for a large-scale action: stocks of artillery ammunition in Versailles were low, with no immediate prospect of their being replenished.[27]

Du Barail's patrol advanced towards Châtillon in the darkness, almost colliding with a force of infantry which an agitated Thiers had sent forward as an extra precaution without telling anyone. The Châtillon redoubt was occupied by Fédérés, but they did not fire, merely calling out to the soldiers to join them. At dawn it was clear that no attack was planned, and Du Barail sent to tell Vinoy that he could proceed. Vinoy warned Mont Valérien that 'une petite opération' was about to take place.[28]

The expedition marched in two columns: one a brigade of Bruat's division (74th *de marche*, a regiment of Marines and a regiment of sailors) accompanied by Vinoy, and the other Daudel's brigade (113th and 114th *de ligne*), thought to be among the most reliable troops. They assembled, in mid-morning, just north of Mont Valérien. Galliffet's cavalry, with half a battery of guns, had been ordered up in support, making a total force of about 9,000. Vinoy had halted a few hundred yards from the Courbevoie crossroads, which was defended by loopholed houses and a barricade of carts and barrels. It was planned to send the 113th to join Galliffet, who would then outflank the Fédérés from the north. Before this could be done the first shots were fired, and the chief surgeon of the army, Dr Pasquier, who had become separated from the main body, was killed. Galliffet placed his guns in battery, and ordered them to open fire. The men made no move. Just as serious, the 113th had stopped their advance at the first shots, and some of the soldiers began to run. Those at the gun battery could hear the shouts of the officers of the 113th as they tried to rally their men, some galloping after them on horseback, with swords raised. 'There was a minute of anguish; I shall remember it all my life': Galliffet and his staff dismounted, their revolvers drawn, and at pistol point the gunners at last opened fire.[29] Hearing Galliffet's cannon, Vinoy ordered his own artillery into action and then, struck by the disarray among the Fédérés, ordered the 74th *de marche* forward. Skirmishers led the advance towards the barricade but, meeting a volley of fire from one of the adjoining houses, turned and ran. The panic spread to the whole battalion and to the artillery: all the gun-crews, even the N C Os, fled with the horses, leaving the officers standing. The soldiers in their panic fired their rifles as they ran away from the Fédérés, sending bullets over the heads of Vinoy and his staff. Vinoy rode up to the regiment of sailors in reserve with the intention of leading them forward in person to try to save the situation.[30] His powers of leadership were not tested, however, for the Fédérés, outnumbered and with their flank threatened, abandoned their position and retreated across the Seine, about thirty being taken prisoner. The Marines and the 74th followed as far as Neuilly bridge, taking its protective barricade which offered no real resistance. Strict orders from Thiers prevented further advance. At 1.15 p.m., Vinoy reported the reconnaissance over. The army losses were three killed (including Pasquier) and twenty-one wounded.[31]

One thing remained to be done before returning to camp. Vinoy ordered Colonel Boulanger to bring forward the 114th, which had taken no part in the fighting. The prisoners were assembled. Wrote Boulanger:

I could not be more satisfied with the attitude and conduct of my regiment. The curses that all those brave fellows hurled in the faces of the captured insurgents, the desire they all showed to measure themselves against the scoundrels, and finally the promptness with which a platoon placed itself at my disposal to shoot five of the wretched murderers whom we were holding . . . permit me to affirm . . . that you can count on them always and everywhere.[32]

Evidence from less interested parties hardly bears out this account of the regiment's loyalty, but where it was a question of demonstrating devotion to his superiors' wishes, Boulanger had few equals.[33] It is not difficult to imagine his stage-management of the spectacle. Five men were shot: the supposed killer of Pasquier, twenty-two-year-old Louis Pesme, a barber from the Faubourg Saint Antoine, two soldiers who had joined the Fédérés, and two other National Guards. The executions were carried out in a field so that the other prisoners could be brought to watch.[34] The incident was soon public knowledge: groups of soldiers discussed it at Versailles and it was being talked about the same day in Paris, where one rumour stated that 200 had been shot.[35] *Le Gaulois* (4 April) reported accurately that the executions were performed on Vinoy's orders. *Le Soir* produced an interpretation which was frequently reapplied over the following weeks and became practically official, for it shifted responsibility from the officers to the men. It described one of the 'assassins' being caught by the soldiers, who, 'without orders . . . fired, and laid him dead on the body of his victim'.[36] The official version in Paris similarly obscured the identity of the true culprits. As it was believed (or at least claimed) that the army as a whole was well disposed towards the Fédérés, it was asserted that those involved in the fighting and the executions on 2 April were men specially chosen for their hostility to the Commune: policemen in army uniform, gendarmes or Papal Zouaves. This became and has remained the accepted version: 'The gendarmes . . . took five . . . and shot them at the foot of Mont Valérien.'[37]

Vinoy's orders were clear:

To confirm my verbal instructions concerning prisoners . . . I again request you to treat according to the laws of war, that is to say to execute immediately by firing squad, all soldiers, Mobiles or sailors taken in the ranks of the insurgents. . . . These men must be considered as deserters to the enemy and consequently shot on the spot. As for the others, they will be sent before the military tribunals.[38]

There is no reason to suppose that the government was necessarily aware beforehand of Vinoy's intentions. His relations with Ministers were not good – he had twice offered his resignation as a protest against their interference – and his powers as Commander-in-Chief in a region under martial law were extensive. By background and temperament he was likely to favour harsh measures against the insurgents. Extremely jealous of his rights, he was capable of taking it upon himself to decide such a policy, and his later conduct shows that shooting Communards was very much a personal concern.[39]

One of the excuses for this first shooting of prisoners was the 'murder' of Dr Pasquier, which was to become one of the mainstays of Versaillais propaganda. This incident, and the reprisals that followed, though only the first of many, helped to bring the developing conflict to a head, particularly in Paris, where feeling against Versailles reached a new intensity. Many said, it was reported, that because Versailles had 'given the order to take no prisoners among the patriots, the cannon must have the last word'.[40] The Versailles press reacted similarly. *Le Gaulois* (4 April) commented, 'Against murderers such as these, pity is inconceivable.' Pessard, in *Le Soir* (Versailles edition, 4 April), wrote: 'Unfortunately, we have no longer to seek peaceful solutions. The facts silence us.'

Vinoy claimed success for the operation: 'Moral effect most satisfactory.'[41] Perhaps he had feared a repetition of 18 March, and was grateful for having avoided it, if only narrowly. The pack had been blooded, as one member of the government put it,[42] but none the less it had bitten feebly and after much hesitation. Both attacking units, the 113th and 74th, had run away, as had Vinoy's gunners, giving, as their commander admitted, 'a poor impression'; the guns they had abandoned had to be hauled back by the sappers.[43] Galliffet's gunners had only obeyed orders at pistol point. The 74th, which had already lost forty-four men through desertion, returned to camp with another seventy missing, though it had suffered only five casualties.[44]

Some of these men were seen later that day with the Fédérés in the Champs Elysées, where a large crowd of sightseers had assembled, drawn by the sound of gunfire. Among those present (as well as the inevitable police agent, who counted twenty-six men of the 74th) were General Cluseret, soon to become the War Delegate of the Commune, the American Minister, Washburne, and a journalist who reported cries of 'Vive la ligne', and the taking of a collection for the deserters. Washburne, however, thought that they 'made no response, nor evinced any desire to fraternize'. Cluseret heard them declaring that 'they did not understand. They had been taken on a route march, then there was shooting: they did not know what it was all about.'[45] They were showing, in short, the bewildered hesitancy that had, since the beginning, been the most general reaction of the rank and file.

An enquiry was ordered into the desertions. The company commanders assumed that the missing men, nearly all young recruits of the Class of 1870, must at first have hidden in the houses because they were frightened, and then given in to the urging of the inhabitants not to take part in the civil war. On the whole, the blame was placed on certain NCOs who were Parisians or had relations in Paris; it was supposed that they must have led their colleagues and subordinates astray. In the case of eight young Bretons – 'they hardly know a word of French' – it was suggested that they must have hidden through fright. The officers of the regiment had a personal interest in explaining away this embarrassing lapse, and their attempts to do so are perhaps more reliable as evidence of their presuppositions (or of their ideas of what their superiors would find plausible) than as true explanations. They assumed that only Parisians, or those with contacts there, would have reason to desert. They explain the disappearance of provincials (the Bretons and a dozen men from the Côte d'Or) and 'bons sujets' as being due to panic or accident.[46] The extent of the unwillingness to become involved in a civil war – whether on the side of Versailles or of Paris – was still not realized.

Misled, perhaps, by the ease with which the Fédérés had been routed at Courbevoie, Vinoy and Galliffet, at his important listening-post, were slow to comprehend the violence of the Parisian reaction to the allegedly unprovoked attack by imaginary Chouan volunteers and Papal Zouaves.[47] The Commune began to prepare its counter offensive at once. A council of war was held that very afternoon at the Place Vendôme, National Guard headquarters, where, according to Rossel, 'nothing important was said', and which he left after having obtained permission to reoccupy Courbevoie.[48] Whether important or not, by 3.47 p.m. National Guard headquarters was able to inform the Executive Commission of the Commune of a plan for a three-pronged attack on Versailles, and by 5 p.m. Duval had left with a column for the Châtillon plateau.[49] His force was to form the left of the attack. The centre, under Eudes, was to take the shorter route through Meudon, and the right, under Bergeret and Flourens, was to advance on Versailles through the Gennevilliers peninsula. The Fédérés began to assemble during the afternoon, and their movements continued all night. Galliffet was unsuspecting: 'Courbevoie and Puteaux have been patrolled. Nothing to report. The inhabitants willingly relate that the Committee will retake tomorrow the positions it lost today. I do not believe it, but I shall keep watch.'[50]

The police gave the first warning: the call to arms had been beaten all over Paris, horses had been requisitioned to pull guns, and there was talk of an attack on Versailles. Late that night, Vinoy ordered Lochner at Mont Valérien to watch for and report on possible movements during the night and the next morning. Soon after, another police report passed on information from someone who had just arrived from Paris and had seen a force of Fédérés (which he estimated at 30,000) with thirty guns at the Porte d'Italie; he had heard a Fédéré captain say that they were going to march on Versailles through Châtillon, while another 60,000 attacked through Rueil. The information was passed to General Faron, with the instruction to have de la Mariouse and Derroja stand to arms and send out scouts.[51] Soon the whole army was alerted: 'it is announced that the call to arms has been beaten in Paris and that the insurgents intend to move on Versailles via Courbevoie and Châtillon'. Garnier's division was to move forward to Vaucresson, about two miles north-east of Versailles (which it did at 4 a.m.), with Wolff's brigade in support. Mounted gendarmes were to scout ahead to watch for an attack over Neuilly bridge. Vergé's division was to be ready to march if needed, as was Susbielle's at Satory, which was ready to move by 5 a.m. A brigade of Bruat's division was to be placed in reserve at the gates of Versailles. As one of its units, the 75th *de marche*, was moving into position through the woods, a watching policeman saw soldiers throwing away their rifles and running off into the trees.[52]

The Fédérés had lost the advantage of surprise; fortunately for Versailles, this was not their only handicap. They had no conception of the reality of the task they faced, believing that the army would come over to their side, and so it was only a question of 'chasing out old Thiers'. The previous day's fighting was officially explained away as the work of a handful of policemen and fanatics. The Fédéré commanders were as confident as their men.[53] Presumably they relied on weight of numbers, which barely materialized, and revolutionary fervour – the *levée en masse*, at last – to compensate for the lack of a detailed plan, reserves or supplies, and of officers experienced enough to turn the crowd into an army should the expedition turn into a battle.

The terrain was against them. The Versaillais had to defend a line of naturally strong wooded heights from Buzenval to Meudon, which the Prussians had fortified to defend their headquarters at Versailles. These defences remained almost intact. There were three routes to Versailles on the south side of Paris: through Châtillon, the longest but the easiest, for it passed through open country – this was Duval's route; the second, through Meudon wood, passed only a few hundred yards from the Prussian-built redoubts and batteries at Meudon, a fortress of trenches, barricades, loopholed walls, dugouts and obstacles; the third and shortest route, through Les Moulineaux, passed close to the Versaillais positions on the high ground overlooking the Pont de Sèvres. Besides, the second and third routes crossed woodland, doubly difficult because of the cover it provided for the defenders, and because the Fédérés were not trained to split up their columns and advance in skirmishing order – impossible for raw troops under raw commanders.[54] These were the routes taken by Eudes's forces. On the northern flank of the attack, the Fédérés would have to pass under the guns of Mont Valérien before even arriving at the first line of Prussian defences on the Buzenval heights – the same defences that had halted the French sortie of 21 October and which 'at this point . . . were at their deepest and thickest'.[55] It was on this flank that the fighting began.

Perhaps because it had taken no part in the fighting of the previous day, and because of the ambiguous answer given by Lochner to a National Guard deputation which came to demand possession of the fortress on 20 March, Mont Valérien was thought on the Parisian side to be neutral.[56] At 6.30 a.m. the Fédéré column reached the Bergères crossroads, and the fortress opened fire with eight guns. 'At the first shell, great panic; the main part of the column . . . has scattered.'[57] The main effect had been one of surprise, for there had only been about thirty casualties,[58] and the attack continued. A second force, on the

2 Prussian dugouts used by the Versaillais.

3   Versaillais sailors on watch.

right of the first, which Lochner estimated at 15,000 men, was already approaching Nanterre, and the fire of the fortress was unable to halt it. Mont Valérien continued to fire throughout the morning, but with less effect: the Fédérés had begun to advance in small groups across the fields and in the ditches, keeping their distance. At 10.05, Lochner reported that he was running short of shells, and after 11 a.m. his fire slackened.[59]

Meanwhile, Vinoy had warned Galliffet of the attack, and told him to do what he could on his side. Galliffet moved up his two regiments of *chasseurs* and the pro-government Saint Germain National Guard on both sides of the river to Marly and Chatou. A sizeable force of Fédérés had already arrived on the east bank, and Mont Valérien reported another 10,000 marching in that direction along the riverside, out of the effective range of its guns. Galliffet at Chatou asked for reinforcements and reported that the 3,000 Fédérés facing him had not pressed their attack. 'Three who had crossed the river in arms were killed' – in fact, captured and shot on the orders of Galliffet,

4 Mont Valérien firing on the Fédéré column.

who thereupon published a proclamation warning of the dangers of rebellion.[60]

The main force of Fédérés continued to move south in the direction of Versailles, only five miles away. By two o'clock, Galliffet's artillery and National Guards were out of ammunition. Vinoy had moved up with reinforcements, however, and the Fédérés, incapable of maintaining the momentum of their advance without plan or reserves, had begun to drift back towards Paris.[61] Boulanger's 114th *de ligne* was the first unit of Vinoy's reserve to be engaged that afternoon, being ordered to clear Flourens's men from the village of Bougival, on the southern bend of the Seine north of Versailles. Boulanger was dubious, having only 1,400 men against 7,000–8,000 said to be with Flourens, but the order was definite. The 114th was to be supported by the 113th on its flank, and a battery of guns in the old Prussian position on the hill of La Jonchère, which Vinoy had remembered from the siege. The troops were to search and disarm the villages they took.[62] Evidently, by this time the Fédérés had given up their attempt to reach

Versailles, for Boulanger was able to reoccupy Bougival in the early afternoon with the loss of only one man wounded. Once more, he showed a murderous zeal: 'the soldiers searched the houses and shot every National Guard who was hidden'. In this case, the shootings cannot be explained as the actions of angry and over-excited soldiers: the 114th hardly fought and its total casualties were one killed and two wounded, out of 1,400 men.[63] Comparison with the 113th, who performed the same task, is enlightening: 'my men, in accordance with instructions, operated with mildness and conciliation'; the town crier of Rueil proclaimed the order to hand in firearms, with 'full success', 400 being collected without difficulty.[64] It seems evident that Boulanger's severity was, in part at least, inspired by his eagerness to curry favour with his superiors. The retreating Fédérés were pursued across the peninsula by General du Preuil's cavalry division, which included a brigade of mounted gendarmes; an officer of the 2nd regiment, Captain Demaret, killed Flourens, who had been taken prisoner.[65]

On the other side of Paris, the Fédérés fared no better. At the beginning of the day, as nothing seemed to be happening, the Versailles forces, which had been on the alert since the early hours, relaxed. Susbielle's division was sent back to camp, and Derroja's brigade withdrew to make their soup. It was then that Duval advanced from Châtillon, and was able to reach Villacoublay, halfway to Versailles. Derroja, with Péchot's brigade (70th and 71st *de marche*) in support, spent most of the day pushing the Fédérés back to Châtillon, taking about fifty prisoners. The fighting was less than fierce: the Versaillais suffered only thirteen casualties, perhaps because Duval had no artillery and ran short of ammunition.[66]

At Meudon, Eudes's men, like their comrades at Courbevoie, advanced lightheartedly, many without ammunition. Some even thought that Mont Valérien's cannonade in the distance must be directed against the Versaillais. Although large numbers of Fédérés arrived on the scene, their advantage was reduced by lack of direction: 'no leaders to give orders; the National Guard officers lost their heads'.[67] The advancing column, marching along the railway line, was broken up by a salvo of shells (probably from the Prussian-built batteries at Meudon), fortunately aimed too high. The rear of the column ran back towards Fort Issy, but the leading units charged into Meudon, only to find themselves mixed up with other units like 'a flock of sheep', with no idea what to do next.[68] A little to the west, at lower Meudon, it was the same, and Cluseret, who was present, had the same impression – 'a flock of sheep'.[69] The gendarmes defending Meudon were outnumbered and hard pressed, firing off 100 rounds per man and having to send for more ammunition. Eudes managed to force them out of the château, which he then occupied. But the gendarmes held on in the village thanks to positions fortified by the Prussians, and support from guns placed in the former Prussian batteries; the confused Fédérés could make no further progress. By early afternoon, de la Mariouse's brigade had reoccupied the château, and a regiment of sailors, one of Marines and two of infantry of the line had arrived – about 9,000 men in all – to support the thousand or so gendarmes and the few hundred policemen, reversing the Fédérés temporary numerical advantage.[70] The Fédérés' attack had totally disintegrated: 'It was all confusion, talking, drinking and panic.'[71]

The loyalty and discipline of the Versailles troops had not therefore been severely tested, in spite of certain problems caused by numbers and shortage of ammunition, the limited stock for artillery in Versailles being exhausted.[72] At 4.10 p.m., Vinoy reported that fighting was over.[73] The small number of casualties testifies to the ease with which the sortie had been contained:[74] even the Versailles troops, raw and unsteady as they were, had been more than a match for the well meaning mob that came against them. The Fédérés had withdrawn: Bergeret was at Asnières with 10,000 men and no food; a crowd of National Guards was settling down for the night at Issy village; Duval had several thousand men in the Châtillon redoubt. At 6.30 Galliffet patrolled forward and found that all was quiet, and at 9 p.m. Thiers telegraphed news of victory to the provincial authorities.[75]

In private he was less confident. The following day, 4 April, he sent an officer to General Pellé warning him that 'tomorrow there is to be a big sortie from Paris against our outposts'. The same day, Vinoy ordered Vergé to send a brigade to reinforce Faron at Meudon, as 'reliable information indicates that the enemy is to attack us today via Châtillon'. Faron reported having taken precautionary measures in case of a sortie from the directions of Meudon and Châtillon. Given these fears on the part of the Versaillais, it seems probable that the attack they themselves carried out on 4 April on the Châtillon redoubt was intended to seize that vital position in order to block an expected Fédéré offensive.[76]

The attack on the redoubt was carried out by units of Péchot's brigade (70th and 71st *de marche*), with the rest of Pellé's division and Derroja's brigade in support. Resistance was slight, and the position was rushed by four companies of the 70th. Derroja's 109th on their flank swung round to the Fédérés' rear. According to one account, Derroja himself was leading them, and he noticed some of the men raise the butts of their rifles (as a sign that they did not intend to fight). Tapping one of the men on the head with his revolver, Derroja called out 'you're making a mistake, comrade, that's not the end you shoot with'. Cluseret refers to the same or a similar incident, as does Elie Reclus, who was told it by a Fédéré captain. The troops, he relates, called out 'Vive la République', to which the Fédérés replied, themselves raising their rifle butts, allowing the troops to approach. But the Fédérés were then ordered to surrender, a shot was fired, and a confused mêlée followed. Naturally, the Fédérés assumed that they had been tricked; it is hardly likely, however, that the Versaillais commanders would risk coaching their men in such a dangerous manoeuvre. Knowing the attitude of the 109th, it seems more likely that it was a genuine attempt to fraternize by some of the men which Derroja, said to be a popular commander, was able to handle.[77]

Lissagaray states that the defenders of the redoubt surrendered because General Pellé offered to guarantee their lives. Nevertheless, Vinoy's orders concerning the treatment of prisoners were carried out, in spite of the objections of one of Pellé's officers who was escorting them to Versailles. Vinoy himself set the example by ordering the execution of Duval and two of his officers.[78] A police officer saw the bodies of five men of the National Guard who had been executed, and those of a sergeant of *zouaves* and a Mobile. Another police officer was told that eighteen prisoners who refused to march had been shot.[79] In an attempt to deter the Versaillais from continuing these shootings, the Commune passed on 7 April its Decree on Hostages, though without putting it into effect. The shootings continued and the arrest of hostages, particularly the Archbishop of Paris, had no other result than further to damage the reputation of the Commune, especially abroad. As if to justify the shooting of prisoners by the army, a report circulated in Versailles that nine soldiers made prisoner by the Fédérés had been shot.[80]

There was no fighting on 5 April. Although the expected sortie did not materialize, the fears of the Versaillais were not allayed. During the afternoon the colonel of gendarmerie at Sèvres reported: 'It is widely believed that a large force of insurgents is coming from Paris along the Versailles road. I urgently request a section of artillery.' The same day came a report of 10,000 Fédérés ready to attack from Asnières.[81] On

6 April, when the army moved to secure its left flank by attacking Neuilly bridge, there were constant alarms. In the early hours of the morning, the colonel of the 45th *de marche*, at Châtillon, reported that a Fédéré battalion was at Choisy-le-Roi (on the Seine south-east of Paris), and that 1,500 men 'are coming silently up between the Seine and the Bièvre' – presumably with the intention of attacking the whole army on their own. At 6.30 a.m., the Commissaire of Police at Charenton, south-east of Paris, reported preparations for another attack on Versailles: 'it is said that there are . . . Fédérés at Orly. It is announced that there will be more than 50,000.' At 9 a.m. came a report that 2,000–3,000 Fédérés had passed through Choisy-le-Roi, on their way to Versailles, requisitioning horses and money on the way, and that they had reached Belle Epine. At 3.05 p.m., General Susbielle reported large enemy forces moving in front of his positions, and said that he was running out of ammunition; he repeated his warning at 5.50.[82] On the night of the 7th, Vinoy informed Faron that a large enemy force was about to attack him at Issy.[83] From then on the alarms became ever more extravagant, and yet were taken seriously. On 9 April, Galliffet – usually contemptuous of the Fédérés' military capacities – passed on information about a 'big sortie with gunboats and floating batteries tomorrow morning. I believe [this] to be genuine.' Vinoy passed the warning on to Faron and Vergé with the order to take precautions. The same day on the other side of Paris, the officer commanding at Châtillon reported his fear of serious attacks, and was sent reinforcements.[84] Most bizarre of all, on 10 April, the Sub-Prefect of Corbeil, about twelve miles south-east of Paris, raised the possibility of a Fédéré sortie by train to his town to raise revolt among the population and 'if not to outflank Versailles, at least to carry out requisitions and even to arrange themselves a line of retreat . . . on the forest of Fontainebleau'; he asked for the railway to be cut. A cavalry force was sent next day to secure the railway line at Juvisy.[85] A cavalry corps was formed under Du Barail to guard the area to the south of Paris as far as the Seine, in case of further attempts by the garrison to break out. Warnings of sorties continued during April. From the 10th to the 19th, troops at Sèvres stood to arms every night 'in expectation of an offensive on the part of the insurgents'.[86] As late as 3 May there were reports of a 'supreme effort' being prepared by the Commune – a four-pronged attack on Versailles.[87] None of this materialized: 3 April had been the high point of the Fédérés' military strength, both in numbers and enthusiasm. Thirty thousand men or more had turned

out to march (if not necessarily to fight) for the Commune. From then on, spirits flagged, as it became evident that a real civil war was in progress. The hard core of the Commune forces was reduced to a few thousand, while those who turned out because they were obliged to do so became steadily less enthusiastic.[88]

The government and the military authorities were never able to comprehend the extent of their enemies' feebleness. This, combined with awareness of the state of their own troops – the fighting of the first days of April had shown that they could not be trusted under pressure – deterred them from taking the slightest risk. Their weakness, not their strength, had led them to take the offensive on 2 April ('an unforeseen accident', claimed Simon),[89] and thereafter the civil war took on a momentum of its own. Their weakness, and the exaggerated fears it engendered, continued to influence the whole conduct of the war, and of the repression that followed.

6

The Army of Versailles

The government, whose security seemed barely improved by the indecisive successes of early April, was concerned to increase the strength of the army. It had reached by that time some 55,000 men, about the same number as the Commune might be expected to muster,[1] though much smaller than the Fédéré hordes imagined by nervous Versaillais observers, both military and civilian. Large reinforcements were considered necessary for the investment and eventual assault of Paris, and might even impress the Fédérés and bring them to terms. The increase in numbers gave rise to difficult and time-consuming problems of administration, supply and training, and it caused friction with the Germans, as the peace preliminaries permitted only 40,000 troops to concentrate north of the Loire. But numbers were not the only concern: the 'spirit' of the troops had constantly to be borne in mind, and much effort was spent in trying to estimate and improve it.

There were two principal sources of manpower: the National Defence Armies of the North and the Loire, composed mainly of young recruits; and the prisoners of war in Germany, the survivors of Sedan and Metz, a mixture of regulars and reservists totalling 310,000.[2] The Army of the East, interned in Switzerland, was of little use, being composed mainly of Gardes Mobiles due for demobilization, while the number of volunteers who answered the call of the Assembly was negligible. Most of the latter were officers of wartime *franc-tireurs* or the Garde Mobile who wanted to be employed as officers, and when they found that no dignified employment was awaiting them at Versailles they held an angry protest meeting, roundly criticized 'that senile old fool' Thiers, and then went home.[3]

The National Defence troops were the only ones immediately available, therefore, and they sent a flow of reinforcements to Versailles. Even the seven divisions existing at the beginning of April were too much for one man to handle and a new command structure was created in anticipation of the increase in the size of the army. By a decree of 6 April, three army corps were set up to form the newly named Army of Versailles. Vinoy was replaced in the chief command by Marshal de MacMahon, as the press had predicted.[4] He was an ideal candidate. One of France's most renowned soldiers, the brilliant reputation of his younger days had not been entirely destroyed at Sedan: his wound early in the battle had, in some eyes, relieved him of responsibility. As a Marshal of France he was placed above most of the other possible candidates, and conferred a prestige on the Versaillais of which they stood greatly in need. A known Legitimist, he had also been associated with the military glories of the July Monarchy and the Empire, but was not, unlike the other available Marshal, Canrobert, sullied by involvement in the 1851 *coup d'état*. Thus politically acceptable to the majority in the Assembly, he was also personally acceptable to Thiers, who found him to be of a striking 'modesty and simplicity', which probably means that Thiers, who persuaded him to accept the appointment, thought that he would be easy to manage.[5] Vinoy was disposed of by being given the separate but subordinate command of the Reserve Army and the Grand Chancellorship of the Legion of Honour. He would not have been an obvious choice for the chief command, lacking the prestige of a famous name and being little known to the provincial troops. He had been active in the 1851 *coup* – no longer a title to the favour of the Assembly or the government – and he bore the responsibility for the failure of 18 March. Finally, for these or for personal reasons, he seems to have attracted Theirs's dislike.[6]

There was a large choice of officers for the corps and divisional commands. 'We have not sought them in one party, but in all', declared Thiers, 'looking to loyalty and ability, not origin. . . . We have taken the men who have proved that, if they had been well directed, they would have made . . . France victorious.'[7] He was indeed able to find men considered to have done well against the Germans,[8] while limiting himself mainly to established military figures rather than choosing Gambetta's discoveries, and at the same time maintaining a political balance – all as elementary military and political prudence required. The command of 1st Corps was given to General de Ladmirault, an aristocrat, Legitimist and friend of MacMahon, who had commanded a corps against the Germans, showing himself fully up to his responsibilities.[9] General de Cissey, an experienced staff officer, not notably Bonapartist, 'très en vue' and already spoken of as

5   Marshal de MacMahon.

a future Minister of War,[10] commanded 2nd Corps, and 3rd Corps (cavalry) was under General Du Barail, an able soldier who had risen through the ranks of the African army; he had supported the Empire, though without being implicated in the *coup d'état*.[11] Two other army corps were formed later from released prisoners of war: 4th Corps, under General Félix Douay, and 5th Corps, under General Clinchant. Douay, a corps commander at Metz, had risen through the ranks, joining the Marines at sixteen and becoming a general at forty-two. He was regarded as a loyal Bonapartist, having been an aide-de-camp to the Emperor.[12] Clinchant, who had commanded a brigade at Metz, been implicated in the plot against Bazaine and escaped to fight under the Government of National Defence, becoming commander *in extremis* of the Army of the East, was the only Gambettist corps commander in the new army.[13] Vinoy's Reserve Army, composed mainly of the old Army of Paris as it stood on 18 March, retained its improvised commanders.[14] Among those refused employment by Thiers were Bazaine, Canrobert, Palikao and Frossard (all Bonapartists),[15] Changarnier (an absurd but influential Orleanist)[16] and Ducrot (of unpredictable but extreme views).[17]

Having found the commanders, Thiers had also to find the men, for the corps, divisions and brigades hardly existed in some cases except on paper. All needed large drafts to bring them up to strength. A brigade of 2nd Corps, for example, had only 1,400 men, instead of the full 4,200;[18] one of the Reserve Army had only 1,500.[19] This meant that they had to be used piecemeal to provide working parties and the like while formations that were reasonably strong, such as Faron's division, bore the brunt of the fighting. All units were constantly asking for more men, and at times there were none immediately available.[20] At the same time, existing strengths were being reduced by demobilization – in the confusion, too many men were sent home – by casualties and sickness, and by odd complications such as the need to release fishermen in time for the season, and to discharge Alsatians and Lorrainers who had become German subjects. In spite of inevitable problems of transport and accommodation, reinforcements continued to arrive in Versailles throughout April and May, and even after the entry of the army into Paris. In fact the Versailles forces never reached their full strength, which is probably one reason for the slow progress of their operations: even though their numbers were to prove adequate, the temptation to wait and make doubly sure must have been strong. As the numbers increased, from about 55,000 in early April to 120,000 in late May, so did problems of supply: 'everything showed the effects of the haste with which we had to act'.[21] Clothing and footwear were short, transport facilities were lacking, and there were even problems with food.[22] Bread had to be brought from as far as Rennes, for Versailles lacked the capacity for baking on the scale necessary for the army.[23] Fortunately for the commissariat, bearing in mind its poor record during the late war, the army was stationary and close to its base, which simplified matters. In addition, Thiers himself took over much of the responsibility for administration, holding 'a sort of council' daily of civilian as well as military officials.[24] One of his measures was to have another railway station built at Versailles to handle supplies. Their task thus simplified, some of the military staff found life easy: 'we relax, we smoke cigarettes, people drop in at the office and crack jokes'.[25]

More difficult to solve was the problem posed by the inexperience of the National Defence troops. As late as 15 May Ladmirault complained that drafts received by his 3rd division consisted of young recruits who had not had 'a single day' of training.[26] Soldiers throughout the army needed basic drill and instruction in the care of their rifles and the 'basics of shooting'; many had never performed target-practice.[27]

Vinoy ordered drill twice a day, even for units in the front line.[28] But there was a shortage of men capable of training the recruits: 'Weakness on the part of some young officers, weakness on the part of many NCOs', reported one regiment.[29] Another unit reported being short of NCOs, and had no suitable men from whom to improvise them. Officers too were needed, especially experienced men. Early in April, for example, one regiment lacked thirteen captains (company commanders) and six lieutenants, although it had fourteen second-lieutenants too many; another lacked five captains and four lieutenants, but had twenty-five second-lieutenants too many.[30] This state of affairs was general, and was more than a matter of administrative untidiness. It was vital to have enough officers if the men were to be properly supervised: two officers per company, reported the Foreign Legion, was the absolute minimum required to 'make the men march under the present circumstances'.[31] It was equally vital to have officers who were experienced – most second-lieutenants had been commissioned only weeks before – and convinced of the necessity of their task. This could not be guaranteed simply by recalling officers with temporary wartime ranks, as had to be done on 6 April. Many of them were incapable of training the men: some months later the Minister had to order 'confidentially' that in such cases junior officers were to be given elementary drill 'out of sight of the public and the troops'.[32]

Many too were suspected of no more than lukewarm devotion to the cause of order. Cissey reported to MacMahon on 13 April that among the recently commissioned officers there were some who were 'utterly worthless', and others who had 'sympathies for the insurgents'; he wanted them to be replaced by 'solid' officers returning from Germany.[33] He told his commanders to 'purge their regiments carefully . . . and to bring about by all means in their power the resignation of certain officers bequeathed to the army by the Tours and Bordeaux delegation [of the Government of National Defence] who have a mediocre military spirit'.[34]

In part, this was simply the prejudice of the professional against the amateur, aggravated by defeat and by resentment at the rapid promotion won by officers of the National Defence armies. But the evidence, fragmentary though it is, suggests that this suspicion had some foundation. Examination of the cases of officers whose attitudes led to their prosecution or dismissal shows that they shared a largely common background: recent promotion from the ranks, recall to the army at the beginning of the war, usually a history of republican loyalty, often ties with Paris.[35] Second-Lieutenant Serres (109th *de ligne*), recalled August 1870 and commissioned November 1870, was said to have been unwilling to fight against the Commune or the Army of Versailles.[36] Lieutenant Touiller (41st), recalled in August and commissioned in October, was a Parisian: 'his opinions are more than advanced'; Second-Lieutenant Bosc (9th lancers), another reservist, commissioned in February 1871, 'affects an exaggerated liberalism, criticizing the generals, the army commanders etc.' – ideas common among the National Defence officers. Common too was the kind of personal resentment against the military establishment that added to Captain Bourgogne's republican fervour: he had been recommended for the Legion of Honour after the battle of Champigny but it had not been awarded. Similarly, Captain Menuet (120th *de ligne*) had been recommended without result for a decoration: he admitted having been 'greatly affected by this disappointment'.[37] These men showed no great sympathy for the insurgents, but rather, like moderate republicans in Paris and elsewhere, they longed to find a means of remaining neutral, being 'neither for one nor the other'.[38] As many National Defence officers serving in the *régiments de marche* of the Army of Versailles shared the background, and to some extent the opinions, of the few who rebelled more openly, it was inevitable and not unreasonable that the senior commanders should be mistrustful.

Their solution to the problem was to give command of the troops to regular officers returning from captivity in Germany. 'Ah! The officers of the army of Metz, those are the good ones!' exclaimed General Lian, himself one of them.[39] There was, however, a limit to the speed with which they could take over. More important than time-wasting formalities with the German and French authorities, and the administrative difficulty of fitting available officers into the right vacancies, was the problem of getting rid of National Defence officers considered unsuitable. However unenthusiastic at the prospect of civil war, few were willing to give up their hard-won ranks and positions. The legal position was not clear. The Loi Soult of 1832 laid down that an officer's rank was his property, of which he could only be deprived by due process, in case of proved misconduct or other unfitness. The title of certain of the National Defence officers to their ranks was disputable – at least in the eyes of the returning prisoners of war – and in flagrant cases swift action was taken to enforce the regulations. But in general, the question of the validity of wartime promotions and appointments was to be decided later by a commission, as *Le Gaulois* (17 March) had suggested.[40]

In the meantime, it was only possible to use unofficial means to persuade officers to resign. In some cases improper pressure was used, and National Defence officers, especially those who had escaped from Metz, met with minor persecution from their less enterprising colleagues.[41] To have been associated with Gambetta was in itself regarded in some quarters as a sign of political untrustworthiness as well as unscrupulous self-seeking; *Le Soir* (Paris edition, 29 March) wondered if the seeming prejudice at the Ministry of War against escaped officers, 'who have paid to the full their debt to their country and to the Republic', was on account of their republican loyalties. Feeling became so intense between the 'new' and 'old' armies that one general suggested placing the officers from each in separate battalions.[42] This was not necessary, however, as the new *régiments provisoires* being formed from prisoners of war were commanded entirely by officers of the old army, while the *régiments de marche* remained for the most part under National Defence officers. Vacancies in these, however, were filled by returned prisoners: 'they were given preference in everything so as to compensate for the sufferings of captivity' (not always very rigorous) 'and the stupid animosity of public opinion'.[43] In particular, full colonels were appointed to command the *régiments de marche*, in spite of the protests of the lieutenant-colonels who had commanded them during the war.[44]

The authorities could not afford to be too high-handed, however, especially as their legal powers were limited. They could not afford the risk of too deeply offending the National Defence officers and their men who formed the majority of the army, and so promises were made to safeguard the ranks of officers who served in the Versailles forces – promises that were not kept.[45] A gesture was made in the case of General Clinchant, whose prestige among the National Defence forces was great.[46] He had been appointed by Thiers to organize an army corps of returning prisoners, and when afterwards offered the command of a mere division under Douay he threatened to resign: 'I regarded myself as one of the representatives of the young army that has just fought throughout five winter months . . . I see that you have judged otherwise. . . . Not one name in the composition of the Army of Versailles recalls the armies that fought in the west, in the north and in the east of France. In the face of this exclusion . . . I feel that I must withdraw.' Four days later he was given command of 5th Corps, and Ducrot was dropped.[47]

Not only, of course, had Thiers to take account of the sentiment of the army, but also of the effect on public opinion of creating an army which appeared wholly reactionary. For both these reasons, the few volunteers who presented themselves were little used. The Marquis de Carbonel was not permitted to form a 'guard of honour' of gentlemen volunteers, Cathelineau's Bretons were kept back at Rambouillet and never armed, and Charette's Volontaires de l'Ouest, mostly former Papal Zouaves, remained inactive at Rennes, on bad terms with the local population.[48] The more eager Mobile officers were allowed to form a company of about 100 men in which they served with 1st Corps as ordinary soldiers under the auspices of the official National Guard of the Seine, but they were not permitted to serve as officers: all available posts, such as aide-de-camp or orderly officer, were to be kept for regular soldiers.[49] In practice, they were reserved for returning prisoners of war, for to have served in the Army of the Rhine and not 'broken parole' by escaping was considered a proof of honourability and constituted, in conservative eyes, a recommendation for appointments and decorations.[50]

During April, regular officers returning from Germany took control of the higher echelons of the army, though still a minority at company level.[51] It may be assumed that their loyalty to Versailles, in spite of occasional grumbles, was unquestionable: unlike many of the National Defence officers, they had little knowledge or understanding of the wounded patriotism of Parisians that had helped produce the insurrection, and were largely ignorant of their other grievances. Their only knowledge of events came from the newspapers: a policeman was asked by 'several officers . . . if it might be possible to have Versailles newspapers, as they knew nothing of what was happening'.[52] In addition, personal interest attached them to a conservative regime that would return to the pre-war military system. This change in the composition of the Versaillais officer corps was among the most important factors that made the army an instrument usable against Paris. Encouraged by the rivalry with the National Defence officers, their determination had, according to Cluseret (whose opinion seems in this instance credible), a noticeable effect on the performance of the army: 'One felt that they were defending their salaries . . . their personal future'; each was fighting for 'his own life . . . for self preservation'.[53]

The authorities hoped to transform the rank and file too with released regular soldiers – a hope that had been nourished since the beginning of the crisis. Thiers, according to Simon, had not been entirely sure of the loyalty of the 'old army': 'Several months of captivity might have altered it, physically and morally.'[54] Perhaps because of this, he ordered the sailors and Marines, generally regarded as the most reliable elements, to be repatriated first.[55] Only about half the 310,000 prisoners were long-service regulars, the rest being reservists and those near the beginning of their military service. The difficulties of repatriating and reorganizing them were at first underestimated. Attempts to transport large numbers early in March had ended in chaos, due to wartime damage to the railway system and shortage of rolling stock.[56] The Germans proved uncooperative. Officers returning to France were stopped at the frontier.[57] The passage of troops overland was repeatedly interrupted as the Germans 'no longer authorize the passage of French troops through their lines'.[58] The number allowed to return by sea was restricted to 24,000, although the navy could have carried 100,000.[59] Moreover, regiments were split up, deliberately it seemed, so as to deprive the troops of 'the character of an organized army'.[60] This encouraged the belief that the Germans were favouring the Commune in the hope of destroying France as a nation – a belief that certain statements from Paris and the conduct of Bismarck, who 'exploited the situation with a bullying acerbity', seemed to confirm.[61] It is possible that the German army took matters into its own hands, going further than the Chancellor intended. Favre protested to General von Goeben against his refusal to permit troop trains to pass, after Bismarck had agreed to an increase in the Versailles forces.[62] There was great bitterness between the German High Command and Bismarck, due to his insistence that political considerations should prevail over military, and particularly that the defeated France should be treated with comparatively less vindictiveness.[63] Moltke, who had wanted to occupy Paris after its fall and continue the war in the south, may not have been averse to intervening in the civil war, rather than permitting Versailles to put its own house in order by rapidly rebuilding its army, and thus threatening German security. It was only after the signature of the Treaty of Frankfurt on 10 May that the Germans became cooperative, particularly by facilitating the return of the remaining prisoners.[64] This change of policy came too late to affect the outcome of the civil war, as a long time was needed to reorganize the prisoners: only two incomplete army corps took part, less than a quarter of the whole army.

The prisoners returned in a state of disorganization, and so the original plan, to send each detachment back to its depot to reform the regiments of the pre-war army, had to be abandoned. It was found necessary to form *régiments provisoires* from the mixed detachments as they arrived.[65] It was hoped that companies could be formed from men of the same unit, no doubt with the intention of minimizing the danger of indiscipline arising from the lack of acquaintance of officers, NCOs and men that was blamed for the breakdown of the army in March. Even this method was slow, for the returning prisoners contained a high proportion of reservists due for demobilization – about half, according to Thiers. There was no question of keeping them: 'they would have been grumblers, not fighters'.[66] Of the 13,452 who had arrived at Cherbourg by 11 April, more than 4,600 had to be demobilized and 1,700 sent back to their depots; only 3,800 had been assigned to regiments. By the middle of April 4th Corps was still only partly formed: its 1st Division had two regiments reasonably up to strength, but the two others consisted of five officers and no men and one officer and no men respectively; similarly, one of the regiments of the 2nd Division consisted of sixty-six officers and six men.[67]

There were shortages of equipment as well as of men. The prisoners returned without arms and frequently without suitable clothing: their boots, for example, were falling to pieces. There were not enough buttons, mess-tins, ammunition pouches and all the small items that smooth the path of the military machine; bugles and drums – as vital as radio sets to a modern army – were in short supply, as were tents, wagons and tools. In the middle of April all the new regiments were still short of rifles. Even when the equipment was available, distribution took time: the 6th *provisoire*, for example, was encamped five miles from the nearest village, from where all the material had to be transported by 'numerous fatigue parties'.[68]

As a result of these difficulties, the prisoners of war took part in the campaign only in its later stages, when the superiority of the Versailles forces was already established. The units of 4th Corps arrived in Versailles during the second half of April, and began operations on 8 May, just as the most serious obstacles to the Versaillais advance, the fort and village of Issy, gave way to the attacks of 2nd Corps and the Reserve Army. 5th Corps, reaching Versailles during the last week in April, assisted in the siege operations only from 13 May.[69] The arrival of the prisoners of war, therefore, although it shortened the campaign and no doubt increased the confidence of the Versaillais commanders, cannot be considered the decisive element in their victory.

Accompanying the organizational problems of strengthening the army was the grave question of the morale of the troops. Known to have been low during the few days following the evacuation of Paris, at first it seemed to have been improved by the fighting at the beginning of April, when the troops had not fraternized with the Fédérés as had been feared. Police reports were optimistic. The sailors seemed delighted by the ovation they received from the Versailles crowd on their return from the first fighting, and 'an immense change' in the spirit of the troops as a whole was reported: 'today they declare themselves to be quite prepared to act against Paris'.[70] The complacency was short lived. The next day it was reported that, according to one of the sailors, they would not have fired if the Fédérés had not fired first. Similarly, men of the 69th *de marche* at Satory declared that they would not fire on the National Guard unless the latter fired on them. It was noted that each time the Line regiments left camp, several soldiers stayed behind so as to 'lose' their units. A corporal of the 69th stated that he would 'almost as soon do ten years in Africa as fire on the people of Paris'.[71] This was to be precisely the choice the troops faced once the disciplinary machinery was re-established.

As fighting continued throughout April, the men frequently expressed their impatience. At first they had wanted a compromise, but if this proved impossible they wanted the rebellion ended 'as quickly as possible and by the most energetic means'. Men newly arrived 'all seem decided to march against Paris to get it over with as quickly as possible'.[72] But the campaign dragged on inconclusively, and discouragement set in, and with it a sullen resentment that could be directed against the government or the Parisians. Men of 2nd Corps were complaining of the length of the siege and the fatigue duties, and threatening to 'turn their coats'; yet a few moments later they threw stones at Fédéré prisoners.[73] At Viroflay, the men of the 35th and 42nd *de ligne* 'showed themselves very little disposed to march, which makes it appear that boredom has set in among them'; drunkenness was increasing.[74] At La Malmaison, men of 1st Corps showed their 'discouragement', and even the Volunteers were complaining: 'Many are disposed to give their resignation.'[75] Reporting the failure of his attack on the Château de Bécon, General de Maud'huy noted that the men 'begin to be weary of the incessant service that is demanded of them'.[76] Troops arriving from the provinces were no more eager: of seven detachments that arrived on 13 April, two made pro-Commune demonstrations, and all the others except the *fusiliers-marins* (sailors) were 'undecided': 'they fear the insurgents' and so were glad to be placed in a reserve unit.[77]

The authorities had hoped to be able to count on the released prisoners of war to stiffen the resolve of the others. They were, of course, noticeably better trained than the *régiments de marche*, and the smartness of 5th Corps marching through Versailles was favourably noted. But soldierliness was no guarantee of reliability in the circumstances of April and May 1871. The characteristics of the old soldier included a show of discipline, and perhaps a belief in its virtues, but accompanied by a cynicism and worldly wisdom that made the veteran harder to manage than the raw recruit. The failures of the war still rankled: soldiers were heard saying that if they were placed under Bazaine's orders they would shoot him.[78] As Thiers had feared, their attitude left much to be desired. 'Confidentially', wrote the military commander of Cherbourg, 'I am warned by the navy that the spirit of the men is bad'; he advised that all measures should be taken to assure order and discipline among the officers and the men.[79] The Prefect of Calvados reported that 'the political spirit and the attitude' of the troops arriving at Cherbourg had provoked unfavourable comment, and that he himself had been able to see 'how far captivity and defeat had demoralized our troops'.[80] Even some of the officers were rebellious, for they had not received compensation for their belongings lost during the war, and some were heard saying that they would refuse to march against Paris.[81]

When the first units left for Versailles, therefore, Le Flô ordered that soldiers of Parisian origin or 'animated by bad spirit' were to stay behind.[82] This prudent measure caused its own difficulties. At Auxerre, when it was time to leave, many men of the 13th *provisoire*, especially NCOs, demanded to stay. It was impossible to check whether they were really Parisians or whether their families were inside the city, something of which they themselves were often uncertain. Other soldiers 'made difficulties' when ordered to entrain.[83] Some claimed to be natives of the annexed provinces, and therefore Prussian subjects due for discharge. Various old soldiers' tricks, such as going into hospital and then getting posted back to the depot, served the same purpose of 'withdrawing from the theatre of fighting': 'It is revolting, but that is how it is.'[84] In several regiments old soldiers were sent to Algeria as their bad influence on the young recruits was feared.

Two things favoured the government, however. First, the hostility with which the troops were received in certain towns aided its efforts to divide them from the population. The 17th *provisoire* complained of their reception at Besançon, Dijon, Le Creusot and Tours, although one battalion joined in the disturbances.[85] The 15th *provisoire* took two days and three nights to travel from Auxerre to Versailles because of the delays deliberately imposed by railway workers, one of whom said that they treated troop trains like cattle trains (with which they were left in a siding); the officers were insulted and stoned.[86] Similarly, some of the old Army of Paris remembered being 'insulted' on their arrival in the capital before 18 March by 'the militants of insurgent quarters' and were ready to take their revenge.[87] Anti-military propaganda must also have created resentment. The term *capitulard* was commonly used with reference to the prisoners of war, and the Communard press was free with insults and threats, eagerly reprinted in Versailles papers for the consumption of the troops. Second, the resentment caused by being obliged to fight in a civil war could turn against Paris, as well as against the government. While on one hand a battalion of *zouaves*, the elite French infantry, had to be sent to Algeria after numerous reports of its indiscipline and sympathy for Paris, other prisoners of war were 'furious with the Parisians'.[88] In short, the returning prisoners were of an uncertain and changeable disposition, and like the rest of the army, they needed careful handling.

The first step was to re-establish the system of military discipline. Vinoy had already begun, and MacMahon took up the matter immediately on arriving. Judicial proceedings were slow. *Conseils de Guerre* had to follow a rigorous procedure and had the disadvantage of requiring evidence. They were also unreliable, as when the court trying Captain Bourgogne for desertion ignored aggravating circumstances and instead of a death sentence let him off with two months' imprisonment, much to MacMahon's annoyance.[89] He therefore introduced the expedient of dispatching undesirables to the *infanterie légère d'Afrique*. Although this was in practice a severe punishment, for these units – the *zéphirs* – were penal battalions where conditions were appalling and where a brutal discipline was maintained by the free use of corporal punishment,[90] no court martial was required to sentence men to them: an order from the Minister sufficed. Three days after his arrival, MacMahon used this method in a case in which he feared a court martial might acquit[91] – a fear he was later to express on several occasions. On 21 April it was announced that in future indisciplined and bad spirited men would receive the same punishment, and this happened many times during the weeks that followed, even when evidence was scanty and the charges vague. Eleven men of the 46th *de marche*, for example, were ordered to the *bataillons d'Afrique* on 2 May because they were reported to exercise a 'bad influence', and on the same day the colonel of the 5th *provisoire* asked for similar punishment for two of his men because of their 'undesirable influence', noting that they could not be put on trial as they had committed no 'offence in law'.[92] Most regiments provided a number of men for this exemplary punishment, and the knowledge that mere suspicion of sympathy for Paris, or a word out of place – let alone overt protest or disobedience – could receive at once a punishment equal to several years' hard labour or worse must have been of enormous importance in imposing obedience on the army.

As well as punishment, the authorities used inducements. Modest rewards for good behaviour were given: double wine rations (half a litre) after even minor skirmishes, extra food and pay for work in the trenches (5 centimes per hour, the regulation sum), and monetary 'gratifications' after successful operations. Such was the 800 francs voted by the National Assembly to the men involved in the taking of Fort Issy, and similarly after the taking of Fort Vanves.[93] Some commanders treated their men: General Lacretelle gave 50 francs to the company that took Issy cemetery. The Versailles crowd gave money to troops passing through the streets. When food stocks were captured from the Fédérés they were distributed to the troops concerned. Complaints about food were quickly remedied.[94] The reaction of the troops to this not very lavish bounty is unrecorded. Official approval was also expressed to the troops in non-material ways. Soon after the first fighting, Thiers and a delegation from the Assembly visited the wounded and distributed medals. Thiers continued to make visits daily to the units. The Assembly passed motions of congratulation to the army, which were read out on parade, and on at least one occasion a detachment was harangued by one of its vice-presidents, Léon de Malville. As might be imagined, 'the ordinary soldiers had little notion of what it was all about'.[95]

More important than these primitive and clumsy attempts to ingratiate themselves with the troops were the measures taken by the authorities to isolate them, though even when the civil war was well advanced it continued to be impossible to do this completely. Contacts with camp followers were maintained, for reasons that had little to do with politics, even though, as MacMahon remarked with unexpected humour, they did put a number of men out of action.[96] Even in the front-line trenches the soldiers 'allow ill-intentioned people to wander about with deplorable freedom', especially women and liquor merchants.[97] The men found ways of slipping away to *cabarets* when on duty. Strict orders were given to prevent them from coming into contact with Fédéré prisoners, but the frequency with which they were renewed suggests their ineffectiveness.[98] Occasionally, through these channels, the men were exposed to the Parisian view of things. At Saint Cloud at the end of April a soldier found reading Rochefort's *Le Mot d'Ordre* said that it was brought every day by a woman selling brandy. Vallès's *Le Cri du Peuple* was said to be available at Meudon. On 10 May, Daily Orders warned of newspapers being brought into camp 'which it is essential to prevent from getting into the hands of the soldiers'.[99] No doubt Parisian opinion also reached the troops orally, through the same intermediaries. The vigilance of the authorities, especially with regard to newspapers, was so great, however, that it is hard to imagine that these contacts with Paris were more than tenuous.

Nevertheless, in spite of all the authorities could do through punishment and inducement, and in spite of the propaganda of Versailles compounded by the inevitable bitterness resulting from the weeks of fighting, a remarkable amount of dissent continued to show itself throughout April and May. Disorders were common in troop trains; no doubt the men felt safe from detection. Several hundred men arriving from Bordeaux on 13 April shouted pro-Commune slogans, and some explained that they would not fight 'because the Parisians had fed them for five months, while the government had let them starve'.[100] In Lille, thirty-five NCOs of the 75th *de ligne* summoned to Versailles paraded through the streets shouting 'Vive Paris! Vive la Commune!'[101] In such manifestations there seems to have been a mixture of class solidarity, traditional popular hatreds, and grievances dating from the war, reinforced in some cases by personal ties with Paris. One soldier was heard telling his comrades that if they were forced to fight it was only for the 'good-for-nothings in power' and the police 'pigs'. Three NCOs of the 3rd *provisoire* told police agents, as late as 17 May, that the regiment should not be counted on: they would not fight 'so as not to kill their relatives', and because although there were bad elements among the Fédérés, 'Henry V must not be put on the throne'. The phrase 'our Paris brothers' became so familiar that it was used ironically in official reports.[102]

The authorities had supposed that such dissent was confined to bad soldiers and could be dealt with as a routine question of military discipline. In fact, some of the most exemplary soldiers were involved, and this gives the matter a significance that goes beyond the number of offenders. In the 110th *de ligne*, Sergeant Dufust refused to accept the Médaille Militaire as a protest against the civil war (and perhaps too against the shooting of a prisoner ordered by his battalion commander): 'he stated that he would no longer march against the insurgents, and sought to make the men share his ideas'. The medal was withdrawn and he was sent to the *zéphirs*.[103] Sergeant-Major Jouën, of the same regiment, was court-martialled for threatening his superiors and making 'seditious statements'.[104] Sergeant Gérard, of the 2nd *provisoire*, had his medal withdrawn for similar reasons. Another holder of the medal, an artillery NCO, was reduced to the ranks for trying to avoid going into action.[105] The influence exerted by such men cannot have been negligible.

Disaffection continued to show itself throughout May, even after the entry of the army into Paris. Soldiers from many different units were involved, from all sections of the army: the provincial National Defence regiments, the old Army of Paris, and the former prisoners of war.[106] Clearly, being of rural origin or having served in the Imperial Army and passed through the prison camps of Germany did not guarantee hostility towards Paris, and still less enthusiasm for Versailles. Yet the broad view of the conflict as being between *ruraux* and townsmen is not without some validity. The fragmentary evidence provided by the surviving dossiers of soldiers court-martialled for desertion or complicity in the insurrection – that is to say, the small minority of extreme cases, further reduced by the unknown number executed without trial – shows (unsurprisingly) that many shared an urban origin and a non-agricultural, often artisan, occupation.[107] Men of similar background, among whom sympathy for Paris and reservations about Versailles appear to have been strongest, were a minority in the army as a whole, but they provided a high proportion of the NCOs.[108] On the other hand, in the most important of these court-martial proceedings, those bearing witness against their comrades were (equally unsurprisingly) of rural origin and, as important perhaps, very young. Of eleven witnesses of whom details are given, ten were under twenty-two years old and eight were agricultural workers.[109] The importance of regional variations is suggested by a sample of soldiers' votes in the Assembly by-election of 2 July, provided by a surviving register of the votes of the garrison of Fort Ivry.[110] In certain departments radical loyalties persisted: for the Hérault, Gambetta and Floquet won nearly all the votes, although they had been openly accused of complicity in the Commune. In the circumstances of 1871, radical sympathies implied an ambiguous and even benevolent attitude towards the Commune and suspicion of the Assembly.[111] But on the whole, no definite political trend is noticeable. On the contrary, a high proportion of the ballot papers were blank or spoilt: in several departments (nearly half the twenty-three recorded) between one-third and one-half, and in Seine-et-Oise all the votes were invalid – surely a sign of ignorance and bewilderment rather than conviction. But the evidence is too slender to sustain weighty conclusions, and even when combined with that of police and army reports on the spirit of the troops can only support tentative and somewhat speculative hypotheses. Above all, no precise idea of the extent of disaffection can be formed: the documentary evidence is incomplete and is moreover based on the judgments of contemporaries who had no way of obtaining any but general impressions. It would be a mistake anyway to demand precision and coherence in this matter, for the opinions and actions of most soldiers were imprecise and incoherent. Not only did their views fluctuate but, more important, their views did not determine their actions. Practically none of the soldiers of March fought; practically all the soldiers of May did. This was not a question of opinion but of circumstance, to which all but the outstandingly courageous or rash submitted. For the mass, their background and opinions merely left them more or less open to the influence of their superiors, more or less easy to manipulate.

Certain definite, though limited, conclusions can nevertheless be reached on the 'spirit' of the troops and its consequences. The army did not suddenly change from a mutinous rabble eager to fraternize with the people, into a hardened instrument of repression. In spite of the measures taken by the government, notably the purging of all those thought to favour the insurgents, there remained to the end soldiers who sympathized with Paris, and a much larger number who were strongly opposed to involvement in civil war. This opposition, rather than any active sympathy for the insurrection, caused the retreat of 18 March, and it continued to manifest itself thereafter. The authorities had to ensure, therefore, that the troops should never again be severely tested, hence the prudence with which the campaign was conducted. Loyalty to Versailles demanded no more than acquiescence in what seemed to be the inevitable. The widespread reluctance to fight, though it reduced the army's efficiency, was prevented from disrupting its functioning. It may even have added to the ferocity of the final stages of the campaign, when resentment at being forced to fight seems to have turned against the stubbornly resisting Fédérés: 'It is the Parisians' fault that we are still not back home.'[112]

7

~~~~~~

Propaganda, myth and the army

That the army of March became the army of May can be explained only in part by the measures of discipline and organization taken by the authorities. These were enough to impose a semblance of order and compel the troops to defend Versailles and finally to attack Paris. But the appalling repression that reached its climax during *la Semaine Sanglante* went far beyond anything that these measures alone could account for. A first step towards further elucidation is to try to understand how the civil war and the Communards came to be seen by the army. The information that the troops received can be examined: the orders, proclamations and speeches they heard, and the newspapers they read. Less simple is the task of gauging the reaction of 'the army' – 120,000 men – to this flood of words, which was accepted, rejected or simply ignored according to the knowledge, prejudices, interests, temperament and intelligence of each. No doubt, the principal agent that formed views within the army was the continuous exchange of news, rumour and opinion among its members. But of this, few traces remain. Information exists on a mere handful of officers and even fewer men: those eminent or eccentric enough to have left memoirs or found biographers, a few whose duties demanded that they record their opinions, and others bold or careless enough to have attracted the attention of the police or their superiors.

There is, however, a source of assistance in fleshing out this incomplete and disparate evidence. Two newspapers, *Le Soir* and *Le Gaulois*, were regularly distributed to the troops. As the attempts of the government to isolate the army from subversive views, though not completely successful, had severely limited its knowledge of the events in which it was made to participate, there was little to contradict the information these papers provided. During March and early April, when Vinoy had tried to keep all newspapers away from the troops, the only regular news came from orders read on parade and govern-

109

ment proclamations posted in the camps – methods of doubtful efficacy. The ignorance of the troops encouraged rumour and speculation, sometimes damaging to the government. Interest in happenings inside Paris was naturally great, and several officers asked to have Versailles newspapers. The request was passed to Thiers's secretary. The Assembly had just voted to give 300 copies of *Le Soir* and *Le Gaulois* to the troops, 120 to 1st and 2nd Corps and 60 to 3rd Corps.[1] At about three copies per battalion, most officers at least would have had an opportunity of reading them regularly, and news from them must also have passed orally. Throughout the campaign, the papers were distributed by the police among the units camping in forward positions. Officers and men 'received the papers with pleasure', though often demand outran supply 'for all wanted to know the news immediately'.[2] The same two papers were also on sale at Satory camp in April, the only ones then available.[3] That they were read with attention is shown by the frequent letters from army officers that appeared, in spite of regulations.[4] Probably by accident, the government had found a means of propaganda far more effective than exhortation: biased reporting, all the more acceptable as it was professionally presented and came from non-official sources.

Le Soir, which had a separate Versailles edition from 22 March, was solidly republican and frequently critical of the Assembly, and especially its monarchist majority. Under its editor, Hector Pessard, it constituted Thiers's 'unofficial newspaper',[5] and concentrated on parliamentary affairs. *Le Gaulois*, concealing for the moment its Bonapartist sympathies, restricted its political line to a general support for 'order'. It concentrated on military affairs, upon which it was well informed, and was said to be the most popular newspaper in army circles.[6] The power of newspapers, however widely read, and even when enjoying a near monopoly of news and comment, should not be overestimated: they reflected opinion as much as they created it, and the views they propagated were certainly not tamely accepted by the whole army, in spite of the restrictions on the expression of other opinions. An analysis of their contents – the attitudes and beliefs they reflected, reinforced and spread, and the very words and phrases they used – does not aim at finding in their influence the cause of the army's actions, but rather at exploring a certain mentality of which other sources give only glimpses. A comparison of the presentation of events by *Le Soir* and *Le Gaulois* with the evidence from army sources, official and unofficial, shows how some within the army accepted the opinions propagated, and also provides a fuller version of the Versaillais view than those sources alone could provide.

For the sake of convenience, though at the risk of making it appear too coherent and immutable,[7] this 'Versaillais view' may be summarized under three broad headings. Each constituted a different argument against the Commune, showing it not as an equally legitimate government but as an impossible and criminal regime necessitating repression, if necessary by armed force. The first theme was that of order against disorder; the second, of nation against faction; the third, of liberty against tyranny.

The contention that Versailles represented order and the Paris regime disorder dates from the beginning of the crisis. In the first days of the insurrection, when the dispute remained political and constitutional, emphasis was placed on legalistic argument: the Assembly, freely elected by universal suffrage, was the only legitimate authority, whatever its faults.[8] Such theorizing carried little weight in the circumstances, even among political journalists: *Le Soir* (Paris edition, 26 March), criticizing the Assembly for its lack of political sense, advised its readers to vote in the elections for the Commune in spite of their theoretical illegality. But as the political insurrection developed into a class-based social revolution, the Versailles concept of order came to mean the defence of property and the existing social hierarchy against 'anarchy'. In the words of Jules Simon, 'one overturns aristocracy, which is a privilege . . . One does not overturn the bourgeoisie, one attains it', for to destroy the bourgeoisie would be to destroy civilization.[9] It became a commonplace to assert that the Commune had no rational programme, and that its aims were impossible and destructive. Claiming that the Commune was abolishing property and liberty, *Le Gaulois* (1 April) asserted that 'no one can doubt any longer that they are for France ruin, misery, disorganization and shame'. From there it was a short step to denying that the Commune had any political motives at all, and claiming that its supporters were motivated solely by the desire for gain. Favre spoke of the 'criminals who have usurped power, not to establish a political principle, but to achieve the satisfaction of the most debasing passions'.[10] The Fédéré leaders, habitually referred to as *ambitieux*, were depicted as cynical and corrupt. *Le Gaulois* ran almost daily a series of articles headed 'Ces Messieurs de la Commune', purporting to disclose the truth about the past and present lives of its leading figures. The more flamboyant figured prominently in the Versailles press, for example, General Eudes and his wife,

Billioray 'the hurdy-gurdy player', and Raoul Rigault. Billioray, 'in less civilized days' a beggar, was so proud of his new position, claimed *Le Soir* (Versailles edition, 28 April), that 'nothing is good enough for him any more'; installed in one of the finest houses in the city, 'he ceaselessly demands improvements'. Raoul Rigault, chief of the Commune police, was reported to have made a fortune selling passports, and it was regularly reported that immunity was for sale, both for refugees from Paris and for those wanting to use the power of the Commune to rob or dispose of an enemy inside the city.[11] 'What disinterest!' commented *Le Soir* (Versailles edition, 19 May) on the decree of the Commune limiting the salaries of functionaries to a maximum of 6,000 francs; in reality, it claimed, they were much higher, quoting 12,000 for that of the Director-General of Artillery. Similarly, pro-Commune journalists were accused of acting from mercenary motives. Vermersch, editor of the popular *Père Duchêne*, was 'a journalistic businessman' who told his readers what they wanted to hear and spiced his banal writing with gutter language simply to maintain circulation – a criticism not confined to the propagandists of Versailles.[12] The ideas expounded in the Commune press were therefore discounted as hypocritical or absurd. Commenting on an article by Henri Rochefort in *Le Mot d'Ordre*, in which he claimed that the aim of the revolution was 'to open up intelligences', *Le Gaulois* (7 May) remarked that 'until now it has done no more than "open up cash-boxes"'. Even those attempting to mediate between Versailles and the Commune were accused of dishonesty: Floquet, a prominent republican Deputy, was reported to accept bribes from the Commune.[13]

The accusation that the Communards, both leaders and led, were *pillards* (plunderers) was a frequent item of Versaillais propaganda. Although their 'theft' of public money was deplored, the most sensational treatment was reserved for accounts of the expropriation of private property, which were given in ways surely calculated to cause a maximum of fear and resentment. The outrage to the privacy of the home was emphasized, with a tinge of disgust at the material and moral sully that was assumed to be the inevitable result of occupation by the Fédérés. *Le Soir* (Versailles edition, 28 April) implied that fumigation would afterwards be necessary. *Le Gaulois* reported that Belleville families had occupied private houses in Passy, making themselves fully 'at home': 'all your cupboards and your wine cellar have been broken into. Your successor behaves as master in your house. Tuesday night was one of frightful debauchery . . . finally, men and women lay in your beds.'[14] General de Cissey summed up these points in his first General Order to 2nd Corps with an adroit addition for the mainly provincial soldiers: 'they steal public funds and . . . everyone's savings; they loot private houses . . . Their Republic is no more than an odious tyranny which would force the provinces to feed them in Paris without working.'[15] The righteous indignation of Versailles propaganda is clearly marked by envy of those who had seized the privileges of the powerful and the wealthy by occupying houses of émigrés, holding important office (and, it was said, enjoying its lavish perquisites), or running successful newspapers. The obscure origins and previous failures of Communard personalities were dwelt upon: they were, it was claimed, the *fruits secs* of Paris bohemia, turned against society by frustrated ambition.[16] One of Cissey's staff officers, Captain Garcin, responsible for collecting intelligence from prisoners, and thus one of the army's experts on the Commune, told the Commission of Inquiry that the rebel leaders were 'generally *déclassés* or men devoured by unhealthy and jealous ambition, or full of coarse appetites'.[17] General Montaudon, commanding a division of 1st Corps, saw as the motives of the Fédérés 'all the envy, all the hatred of social superiority, and above all the desire to conquer by armed force and at other people's expense, material pleasure and the right to idleness, without having to submit to the daily toil and the regular life of honest men'.[18] General Appert, responsible for the judicial proceedings against the Fédérés, used similar terms: 'The lower classes wanted to succeed in possessing material pleasures that they saw above them.'[19] It is not surprising that soldiers whose political ideas were less than subtle should seize upon the crudest explanations of events of whose origins they were generally uninformed: Montaudon, for example, knew only what he had read 'with the keenest interest' in the newspapers of the organization of the Commune and 'the misdeeds its leaders were committing'.[20]

As if to support their arguments that the Commune was disorderly, destructive and dishonest, the Versailles press emphasized the participation of criminals in the insurrection. *Le Soir* stated that, according to the Prefect of Police, there were 30,000–35,000 ex-convicts in Paris, and that more were arriving from the provinces and abroad.[21] These, according to Captain Garcin, were the 'direct agents' of the Commune, 'all vagabonds, all people out of prison, all that is worst in Paris'.[22] When Fédéré prisoners were taken, they were checked by police and prison officers looking for known criminals. Among 300 captured at the Moulin Saquet, the police 'thought they recognized many ex-convicts and dangerous people', reported Cissey.[23] Garcin examined the same batch, finding many 'dangerous people . . . most abominable blackguards': ex-convicts, thieves and 'people of the lowest class that makes up the dregs of the present population of the 13th *arrondissement*, the Fontainebleau gate, the Mouffetard quarter'.[24] These were then among the poorest districts of the city, with a large floating population – the traditional *classes dangereuses*. Prisoners were questioned on arrival at Versailles by Police Commissaire Macé, who later stated that one-fifth were ex-convicts.[25] Such ideas spread within the army. Montaudon wrote that the Commune made use of 'ex-convicts, drunkards, pimps, *déclassés*, in short, all the vermin of the *faubourgs*', and men of the 55th *de marche* at Satory said that the Fédérés were 'rogues . . . who only fight to loot'.[26]

As well as a concern for order as a safeguard for property, the conservative and particularly the military mind believed that order in the nation was necessary for its post-war recovery. The Prussian victory seemed to demonstrate the value of order: 'Those people are trained to be cogs, they are cogs, nothing more', wrote *Le Soir* (7 March), quoting 'a Russian Colonel'. 'Among you there are people who always want to do the opposite of what is . . . rule and law; do not be afraid to force them . . . It is thus that France will rise again; she must rise again.' Many in the army agreed. MacMahon, in his first General Order to the army, spoke of its duty to re-establish order so as to preserve 'the territorial unity that alone can maintain the independence of the Nation, and restore it to the rank that it has so long occupied in the world'.[27] The police reported several NCOs of the 26th and 94th *de ligne* (4th Corps) saying that they had learned as prisoners of war that discipline was the strength of the Prussians, and that they had decided to establish it in the French army: 'the first who steps an inch out of line will be shot on the spot'.[28] The disorder created by the insurrection came as a blow to such hopes. The very existence of the nation seemed threatened by civil turmoil following military defeat: 'The ancient world in its darkest hours affords us no spectacle of such a collapse.' The result appeared obvious: 'It is Germany who profits from the anarchy . . . She waits, eyeing her prey.'[29]

So enormous were the advantages that Germany stood to gain from the civil war that it was taken for granted that Bismarck was active behind the scenes, using foreign revolutionary forces, and particularly the International, as his instrument. The Bonapartists, too, were suspected in republican and monarchist circles of trying to fish in troubled waters.[30] The idea that the nation (represented by Versailles) was fighting for its life against a treacherous faction aided from abroad became one of the most important themes of Versailles propaganda and, perhaps, the most telling for the army, still smarting from its defeat. General Lian, a brigadier of 2nd Corps, thought that the insurrection had occurred 'thanks to secret influences, strongly supported by foreign encouragement and perhaps too by foreign money'.[31] Evidence was sought. Garcin questioned hundreds of prisoners (and his relatives in Alsace), offering parole in exchange for information concerning Prussian complicity, but 'could grasp nothing'. He concluded that apart from allowing food into Paris to prolong the resistance ('Saint Denis is said to be full of German Jews'), they had 'rather given moral support'.[32] Jourde, the Finance Delegate of the Commune, was saved from a firing squad to be interrogated on the same subject by Cissey. 'Naturally, Jourde absolutely denies the subsidies provided by . . . the International or by a foreign power', but on the subject of whether 'the leaders of the Commune, or at least the main ones, had received foreign money, his denials were not so definite'.[33] Certain actions of the Fédérés, most spectacularly the demolition of the Vendôme Column, seemed to confirm these suspicions. *Le Gaulois* (20 May) wrote, 'the descendents of Blucher are there, crushing us with their vengeance . . . The Vendôme column . . . was all that was left us of glory . . . while awaiting the day of revenge . . . How much were they paid to earn the Prussians' applause?' *Le Soir* (19 May) agreed: 'One feels instinctively that there was foreign gold in the wreckers' pockets.' MacMahon, in a General Order, spoke of 'that witness of our fathers' victories . . . this attack on national glory . . . under the eyes of the Germans'.[34]

If the insurrection served foreign interests, it followed that its leaders were traitors or foreign agents: 'That scum . . . have nothing in their hearts, not even love of their country . . . They boast of having no country.' The participation of foreigners was emphasized: 'the movement is no longer essentially Parisian, it has become cosmopolitan . . . the adventurers of every country, dedicated makers of European revolutions, have come together in Paris'.[35] The prominence of certain foreigners (and others assumed to be foreigners) in the National Guard gave substance to these accusations. 'A degenerate Pole is commander-in-chief; a second-hand American is the Carnot of the insurrection . . . La Cécilia . . . must be Italian. So Paris is in the power of the insurrection, but the insurrection is in the power of the foreigner.'[36] Cissey, in his first General Order, referred to the Fédérés as 'a gang of criminals from Paris and every country'.[37] Such statements were not mere propaganda, for they occur in documents not intended for publication. For example, 1st Corps intelligence section reported to Ladmirault on 1 May that, with the exception of the 'very numerous foreigners and some fanatics', most National Guards tried to avoid service; patrols rounding up the *refractaires* were 'nearly always composed of foreigners'; the main reason why the population did not rebel against the Commune was 'the terror inspired by these foreigners'.[38] Such beliefs filtered through to the troops. Men of the 67th, 68th and 69th *de marche* told bystanders that they were fighting 'the Prussians of Paris', and soldiers of the 55th at Satory said that the Fédérés were 'rogues who are mostly foreigners'.[39] Colonel Davoût's orderly, who would no doubt hear much talk, wrote home that 'the general who commands them is an American, a good for nothing'.[40] Early in May the army began to shoot foreigners taken prisoner among the Fédérés.

The third theme of Versaillais propaganda was that of liberty against tyranny. It was not a question of pointing out that the Communards were a minority inside France, which seemed evident, but that they were a minority inside Paris, where they imposed their will by force or fraud. Far from presenting the conflict as one between Paris and France (though there were criticisms of Parisians for feebleness in tolerating the Commune, and suggestions that Paris was unhealthily predominant in France), the official and semi-official Versailles version denied, for political and perhaps psychological reasons, that the Commune represented the capital. The Commune by-elections of 16 April were held to confirm this view by their low poll; the election of 26 March, when far more people had voted, was dismissed as fraudulent. Parisians in general were said not to be involved, or else involved unwillingly or unknowingly, in the acts of the insurgent leaders – *déclassés*, foreigners and criminals – who coerced or misled them. Thiers led the way in a speech to the Assembly on 3 April, the day after fighting began, when he referred to 'unfortunates led astray by criminals' to whom 'indulgence' would be shown if they asked for it.[41] *Le Soir* found this distinction between the misleaders and the misled 'very just and very politic', and noted with approval that Thiers had rejected the protests of the Right against the idea of clemency.[42] This became an almost official theme. According to *Le Gaulois* (3 May), 'three-quarters of the people who are getting themselves killed, maimed or imprisoned for the Commune are equally enthusiastic – that is, not at all'. Apart from foreigners and criminals, most were 'intellectually feeble or totally ignorant', and fought 'either to do as their friends do, or because forced, or because tempted by the pay'.[43] There was some understanding of the economic pressures that made service in the National Guard necessary. 'How will they be able to live soon without the public subsidy [of National Guard pay] and without work?' wrote General Appert. 'Who would feed the wife and children?'[44] According to General Lian, 'there are more than 80,000 workers without jobs and who, without this daily pay, would be without bread'.[45] Among the prisoners, 'we could recognize those led astray by poverty', claimed Captain Garcin, 'we showed them the greatest indulgence, we fed them and put them into a special category'.[46] Even Cissey on one occasion requested 'benevolence' for a prisoner who 'seemed honest'.[47] The press commented favourably on the humane treatment of prisoners, described of course in idealized terms.[48] The conditions in which they were held were apparently tolerable (at least until thousands were brought towards the end of the campaign and crammed into makeshift pens), for the Minister of War, after examining prisoners' letters, allowed them to be sent on to Paris, as the men 'generally express satisfaction with the treatment they receive'.[49]

When, for whatever 'just' or 'politic' reason, excuses were made for the majority of Fédérés, the militant minority – the 'ringleaders' (*meneurs*), a key word – were inevitably made the target of all blame and hatred: 'one learns to become merciful towards the wretches who obey, and pitiless towards the ringleaders who command'.[50] Wrote a Versaillais volunteer, 'I would gladly have seen the ringleaders shot . . . those whose writings and speeches have undermined the people . . . those who have taken advantage of the country's disasters to push so many unfortunates over the precipice.'[51] Journalists were counted among the truly guilty, for inciting the people to violence and misleading them as to the hopelessness of the insurrection. Déroulède's reaction is surely typical of a soldier: 'Even in a civil war I have always preferred those who fight to those who get others to fight.'[52] Sesmaisons felt the same: 'I feel no animosity towards those whose mistaken beliefs led them to fight against us; I only felt it for the crimes that were committed and for those who counselled them.'[53] But these men, 'the Pyats, the Rocheforts, the Pascal Groussets, were not to be found on the barricades'.[54] The same contempt appears in Cissey's dispatch announcing the arrest of 'Citizen Rochefort, cravenly fleeing from Paris at the moment of danger'.[55] Such reproaches were not without justification, and their bitterest expression came not from a Versaillais but from one of the most courageous Fédérés, the dying Vermorel: 'l'homme qui pousse et l'homme qui fuit, lâche et sinistre personnage'.

An allegation that formed a necessary complement to this theme of Versaillais propaganda was that the sway of the 'ringleaders', though aided by propaganda and deception, was in the last resort based on violence and intimidation; this showed that they were indeed as un-principled and vicious as had been said. The impression was given that they had a callous and frivolous disregard for human life. The 'murder' of Clément Thomas and General Lecomte and the 'massacre' in the Rue de la Paix on 22 March were endlessly dwelt upon. Numerous reports appeared of death sentences, and even executions, for spying or for trivial reasons, of the alleged execution of captured gendarmes and policemen, and of the killing of an unknown number of hostages. The Fédérés' bombardment of the suburbs was held up as an example of their 'savagery'.[56] Much was made of the terrorizing of the Church, both clergy and laity, especially the more pathetic incidents: nuns and their pupils being thrown on to the streets, children making their first Communion being bullied by loutish Fédérés, or nuns being ejected from hospitals. Descriptions were given of the desecration and looting of churches, among them Notre Dame des Victoires, a popular shrine of patriotic and religious devotion. Most serious of all for the reputa-tion of the Commune were the arrests of Archbishop Darboy and other members of the clergy.[57] Frequent reference, too, was made to the measures taken against *refractaires*: young men were reported to be dragged away by force, and made to fight under threat of death; whole battalions were said to have been sent to the front line by threat or trickery.[58] Rossel's order of 9 May, prescribing harsh disciplinary measures, seemed to confirm these accusations, and it was read and discussed in the Versaillais camp.[59]

Such reports and accusations helped to create a polemical tone far more strident than that of the early days of the crisis. Once thoughts of compromise were abandoned, Versailles propaganda tried to present the Communards as being beyond the pale of political discussion. The culmination of this polemic was the denial of any political character to the war: 'They say that it is a civil war, a war between Frenchmen. No! It is a war between honest men and scoundrels; it is a war between bandits and gendarmes; crime has no country!'[60] Indeed, the specific causes of the conflict were ignored, and its real nature was over-shadowed in the Versaillais presentation of events by a version empha-sizing the international and historical aspects of a supposedly eternal struggle between existing society and revolution, not only in France but throughout Europe.[61] Quotations from the foreign press were frequently used to give credence to the idea. National pride and political expediency were at the root of the argument,[62] the importance of which in this context is that it encouraged hatred for the insurgents and gave a theoretical and perhaps also a moral and psychological justification for the harshest of measures against enemies no longer seen as compatriots, but as stereotyped aliens, outlaws and bar-barians.

This tendency was reinforced, especially in the army, by aspects of the fighting itself that seemed to prove that the conflict was a particu-larly savage one. Most striking was the use, or threat, of new and terrible weapons. The Commune set up a Scientific Delegation to advise on their deployment, and the press boasted that the means existed to prevent the army from entering Paris. The forts, the gates and the city itself were believed to be mined, and the progress of the siege was seriously hindered in consequence; the morale of the troops was affected. Petroleum shells, probably left over from the first siege, were used by the Fédérés, and a number of men were wounded by them.[63] Exploding bullets were thought to be in use: General Pellé reported having found a quantity of them at Châtillon.[64] Poison too seemed to form part of the Fédéré arsenal. Four phials of an unknown liquid were found by troops at Dombrowski's headquarters, probably on 22 May. Tests showed it to be 'a violently effective poison . . . A few drops put into any drink could cause immediate death. The quantities found would have been enough to poison 100,000 men.'[65] Warnings were immediately dispatched to the whole army: General Susbielle forbade his men to accept 'anything at all' from strangers, especially drinks, following 'barbarous acts' by the Fédérés; Vinoy warned of poisoned wine, and Cissey of women offering poisoned drinks.[66] Thiers referred to the Fédérés having 'collected toxic liquids to poison our soldiers'.[67] *Le Soir* and *Le Gaulois* reported, falsely, that soldiers had actually been poisoned. Other stories of atrocities circulated. Several that can be traced appear to have originated within the army, although later recounted in the press and elsewhere; it may therefore be sup-posed that their main effect took place on the level of rumour. One, of obscure origin, is a story of soldiers hung by their feet, of which one version refers to the discovery near Châtillon of nine soldiers thus treated. The idea persisted, for a naval officer told his men, just before they reentered Paris, of one of their number 'captured by the Fédérés and hung by the feet until he was dead'.[68]

A factual incident that was transformed into myth concerned a soldier of the 82nd *de marche* captured after an abortive attack on Fort Vanves on 11 May. When the fort was occupied three days later, his body was found, with the feet tied, apparently indicating that he had been executed.[69] *Le Gaulois* (17 May) reported that the body had been found with 'the feet bound, hacked with bayonets, and having paid with a long martyrdom the honour of remaining loyal to his flag'. A final version of this incident was that 'worthy imitators of the savages of Lake Chad, the insurgents . . . had nailed one of our men to a post'.[70] There were other grievances. It was said that the Fédérés used the Red Cross flag as a cover for spying and even to launch surprise attacks; that they neglected army wounded; that they fired on the flag of truce; and that they drugged their men to make them fight.[71] In such an atmosphere of near hysteria, shared by both sides, it is not surprising that the fires that broke out in Paris during the street fighting gave rise to the wildest of rumours concerning plots to destroy the city involving armies of *pétroleuses* and *fuséens*. The fear inspired by largely imaginary secret weapons imposed caution on the army and increased the troops' nervousness; but the belief that they fostered in the ruthlessness and barbarity of the Fédérés cannot but have added to the excesses and deliberate vengefulness of the final battle. Cissey, one of the most important directors of the repression, wrote to MacMahon after receiving the medical reports concerning wounds from petroleum shells, 'it seems to me unthinkable to continue any longer to treat with consideration enemies who use such methods . . . I believe it necessary to give instructions to carry out the most energetic repression of insurgents captured carrying arms.'[72] In the context the meaning is clear: that prisoners taken in action should be shot – a course of action that Cissey was to follow during *la Semaine Sanglante*.

The propaganda of the Versailles press and the anti-Communard stories originating within the army no doubt contributed to the increasing bitterness evident in certain actions of the siege, such as the attack on the Moulin Saquet on 3 May, in which about 300 Fédérés were killed, at a cost to the army of only thirty-four casualties. It was reported that many of the Fédéré dead had been mutilated. There is no doubt that such atrocities did occur, for there survive eleven burial certificates of Fédérés interred at Montparnasse on 20 May. The bodies came from the south-western sector, and all had multiple wounds: one had seven bayonet thrusts in the right breast; another, twenty in the armpit; another, twenty-two, and a bullet in the thigh; another, unidentified, had twenty knife-wounds in the face, and a fractured skull; another, thirty-seven bayonet wounds in the face and body, and a fractured skull.[73] This was but a foretaste of horrors to come. Nevertheless, it does not seem that the whole army had adopted the Versaillais version of events and turned savagely against the Fédérés. Dissent continued to manifest itself among the rank and file, and some observers thought that the efforts of the propagandists had had little effect. The soldiers 'find it hard to believe that they are only led into action to repress an insurrection. They are little disposed to understand that they are only marching against rebels and murderers.'[74] Some of the 'crimes' of the Commune, so shocking to bourgeois opinion, seemed less than appalling to the men. 'Our poor soldier had as yet no very clear idea of order and right principles. He had been so demoralized.'[75] Many of the troops took part with gusto in acts for which Versailles condemned the Fédérés. Looting was widespread at Issy, Vanves and Saint Cloud, with the connivance of some officers, and drunkenness, said by Versaillais propagandists to be a characteristic of the Fédérés, was no less rife among their own men. Leperche tried to restore order in his sector because, he wrote, the troops' conduct must not lead the Parisians to compare them with 'the mobs from which we are to rescue them'.[76]

However indifferent, confused or sceptical many of the rank and file remained about the Versailles cause, few officers can have been untouched by the propaganda to which they were exposed, appealing as it did to notions of social order and national prestige which were important to them. Although for a short time the loyalty of part of the officer corps seemed in doubt, the real question once the civil war had begun was not whether they would remain in the Versailles camp, but rather with how much enthusiasm they would take part in the campaign and (it may be asked in retrospect) with how much severity they would conduct the repression. Here there were to be differences due as much to personality as to ideology, but as always ideology provided a comforting justification for acts undertaken as much for unavowable reasons of fear, ambition or wounded pride, as for principle, and overcame the doubts that many at first entertained concerning the rightness of their cause. The majority of the Versaillais probably believed their own version of events. The staples of their propaganda were less inventions than exaggerations of half truths: the Commune was indeed opposed to the liberalism dear to moderate republicans and Orleanists; it was, in spite of its patriotic rhetoric, damaging to the nation and its interests as most men saw them; it did become noticeably less popular with Parisians and irksome to the middle classes at least; its leaders did include foreigners and men of dubious character. The view of the mass of Fédérés as 'misled' by a hard core of schemers, fanatics, foreigners and criminals influenced the actions of the whole army, because it influenced a number of men in key positions whose views prevailed.

Their attitude can be seen in Captain Garcin's report on a batch of prisoners he interrogated. Many were simply 'wretches', but among them were 'dangerous people' requiring special attention: volunteers under or over the age of compulsory National Guard service, the latter 'picked agents let in by the Commune'; criminal types, 'people of the lowest class [whose] faces show at once what we could expect of them if they were free to do evil'; artillerymen, volunteers and therefore 'raving *communeux*'; immigrant workers liable to suspicion of being agents of international revolution; 'inexcusable' army deserters; the better educated, such as one officer trained at an Ecole Normale, a 'follower of Jules Simon, freemason, Commune republican . . . Their presence in the country is harmful.' Garcin believed that apart from this hard core, the population would greet the army 'not only . . . with satisfaction, but would even lend assistance'.[77] Cissey agreed. He found most prisoners 'quite inoffensive . . . the mass of National Guards do not want to fight; there is only a hard core of fanatics recruited among the vagabonds and idle workers, and ready for anything'. Some had 'most ugly faces', which seemed to indicate 'a long habit of evildoing'; these were assumed to include ex-convicts.[78] The practical effect of these views was soon manifest. The 'hard core of fanatics' was singled out for special treatment, though until after the entry into Paris this did not mean that they were systematically killed. Certain officers in particular, and perhaps even the majority of the army, had formed a clear if fantastic idea of who the main enemy was: not the whole population of Paris, not even the ordinary Fédérés, but the dangerous minority behind the insurrection. These were to be eliminated at the 'great clean-up'.[79] The task of the repression was therefore to 'separate the wheat from the chaff', for the government did not want equal treatment for those with different degrees of guilt.[80]

Many officers, with the support of a current of public opinion as yet barely formulated,[81] wanted a final reckoning with the 'reds'. One of them, Colonel Quinel, expressed this intention unambiguously in a letter to his friend Colonel Leperche:[82]

While waiting for time to heal our wounds, it seems to me that we should not lose the opportunity to purge the country of all the scum that is spreading grief and ruin everywhere; in the present case the government should not have the right of mercy, that would be a crime; military regulations must be in force and a court martial must function at once, otherwise they will tell us that it is too late to execute the guilty, and we shall have to start all over again with the same men . . . I demand that military law should be applied in all its rigour, and if the Chief of the Executive Power hampers it, it means that he is not up to the mission he must fulfil for the future of our country . . . I hope that in a few days this monstrous insurrection will have been settled with in Paris in such a way as to break with the revolutionaries for good.

The events of the siege and, to a far greater degree, of *la Semaine Sanglante* show that such intentions were exactly and pitilessly fulfilled.

8

The second siege

The effect of the tension within the army between widespread reluctance to engage in civil war on the one hand and the pressures of military discipline reinforced by propaganda on the other can be seen in the way in which the army performed its task of attacking Paris. There were moments during the campaign when an exceptional ferocity was displayed – a complement of the verbal violence described in the preceding chapter. Even before the troops entered Paris the first steps towards *la Semaine Sanglante* had been taken. But most of the campaign consisted of routine siege warfare, the slowness of which was a symptom of the malaise that still existed in the army, causing military, political and diplomatic problems to the government and High Command.

From late March onwards there were those in the Assembly, the press and even the army who urged rapid and decisive action against Paris.[1] Common sense seemed to show its feasibility: on 12 April, a civil servant arriving in Versailles from Paris reported that the Fédérés were weak in numbers and morale, that the western part of Paris was not barricaded, and that the Passy, Auteuil and Dauphine gates were 'hardly defended'; if the Fédérés were forced back by shellfire, the gates could be seized and a quarter of Paris occupied 'at the double'.[2] On 21 May, the army did exactly this, after a delay that many found inexplicable and inexcusable. Contemporary Right-wing opinion accused Thiers of weakness and even suspected a lingering desire on his part to come to terms with the insurgents.[3] The Germans, as will be seen, thought this too, and feared that the French government was using the civil war as an excuse to rebuild its forces faster than the preliminary peace terms stipulated[4] – a belief echoed by *The Times* (19 May), which feared that the strength of the Army of Versailles would lead to a rebirth of French aggressiveness: there was already talk of 'revenge'. On the Left, it has been suggested that Thiers was prolonging the war as an excuse for harsh repression.[5] More plausibly, Jules Simon explained the delay as being due simply to prudence: 'The advance could be slow, without too much danger from the political point of view; but the least reverse would carry everything away. It was necessary to take account of the spirit of the army, of that of the cities, of the extremism in the other direction of part of the Assembly, and finally and above all, of the presence of the Prussians.'[6] In other words, a false step might cause the army to disintegrate, the cities to revolt, the Right in the Assembly to overturn the government, and the Prussians to intervene. Any military action had as nearly as possible to entail no risk. Given the weakness of the defence, a surprise attack might have been possible with an experienced, disciplined and determined force, though with the risk of being caught in the open under heavy fire if the gates were not secured and the drawbridges lowered – the only way of passing the army and its equipment through the intact fortifications. But the government possessed no such force, and its decision to undertake a formal siege is understandable.

6   The western ramparts and the effects of bombardment.

A siege required time and effort. Although obsolescent and imperfect in design, the Paris fortifications were a formidable barrier. Surrounding the city was a continuous rampart or *enceinte*, faced with masonry and protected by a ditch thirty feet deep and forty-five feet wide. Its ninety-four bastions could mount cannon and machine guns. The gates were protected by drawbridges. These permanent defences had been strengthened during the Prussian siege with additional earthworks and obstacles, and a second line of defence had been improvised inside the ramparts on the south-western side using the viaduct and embankment of the circular railway serving the fortifications. The fixed defences were supported by gunboats and armoured trains, built during the war. About a mile south of the *enceinte* were five detached forts, Issy, Vanves, Montrouge, Bicêtre and Ivry. During the war they had been linked by a network of trenches, redoubts and batteries running from the hamlet of Les Moulineaux, on the banks of the Seine south-west of Issy, through the park of Issy château, through Châtillon, where a redoubt had been built on the dominating plateau, and lastly to two powerful earthworks, Hautes Bruyères and the Moulin Saquet, south of Forts Bicêtre and Ivry.[7] These defences had fallen into the hands of the Fédérés, though the Châtillon redoubt had been retaken by the army on 4 April. On the western side of the city the fortress of Mont Valérien had remained in Versaillais hands from the beginning, giving the army an important advantage.

The northern and eastern sides were neutral ground: the Prussians held a line from Saint Denis to Charenton and occupied all the forts except that of Vincennes, which was in the possession of the Fédérés. It is hard to say which side benefited more from their presence. Though Cluseret, the Commune War Delegate, feared that they would allow the Versaillais to take over their positions,[8] it is unlikely that the army would have had the strength to invest the whole city securely, let alone attack; in such a case it might have been forced to rely on the slow and uncertain means of a blockade, with unforeseeable consequences in Paris, the Assembly, the provinces and Berlin. On the other hand, the Fédérés would have had just as much difficulty in defending the whole perimeter, whereas the German presence enabled them to concentrate their meagre forces in the south-west, and the refusal of the Germans to enforce a blockade meant that food supplies in Paris never ran seriously short.[9]

The first move in the siege took place on 11 April, when a brigade of General de Cissey's 2nd Corps took up position uncomfortably on the

Châtillon plateau. There were no trenches to shelter them from the fire of the forts, which had already caused the evacuation of the plateau on 5 April. Cissey complained that the number of troops was insufficient, the cadres were incomplete, and nearly all the soldiers of the Class of 1870 were inexperienced and barely trained.[10] This was the unpromising beginning of operations against Forts Issy and Vanves, which had to be neutralized in order to permit a siege attack to begin on the other bank of the Seine. Otherwise, Fort Issy would have been able to enfilade the siege works from its high position above the river. Fort Vanves too had to be silenced, as it was able to give artillery support to its neighbour. Once these forts had been taken, the main attack would begin against the south-western corner of the defences, the Point du Jour, where the *enceinte* formed a salient. Thiers, who, as General Du Barail put it, 'would not have chatted five minutes with a potato chip vendor without trying to teach him the secrets of frying', pointed out to the generals the weakness of this sector of the defences.[11] A weightier reason for attacking there, however, was that it permitted the main force of the army to remain in position in front of Versailles, in case of another Fédéré sortie.[12] Supply and relief of troops in the line was simplified by their nearness to base. The terrain too was favourable: high ground on both sides of the Seine at Châtillon, Meudon, Saint Cloud and Montretout offered artillery positions commanding the Paris defences, some already built by the Germans. While 2nd Corps began its attack on Issy and Vanves, with its main body encamped along the River Bièvre where it could prevent a surprise attack on Versailles, the rest of the army remained on the defensive. Du Barail's 3rd (cavalry) Corps covered the right flank as far as the Seine at Choisy-le-Roi, Vinoy's Reserve Army held the centre, and on the left, Ladmirault's 1st Corps continued skirmishing among the houses and gardens of Neuilly, Asnières and Bécon. The fighting here absorbed a large part of the Fédérés' resources, for they believed wrongly that it was the main threat to Paris. In fact, both sides were concerned with holding their ground, although there were many minor battles for tactical positions.[13]

The first objective, then, was Fort Issy. On 18 April, General Rivière, commanding 2nd Corps engineers, produced a plan for its reduction demanding at least twenty and probably thirty days: four for building batteries, six for bombarding and ten for sapping.[14] He therefore expected the fort to fall between 8 and 18 May, and in fact it was to fall on the 9th, after being abandoned by its garrison the previous night.

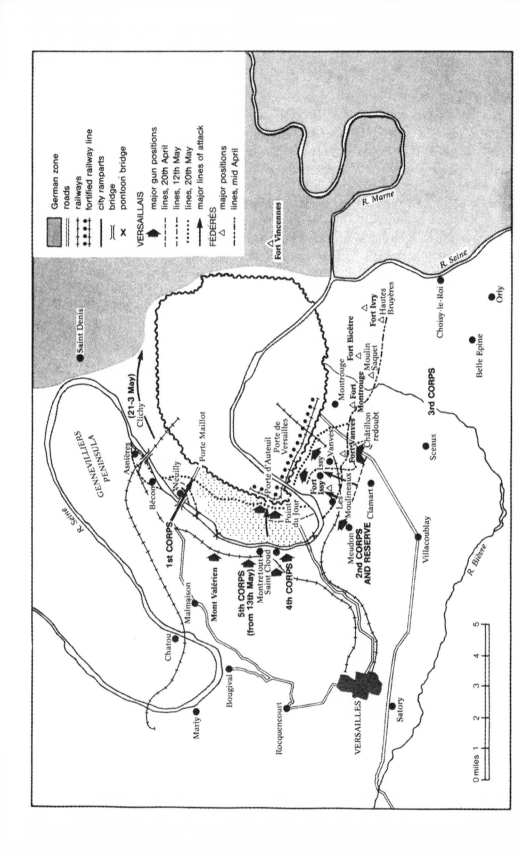

Meanwhile, preparations were being made for the reoccupation of Paris. Maps of the city were issued. The Commission pour L'Attaque de Paris reported on the state of bridges and barricades. The Intendance (commissariat) started to plan the feeding of the troops once in Paris and the care of the wounded. On 23 April, MacMahon issued instructions for the conduct of operations inside Paris: barricades were not to be attacked frontally, but outflanked through the houses; the lessons of 1848 were cited. The troops' loyalty was not taken for granted: commanders were not, 'under any pretext', to leave the troops in contact with the population, who were to be kept at a distance by skirmishers and sentries.[15]

These preparations were, of course, unknown to the public, whose impatience and concern at the seeming lack of progress caused Thiers to explain that 'the government is pursuing its plan', wishing to waste 'neither the powder nor the blood of our soldiers'. Its 'waiting strategy' had two aims: to build up forces so imposing that resistance would be impossible, and to allow 'misguided men' the time to come to their senses.[16] This may have been part of the explanation,[17] but more important was the sheer inability of the army to go any faster. Thiers had his own ways of accelerating its progress. With typical dogmatism he had decided that artillery could force a way into Paris unaided. Most generals were dubious. Their doubts were partly justified: the Fédéré artillery was far harder to silence than Thiers had supposed, and remained troublesome to the end. Consequently, progress had always to be made by the slow methods of siege warfare. Indeed, Thiers's hobby horse caused further delay, for a week was lost, according to Seré de Rivière, in waiting for the completion of the Montretout battery, Thiers's brainchild. This huge construction, mounting eighty naval guns, went into action on 8 May, directing its fire (as a rival battery commander reported with relish) against bastions 65, 66 and 67 (Point du Jour), 'abandoned by the enemy a week ago'.[18]

While building up his artillery, Thiers tried simpler means of overcoming the defences, attempting to arrange through agents the surrender or purchase of one of the gates. On 2 and 12 May, as a result of these intrigues, large forces were moved by night into the Bois de Boulogne, but the gates were not opened. Such manoeuvres were dangerous, for the troops would have been exposed to the fire of the Fédérés had these been warned, and the army risked being split in two by the Seine, crossed only by one sheltered pontoon bridge which a single division took two or three hours to cross.[19]

Negotiations, probably instigated by Thiers with the agreement of MacMahon and Cissey, were carried on with the defenders of Fort Issy.[20] Their resistance appeared so feeble that, on Thiers's orders, Cissey summoned it to surrender on 30 April – not realizing that the fort was at that moment almost entirely abandoned. The offer of 'life and liberty' for the garrison seemed to make a favourable impression, and it was expected that they would surrender the following day. Otherwise an attempt was to be made to place a breaching battery on the glacis, when it was supposed that the Fédérés would retire and perhaps blow up the fort, which 'would not bother us much'.[21] Meanwhile, every encouragement was to be offered to them to surrender. 'The Chief of the Executive Power approves the conditions I have laid down: life, liberty and personal baggage, and would even agree if absolutely necessary to let them keep their arms and return to Paris.'[22] It may have been Colonel Leperche's idea to add – for the Fédérés had spent hours trying to decide – that unless they replied in fifteen minutes they would all be shot.[23]

7   Mont Valérien firing on Paris.

This was evidently not taken seriously, for next morning, 1 May, the negotiations were resumed. The Versaillais then realized, however, that the garrison had been changed during the night and had a new and more determined commander, 'the self-styled General Eudes'. He, clearly intending to interrupt negotiations and spare his men temptation, replied in writing, 'We do not treat with murderers.'[24] Probably with the same intention Rossel, the new War Delegate, sent and published a coolly insulting message to his old Metz comrade and fellow plotter, Leperche.[25] In spite of the failure of negotiations at Fort Issy – though the following day part of the garrison tried to resume them when several hundred men appeared on the glacis waving white handkerchiefs and the fort temporarily hoisted the white flag[26] – similar proposals were made at Issy village and Fort Vanves on 7 May, and at Fort Montrouge on 24 May.[27]

While these vain attempts were being made to shorten the siege, normal operations continued. Cissey was in command of the Issy attack, and by 20 April his 2nd Corps was 23,000 strong. As they lacked experience and training, General Faron's division of the Reserve Army was placed in the forefront of the attack, where it remained from 25 April to 11 May, the period of the most strenuous fighting. Twenty thousand men were engaged in digging trenches, making gabions, building batteries and carrying supplies and ammunition. It was a form of warfare that did not expose the troops to great hardship or danger. Few were involved in serious fighting – casualties were about fifteen to forty a day among over 20,000 men – and the labourers received extra pay and rations.[28]

Fort Issy stands on high ground east of the Seine. The position had three serious disadvantages: it was overlooked by guns on the heights of Meudon and Châtillon, there was an area of dead ground on the western side, where the park and château of Issy were situated, due to a steep slope down towards the Seine, and on the southern and eastern sides a railway cutting and embankment close to the glacis provided cover for an attacking force. The Versaillais hoped that the Fédérés, once surrounded by means of these two weak points, would abandon the fort.[29]

Hostilities were confined to minor skirmishes and noisy but harmless artillery actions until the last week in April. On the 25th, fifty-two guns opened fire on Forts Issy and Vanves, and during the night of the 26th, units of the Reserve Army – 100 sailors and 300 men of the 110th, with four companies of the 35th in support – captured Les Moulineaux,

8 Inside Fort Issy, with Mont Valérien in the background.

believed to be defended by two Fédéré battalions. A 'fairly large number' of the latter were killed, and the Versaillais suffered about thirty casualties. The weakness of the defence seemed to indicate 'great discouragement' among the Fédérés, and so it was decided to press on quickly, without sapping. On the night of the 29th, General Paturel entered Issy park, taking 100 prisoners, eight guns and much ammunition; Colonel Lespiau, with his 109th *de ligne*, took the walled cemetery 350 yards from the fort; and men of the 70th *de marche* raided a Fédéré outpost at Bonamy Farm, capturing two officers and eight men and leaving 'many killed and wounded' among the enemy. Covered by artillery fire, 1,000 labourers dug trenches linking the new positions with those previously held.[30] Limited, well coordinated night attacks of this kind, using surprise, became the usual operational method. Risks were few and the raw and unsteady troops were not unduly tested. The Fédérés had neither the numbers nor the organization to counter them. Nevertheless, there were always dangers. During an attack on 1 May, a company of Boulanger's 114th *de ligne* panicked and ran, firing in all directions and killing at least one of their own side:

'with men who are so nervous and officers who bother so little about them, one cannot take too many precautions'.[31]

The first successes and the seeming demoralization of the Fédérés prompted the attempts to negotiate the evacuation of Fort Issy. Their failure caused the attacks to be resumed. During the night of 1 May, two battalions of the 42nd *de ligne* and one of the 35th occupied Issy château, taking 300 prisoners. Simultaneously, the 22nd battalion of *chasseurs* seized Clamart station, taking sixty prisoners.[32] Among them were several men in army uniform and a Belgian. These were tried by a drumhead court martial, and twelve deserters and the Belgian were condemned to death.[33] Deserters taken among the Fédérés had been shot since the beginning of the campaign. The killing of the Belgian accompanied the growing tendency in the press to blame foreigners for the insurrection.[34]

Although by 1 May the attackers had extended their positions round the flanks of Fort Issy, reinforcements for the garrison still managed to arrive, and from 2 May the Versaillais noted a 'redoubled energy' in the defence. A trench-digging party was routed and part of Clamart station had to be abandoned. When the fort hoisted the white flag, it was assumed to be a trick and the men were forbidden to leave their trenches.[35] A journalist visiting the fort was told that there were 1,500 men defending it. Preparations were nevertheless being made for its loss, heavy guns being mounted on the *enceinte* behind the fort so as to make it untenable.[36]

Continuing the outflanking movements, two companies of the 64th *de marche* and a detachment of sailors took the railway arch between Forts Issy and Vanves during the night of 3 May. The position was important as it gave some protection from the fire of Fort Vanves. A heavy cannonade and counter-attacks, often by mere handfuls of men, prevented the Versaillais from consolidating their gains. There was no progress until the night of 5 May, when 240 hesitant sailors and the 17th battalion of *chasseurs* advanced along the railway to a walled park in the rear of the fort.[37] On the other flank, in Issy village, resistance was equally stubborn. The Fédérés retreated from house to house, building barricades with furniture thrown from the windows. They were solidly installed in the larger buildings in the village: the church and adjoining houses, the Saint Esprit seminary, the Couvent des Oiseaux, the Petits Manèges hospital (containing 1,500 old people) and the dominating *lycée* in the rear, where Eudes established his head-quarters. Faron reported that he was having difficulty in holding his positions, due to heavy fire from the fort and village of Vanves, which the Versaillais gunners were unable to silence.[38] His men, in the forefront of operations since 18 March, were nearing their limits: the trench brigades were suffering 'fairly considerable' losses; the sailors, considered more reliable and so frequently used as a spearhead, had been 'more than feeble' in the trenches; and Derroja's brigade had to be withdrawn a few days later because to keep it any longer in the line would have produced 'an impression on the men the possible outward expression of which had to be avoided'.[39] It was difficult to relieve Faron, however, as his men knew the terrain and the enemy positions. Thiers again ordered emissaries to be sent to the defenders of Vanves to try to persuade them to surrender, by bribery if necessary.[40] Preparations were begun for an assault on Fort Issy, but it was known that although it had suffered much superficial damage, the breach in the ramparts was not practicable, and the outer defences of trenches, palisades and *abattis* were intact.[41]

At this critical moment the defence weakened, and several hundred Fédérés were seen re-entering Paris. Although the struggle continued during 7 May, that night was quiet and the next morning saw 'almost complete calm all along the line'. The fall of Issy church during the morning of 8 May almost closed the circle round the fort, which fired its last shots at 1 p.m. Fifty Fédérés were seen escaping from it during the afternoon, and reinforcements from Paris trying to reach it during the night were forced to retire. It was not occupied until the following afternoon, when Colonel Biadelli and a party of the 38th *de marche* entered cautiously, and found it free of defenders and mines. More than a hundred cannon and plentiful supplies of food, drink, ammunition and equipment were captured. At Thiers's suggestion, the food was distributed among the soldiers who had taken part in the operations.[42]

The fall of Fort Issy was timely for diplomatic as well as military reasons. During the previous weeks, as the campaign had shown no signs of reaching a conclusion, the Germans had begun to doubt the ability of Versailles to win,[43] and indeed its will to do so. Bismarck suspected that Thiers still hoped to come to an agreement with Paris and was using the insurrection as an excuse to break the preliminary peace terms and rebuild an army – suspicions encouraged by the secretiveness of the French War Ministry.[44] The French government was no doubt aware of the advantages of a rapid reorganization of the army, though it is most unlikely that its ambitions went any further.[45]

There was careless talk, however, 'even in the corridors of the Assembly', of using the threat of the army to modify the peace terms, and this was repeated in Berlin.[46] Bismarck suspected that the French negotiators in Brussels were deliberately delaying agreement with this intention. Some believed that renewal of hostilities was likely, and General von Fabrice, the governor-general of the occupied territories, warned Favre to do nothing to encourage German fears, for the army, angry at not having been allowed to occupy Paris fully, 'would consider the insurrection . . . an excellent opportunity to take spectacular revenge'.[47]

Though Thiers and Favre, for their part, disbelieved the stories of German involvement in the insurrection, they realized that Bismarck intended to exploit their difficulties: 'he feels himself the stronger, and will take the utmost advantage of it'.[48] He and the German army seemed to be deliberately hampering their efforts to subdue Paris, with the intention of prolonging a burdensome occupation, increasing German

9   Fighting in Issy village.

influence in France's domestic affairs, weakening her bargaining position, and discrediting her in the eyes of Europe. Protesting against 'decisive support given to the insurrection and an act of hostility against the legitimate government of France' on the part of the German government, Favre added cryptically that it had 'excellent reasons for acting thus'.[49] Bismarck indeed considered playing off Paris against Versailles by mediating or by occupying Paris with the consent of the Commune to protect its liberties – 'after all, not so unreasonable' – which would 'guarantee us against the bad faith of the Versailles government'.[50] He was aware too of the diplomatic advantages to be gained from disorder in France, or from a German intervention demonstrating the impotence of the French government. It provided a 'pretext' for promoting the solidarity of the conservative monarchies against revolution, and made less likely a rapprochement between France and Russia.[51] His short-term interest, the signature of a full peace treaty and the consequent withdrawal of German troops, demanded a rapid execution of whatever policy he adopted.

On 30 April, Friedrich von Holstein, attached to Fabrice's staff, met Cluseret, War Delegate of the Commune, at Fort Aubervilliers.[52] Bismarck wished to know the reaction of the Commune to the possibility of mediation, and to find out if the regime was solvent.[53] Cluseret wished to obtain an assurance that the German army would not hand over its positions to Versailles or impose a blockade. This Holstein, who was favourably impressed by Cluseret, was willing to promise, though he refused to consider selling arms to the Fédérés.[54] Bismarck, finding the Parisian regime apparently more moderate than he had expected, instructed Fabrice to maintain relations with Cluseret. If he agreed to the occupation of Paris by German troops, 'it would be desirable to make a serious endeavour to mediate'.[55] Before a second meeting could take place, however, Cluseret was arrested, and this reduced the likelihood of mediation.[56]

Relations between Bismarck and the French government remained tense. On 7 May he presented an ultimatum to Favre: the insurrection had altered the situation, and made it necessary for Germany to demand guarantees, principally an extended period of occupation. Otherwise, he would insist on the French army withdrawing beyond the Loire, and would occupy Paris until order was 'completely re-established'[57] – a step that would carry the risk of hostilities with the army, the Commune, or both. At the same time, new demands were being made in Brussels concerning the property of the Eastern Railway

Company and trade concessions, and Bismarck was continually harassing the French with accusations that they were failing to fulfil their obligations under the preliminary peace agreement.[58] Favre feared worse: he reported Bismark's statement that if the Germans occupied Paris, they might 'give France a government' – clearly the Empire – and that would mean 'the end of our unhappy country'.[59] French resistance collapsed. Favre offered to sign the treaty immediately, to the surprise and satisfaction of Bismarck, who had seriously considered the resumption of hostilities.[60] A convention was drafted permitting the Germans to continue their occupation, and giving them most favoured nation status. In return, Bismarck agreed to the return of French prisoners and the passage of Versailles forces through the German lines to out-flank the Fédéré defences. He also offered to summon the Commune to disarm the ramparts, thus offering an easy entrance for the Versaillais. Favre thought, and Thiers agreed, that there was no choice but to sign, thus 'saving Paris and perhaps France'. He feared, however, that the German army would bombard the city to enforce the disarmament of the ramparts, 'something that unfortunately I cannot prevent'.[61] This would be a political disaster, and would expose them to further German blackmail. Favre thought the situation so grave that he suggested either 'a decisive blow' or a 'settlement' with Paris, so as to escape from Bismarck's clutches.[62] The fall of Fort Issy, tangible proof that Versailles was winning, offered them the 'priceless advantage' of being able to 'manage our business without asking Prussia to let us through'. Favre felt 'great satisfaction' in being able to give the news to Bismarck, who seemed 'fairly impressed', and became more tractable. On 10 May, the treaty was signed.[63]

After the capture of Fort Issy the final stage of the siege, the attack on the Point du Jour, could begin. Siege trenches and batteries were constructed in and near the Bois de Boulogne, under the direction of General Douay.[64] While this work continued, he was preparing to enter the city by surprise if the opportunity arose. Night reconnaissances were made and a spy, Ducatel, furnished detailed reports on the state of the defences within.[65] Dombrowski's Fédérés, nearing the end of their resources, tried to disrupt the besiegers' progress, making counter-attacks on the Versaillais flank at Neuilly and Clichy, and even sorties into the Bois de Boulogne.[66] But their success could not last; the weight of numbers was too great.

Inside the city, the Communards neglected to build a system of defences in preparation for an assault. Cluseret, under arrest since 30

April, wrote on 16 May to Delescluze, the War Delegate, urging the construction of a line of defence from the Porte de Passy to the Pont de Grenelle and of strong points at the Trocadéro, Etoile and Place d'Eylau, forming a 'natural citadel' because of their height and the field of fire offered by the avenues radiating from them.[67] Very little was done, and western Paris remained exposed to a Versaillais incursion. By 20 May, 4th Corps had reached the glacis opposite bastions 63, 64 and 65 (Autueil–Point du Jour), and its artillery, with that of Montretout, had broken down the gates of Auteuil and Saint Cloud, causing one of the drawbridges of the latter to fall. Douay sent Ducatel into Paris to discover the state of the defences and the disposition of the Fédéré forces, and on 21 May moved another brigade forward in case of need.[68]

On the other side of the Seine, 2nd Corps too was preparing its assault. Cissey had occupied Vanves cautiously, being unwilling to over-extend his tired men, especially as there were rumours that the Fédérés were planning a last desperate sortie.[69] Faron's division was at last withdrawn on 11 May, and neither officers nor men replacing it were acquainted with their duties – a failing compounded by negligence. The failure of the engineer and artillery officers to reconnoitre the positions and supervise the work caused confusion among the working parties. The infantry was no better. One of Leperche's assistants reported being 'extremely dissatisfied with the manner in which duties are performed in the 114th' (Boulanger's regiment).[70] In general, discipline was slack. Civilians were allowed into the trenches, and looting had reached 'worrying proportions'.[71] Further delay was caused by the fear that the Fédérés had mined Fort Vanves: Thiers ordered prudence.[72] An unauthorized attempt to storm the gate on 11 May, led by a junior officer, ended in minor catastrophe when a burst of fire from the Fédérés routed the attackers, causing several casualties. On 14 May a similarly unauthorized and 'very imprudent' initiative by a captain of the 71st succeeded; this enterprising officer proceeded to remove and sell equipment found in the fort, greatly to the disapproval of Leperche, who wondered whether his daring was born of 'the excusable recklessness of youth' or 'an immoderate love of lucre'.[73]

The siege continued after the fall of the fort; renewed attempts to persuade the defenders of the remaining Fédéré positions outside the walls to surrender always seemed about to succeed but never did. On 19 May, a parallel was dug only 100 yards from the ramparts of

Paris. The next day close-range batteries began to make a breach in one of the bastions, and the drawbridge of the Porte de Sèvres was brought down. The operations were costing 100 casualties per day. Scaling ladders were assembled for an assault planned for 22 or 23 May.[74]

If Cissey and Douay were competing to be first to make the assault, MacMahon felt less urgency. On 21 May he asked the Minister to publish a list of decorations to raise the army's morale before the final attack, which he evidently expected to be several days away. Thier's secretary, Barthélémy Saint-Hilaire, even suggested a truce on 21 May, the day of the army's entry into Paris, so that the 16th *arrondissement* could be evacuated. Both Thiers and MacMahon were taken by surprise when Douay's troops slipped into Paris that afternoon.[75] The recently made plan for the occupation of the city had to be abandoned.[76] By nightfall, the Versaillais were established inside the ramparts, and the five-week siege, during which 2nd Corps alone had dug fourteen miles of trenches, built thirty gun batteries and fired

10   The gate of Fort Vanves after the battle.

66,000 rounds of artillery, at a cost of 149 killed, 1,109 wounded and 32 missing, ended without a full-scale assault being needed.[77]

The threat of German intervention was thereby removed. Since the signature of the peace treaty on 10 May, Bismarck, Fabrice and the Crown Prince of Saxony, commanding the forces round Paris, had become embarrassingly helpful. They wanted a meeting with French staff officers to concert measures against Paris, offering to impose a blockade, order the defenders to disarm the ramparts, bombard if necessary, and fire on the Fédérés if a French attack were repulsed.[78] Thiers was unenthusiastic, but Favre and Colonel de la Haye, French liaison officer at German headquarters, felt it impossible to refuse, both for military and diplomatic reasons. Nevertheless, the French intention was to limit German involvement, and when General Borel, MacMahon's chief of staff, met his counterpart on 15 May, no definite action was agreed upon.[79] Favre told Bismarck that all they wanted was passage for their troops, a summons to the Fédérés to disarm the northern ramparts, but without use of force, and the occupation of Saint Ouen. There seems to have been hesitation over asking the Germans to blockade Paris.[80] On 21 May, Favre met Bismarck at Frankfurt and pleaded that under no circumstances should German troops enter the city. He also asked Bismarck to refuse requests to mediate, though he considered it unlikely that any would be made. Thiers made the same plea: 'I beseech M. de Bismarck, in the name of the cause of order, to let us carry out this repression of banditry ourselves. . . . To act otherwise would be to do a further disservice to the party of order in France, and hence in Europe.'[81] It would also, though of course Thiers could not say so, weaken France diplomatically, particularly with regard to Russia.[82] Bismarck would not promise. While offering to consult the French government before taking military action, he reminded Favre that the Germans had 'a thousand times over the right to take strong action' against the brigands of the Commune. The King was worried, and 'our inactivity is no longer understood'.[83] The entry of the army into Paris that same day removed the difficulty.

The events of the siege reveal much about both belligerents: the Fédérés by their powerlessness to disrupt the slow and cautious operations of the army, and the Versaillais by their inability to hasten the end of the campaign. The forces of the Commune were numerous on paper, but far less so in reality. Thirty or forty thousand men had mustered for the sortie of 3 April, the largest number ever gathered.[84]

Thereafter, they lost several thousand casualties and prisoners, [85] and more through desertion, which reflected the gradual abandonment of the Commune by the population of Paris. Many thousands of men turned out for duty inside the city, such as guarding public buildings, and of course to draw their pay and rations. Service in the trenches was a different matter. For example, the 85th battalion, whose activity had been limited to guarding the Place Vendôme and the Hôtel de Ville, was ordered to Neuilly in April. Only 257 men left, out of a nominal 700, and half of these soon went home. Cluseret stated that he only ever had about 6,500 men in the front line.[86] His order of 8 April making service in the *compagnies de guerre* compulsory for men between nineteen and forty years of age at best swelled the number of men in uniform; it could not make them into resolute defenders of the Commune, as droves of surrendering prisoners were eager to point out.[87] The attempts by the garrison of Fort Issy to negotiate its surrender failed only because a minority of officers and men held firm, and at Fort Vanves part of the garrison was ready to mutiny and abandon the fort on 12 May.[88] The defence of Paris rested upon a few dozen dependable battalions and a handful of determined commanders. Such troops were often superior man for man to the Versaillais. They were more experienced than most of the regulars, having endured the first siege and in many cases taken part in the battles of Champigny and Buzenval. Many, especially the officers, were old soldiers, and there was a sprinkling of deserters and soldiers of fortune, some of whom proved invaluable. Some units were hardened by long spells of fighting during April and May, they knew their officers and each other, and the best of them were far more committed to their cause than were the conscripts of Versailles. Their resistance was strengthened by the formidable defences of Paris and the immense quantity of armaments at the Fédérés' disposal, greater than was ever used, which permitted a heavy fire to be maintained. Though not often deadly, it kept the Versaillais at a distance.[89]

The latter, paying them the compliment of exaggerating their numbers and enterprise, proceeded with the utmost caution, regularly taking precautions against sorties and counter-attacks that the Fédérés were incapable of mounting, and secret weapons that they were incapable of constructing. Forts Vanves and Issy were only occupied after lengthy inspections and much tracing and cutting of wires thought to lead to explosive charges, and the tunnels beneath Fort Vanves were immediately blocked for fear of counter-attacks and mines.[90] Thiers urged prudence. 'It was said that all Paris was mined . . . We were most concerned.'[91] In spite of their threats, the Fédérés had in fact set no mines; there were perhaps a few dummies.

However long the army might hesitate, the Fédérés were never able to seize the initiative and seriously interrupt the attack: they lacked the manpower. When Rossel tried to mount a counter-attack after the fall of Fort Issy, only 7,000 or 8,000 men could be collected, and he abandoned the attempt.[92] During the last few days of the siege, when the Committee of Public Safety ordered the offensive at all cost, only handfuls of men were available to be thrown into the battle.[93] Numerical weakness left the Fédérés with no margin of error, making their other shortcomings fatal. There was, of course, indiscipline and drunkenness among the men and culpable ignorance among the officers, combined with frivolous self-seeking and jealousy, even at the highest levels. The same was true to an equal, and perhaps greater, extent in the Army of Versailles,[94] but the Versaillais could afford mistakes. Cluseret, though arrogant and complacent, had a grasp of this reality. While many in Paris were talking of sorties, victories and risings in the provinces, he realized after the fiasco of 3 April that the only hope lay in systematic defence, taking advantage of the strength of the fortifications, 'substituting machines for men', neutralizing the numerical superiority of the Versaillais and forcing them into a long and costly siege. On 5 April he told the Executive Commission that 'if our troops keep cool and spare their ammunition, the enemy will tire before we do'. He hoped that the morale of the army would weaken – by no means a forlorn hope – and that the Prussians or public opinion would intervene.[95] These possibilities disquieted the Versailles government. They would only have become grave dangers, however, if the army's ponderous and uncertain progress had been seriously interrupted: 'if a mishap had occurred under the walls of Paris', admitted Thiers, 'we could have counted on nothing'.[96] Such a result would have required thoughtful planning and disciplined execution from the Fédérés. Widespread ignorance and indifference, aggravated by a pernicious taste for reassuring propaganda, were responsible for the failure to prepare for a blow that was clearly imminent,[97] and that had been delayed less by Fédéré strength than by Versaillais weakness.

The army was clearly not the overwhelming force that its numbers suggested, even after the time-consuming problems of reorganization and supply had been surmounted. The inexperience of the troops imposed delays. The army gunners were frequently outclassed by those of the Commune, whose shooting was at times 'extraordinary'.[98] The Issy attack was held up by fire from Fort Vanves and the ramparts, which the besiegers could not silence, to Faron's impatience.[99] The failings of the artillery were not compensated for by the infantry: Cissey had few men well enough trained to be able to snipe at the Fédéré gunners to interrupt their fire.[100] Panics were frequent. Negligence and indiscipline were widespread. Staff work, which should have presented few problems, produced blunders that showed that incapacity was not confined to the lower ranks.[101] Doubts about the troops' morale were ever present. For all these reasons, the generals relied disproportionately on certain units, thus reducing the effect of their numerical superiority. The gendarmes, of whom there were about 3,500 with the army, were invariably used to stiffen other troops from 18 March until early May, seeing action on 2 and 3 April, leading the attack on Neuilly bridge on 6 April, and then being kept in the line at Courbevoie and Asnières, in spite of their mature age, married status and proverbial caution. The Volunteers took over as the spearhead of 1st Corps, remaining almost permanently in the line, where it was hoped that their example would encourage the others. On the southern front, Faron's division and detachments of sailors from the Reserve Army supplemented 2nd Corps. The sailors, considered to be better disciplined and more reliable than the troops of the Line, were frequently used to lead attacks until 6 May, when they were unwilling to attack and had to be withdrawn. Picked companies of scouts, all volunteers, were used in the successful attacks on the Moulin Saquet redoubt on 3 May, and on an armoured train at Choisy on 15 May. Even ordinary policemen were used to lead the troops forward. On 4 April, a lone police sergeant explored the streets and courtyards of Clamart, 'making sure that they were empty of insurgents', before the 35th *de ligne* advanced,[102] and policemen were among the first to enter Paris on 21 May.

If the army had been altered by purges, reinforcement, propaganda and by the fact of fighting, its mood had still not been completely transformed. The fighting was at times savage. The attack on the Moulin Saquet turned into a massacre. The shooting of prisoners after the capture of Clamart station on 2 May marked 'a cruel page in our civil war'.[103] There were other cases which were barely noticed. It cannot be assumed that these incidents show a changing attitude in the army as a whole, for there were moments, circumstances permitting, when the reluctance to fight that had been so noticeable in March continued to show itself. On 29 April, a delegation of freemasons appeared at Neuilly from Paris with the intention of going to see Thiers, and an unofficial truce of one and a half days ensued. Ladmirault gave orders not to open fire until the Fédérés had done so.[104] For once, the two sides could see each other at close quarters without danger: 'the line soldiers waved to us timidly, taking great care that their commanders should not see them. A few National Guards beckoned to them to come over to us, but they replied by vigorous gestures that they could not, pointing to their captains.'[105] Lefrançais, wearing his red sash of the Commune, stood on a barricade to see what was going on: three times an old Versaillais N C O ordered his men to fire, but they did nothing.[106] 'A vague hope was in the air that perhaps this truce would lead to conciliation', noted an officer of the 67th *de marche*.[107] But on both sides, authority prevailed, and firing began again early in the evening of 30 April.[108]

Even in the middle of the fighting, therefore, the generals could never be sure of the reactions of their men. This was surely the main reason why the campaign was conducted with such caution. There were certainly many in the army who hated the Commune, and who for reasons of conviction and ambition were willing to do their best to destroy it. But the generals knew that the whole army was not like this. The day before the entry into Paris, MacMahon issued another circular warning of the dangers of sedition, lamenting the inadequacy of the military police, and urging all officers to be vigilant 'in order to prevent their men from being won over and led away from their duties'.[109] But the fighting in Paris was not to prove as severe a test as the authorities had feared.

9

vvvvvvvvvvvvvvvvvvvvvvvvvvvvvvvvvvvvvvvvvvvvvvvvvvvvvvvvvvvvvvvvvvvvvv

The battle of Paris

At 1 p.m. on Sunday 21 May, Douay's agent, Ducatel, noticed that
bastions 65 and 66 were empty of defenders. He set off by omnibus for
Saint Denis, intending to make his way to Versailles and report.
Deciding that this would be too slow, he alighted at the Place de la
Concorde and returned to the Point du Jour ramparts. The siege
trenches having by this time reached the top of the glacis of bastion 65,
Ducatel was able to signal to a bystander in the trench, a naval officer,
Lieutenant Trèves, who went forward to reconnoitre. Meanwhile, two
army officers had also noticed the absence of defenders, which they
reported to their superiors who ordered scaling ladders forward.[1] At
about 3 p.m., when Ducatel had been identified and his information
checked, a company of the 37th *de marche* on guard in the trenches was
led over the wreckage of the Porte de Saint Cloud drawbridge, from
which the sappers improvised a catwalk. They were supported by a
working party of the 91st *de marche* and a few gunners, who were able
to use two abandoned Fédéré cannon to hold off counter-attacks.
About an hour later, other troops on the spot were sent in and some
light mortars brought up. A staff officer checked for mines. Telegrams
were sent to Douay and General Vergé, whose division was encamped
round Sèvres. By about 6.30, units of Vergé's division and Gandil's
brigade, moved forward that morning by Douay in anticipation of
events, were inside the city.[2]
This was not simply a stroke of luck for Versailles, or the result of
momentary negligence on the part of the Fédérés. The ramparts seem
always to have been weakly or erratically manned.[3] On this occasion,
however, the army was able to take advantage of the fact because its
siege operations were almost complete, enabling the troops to
approach the ramparts without danger. Ducatel's dramatic intervention was of marginal importance.
The news that the Versaillais were inside the ramparts and that the

defenders had been thrown back reached Dombrowski, the Fédéré general commanding the sector, at his headquarters at the château of La Muette, just inside the western ramparts.[4] He informed the War Ministry, calmly sent for reinforcements and announced that he would lead a counter-attack at 7 o'clock, when he expected that the Versaillais would fall back. The delay permitted them to consolidate, however, and when he did lead forward his assembled forces, in response to urgent appeals from the hard pressed outposts along the *petite ceinture* railway, they could make no headway against the invaders, who were able to bring a 'hot and close fire' to bear on them. Dombrowski was lost to sight, and the rumour spread that he had been killed. By 10 o'clock 'the fight was nearly out of the Communists', who withdrew behind the railway viaduct. An hour later all was quiet, and it seemed that the fighting was over for the night. 'The pause was deceptive. The Versaillists must have been holding their hands for a time to make the blow heavier when it should fall.'[5] Most of Paris was still unaware of what had occurred; Delescluze had denied that the Versaillais had entered, and had forbidden the beating of the *rappel*.[6]

Douay himself had been at the Point du Jour since about 6 p.m. Berthaut's Division took the Auteuil gate from the rear at 9 p.m. The artillery had arrived. The information given by Ducatel induced Douay to send Vergé's division to take the dominating height of the Trocadéro, a park overlooking the Seine.[7] Except for one barricade at the end of the Rue Guillon, Douay knew that it was undefended on the side nearest the river.[8] Colonel Piquemal, Vergé's chief of staff, a section of policemen and a company of scouts of the 90th *de marche* approached the Rue Guillon barricade stealthily in the dark, and seized its commander as he came out to begin his rounds. Taken to Vergé, he gave all information, including the passwords, and went back with the scouts to order his men to surrender. They did so immediately. Thirty scouts went on to surprise the guards of the huge underground powder magazine in the Rue Beethoven and took 100 prisoners, including a member of the Commune, Assi. Another section took the Pont d'Iéna and its defenders, and picked up two senior Fédéré officers who had come to investigate in a cab. By 3 a.m. the whole brigade had occupied the Trocadéro, defended only by a few half-built barricades: 1,500 prisoners and a battery of guns were taken. The artillery sited cannon to enfilade the approaching avenues and to fire on the Place de la Concorde and the Left Bank *quais*; early next morning they opened fire

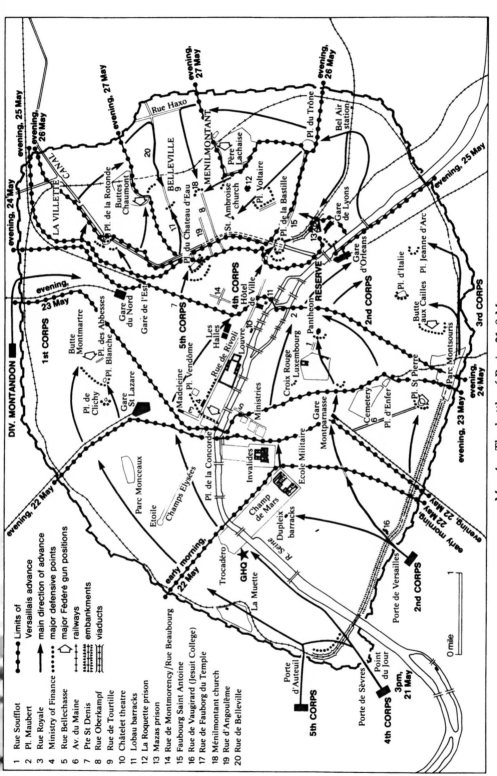

Map 4.   The battle of Paris, 21–8 May.

Key:

1 Rue Soufflot
2 Pl. Maubert
3 Rue Royale
4 Ministry of Finance
5 Rue Bellechasse
6 Av. du Maine
7 Pte St Denis
8 Rue Oberkampf
9 Rue de Tourtille
10 Châtelet theatre
11 Lobau barracks
12 La Roquette prison
13 Mazas prison
14 Rue de Montmorency/Rue Beaubourg
15 Faubourg Saint Antoine
16 Rue de Vaugirard (Jesuit College)
17 Rue du Faborg du Temple
18 Ménilmontant church
19 Rue d'Angoulême
20 Rue de Belleville

Legend:
•—• Limits of
••• Versaillais advance
→ main direction of advance
•••• major Federé gun positions
——— railways
†††† embankments
▓▓▓ viaducts

on the Champ de Mars and the Ecole Militaire, where the Fédéré reserves were sleeping.[9]

On the Versaillais left, 5th Corps had streamed into Paris through the gates of Auteuil, Passy and La Muette, opened as the Fédéré positions along the ramparts were rolled up. A handful of defenders at the château of La Muette were surrounded. Early in the morning, the troops reached the Champs Elysées. On the right, 2nd Corps had entered Paris on the other side of the Seine: small groups of men had been able to pass the defences and open the gates to the others. After a minor battle with the defenders of the Jesuit school and adjacent barricades in the Rue de Vaugirard, Cissey's troops were able to advance rapidly on the Ecole Militaire and the Invalides, aided no doubt by the fire from Vergé's guns at the Trocadéro. By 9.30 a.m. on the 22nd, Cissey had set up his headquarters at the Ecole Militaire.[10]

The Fédéré position in the western districts of Paris completely collapsed, as National Guard units posted there fled or surrendered *en masse*. Fifty thousand Versaillais troops had passed the ramparts within a few hours, and the hastily prepared and poorly manned second and third lines of defence cutting off the south-western salient of the fortifications had been broken at once. The key defensive position of the Trocadéro heights had fallen within hours, and the army was set to advance on both sides of the Seine. The battle of Paris was already lost, for the defenders' only hope would have been to contain the Versaillais incursion, so long anticipated and so little prepared for, by building strong defences in the south-west of the city.

During the day of 22 May, the army moved into position for an attack on the formidable defensive position of Montmartre, planned for the following morning. Elements of five army corps were inside Paris: 1st Corps were on the left, with one division, Montaudon's, advancing outside the fortifications through Clichy; 5th Corps, ahead and to their right, occupied a line along the railway from the Porte d'Asnières to the Gare Saint Lazare, with Clinchant's headquarters at the Parc Monceau; 4th Corps had almost reached the Madeleine; Vergé's division of the Reserve was in the Faubourg Saint Honoré and the Champs Elysées, facing the Fédéré positions adjoining the Tuileries terrace and the Place Vendôme; Bruat's division of the Reserve was on the Left Bank, in the area of the Champ de Mars; 2nd Corps was spreading rapidly through the southern districts of the city, occupying the Gare Montparnasse and the railway line up to the fortifications. MacMahon established his headquarters near the Trocadéro, where he was visited that afternoon by Thiers.

Progress was deliberately slow. There was no plan for the surprise advance, and attempts to increase speed could only have increased confusion. As it was, the roads into Paris were crammed with men and guns, and the Trocadéro itself had been dangerously congested. Fear of mines produced caution. There was also fear of counter-attack by the Fédérés, and leading units were forbidden to advance too far.[11] In order not to leave potential enemies unaccounted for, searches were carried out and many people arrested. A depot for prisoners was set up at the Parc Monceau on 22 May. All available gendarmes were ordered to the Point du Jour to escort prisoners to Versailles, where the first convoy arrived that same morning.[12] Barricades were demolished in the rear of the troops and new ones built as the army advanced, to protect the forward troops whenever they halted.[13] Orders had already been given to avoid frontal attacks on Fédéré positions by sapping through buildings, and the troops 'seemed to take things very deliberately, and to be making quite sure of their ground before advancing further'.[14] This gave breathing space to the Fédérés, who used it to throw up hundreds of barricades all over the city, though seemingly without planning a defence.

The news of the Versaillais entry was officially disclosed on the morning of 22 May. The tocsin was rung and the *générale* at last beaten.[15] At Montmartre, the citadel of the insurrection and the first major obstacle in the army's path, the reaction was feeble.[16] Many of the most active elements of the National Guard had been at the front line, and some must have been cut off or dispersed by the advance of the army. Other units were not armed; others still were disorganized by personal quarrels and perhaps even by treachery. The artillery had been ordered to fire on the advancing troops at the Trocadéro, but it failed to do so.[17] During the night of the 22nd, certain Communard leaders, notably La Cécilia, Lefrançais and Vermorel, with a handful of men, tried to organize the defence of the hill, but in vain.[18] No large reinforcements were sent. Indeed, Delescluze seems to have abandoned all idea of restoring an organized defence, calling for 'revolutionary war':[19] 'Enough of militarism! No more staff officers braided and gilded on every seam! Make way for the people, for the fighters with bare arms! . . . The people know nothing of clever manoeuvres. But when they have rifles in their hands and cobblestones under their feet, they have no fear of all the strategists of the monarchical school.'

If Delescluze believed this, he was seriously mistaken: 'militarism' and clever manoeuvres were soon to show their value, as will be seen, but to the Versaillais. No doubt in part he was making a virtue of necessity and, however unwise the wording, the proclamation can have had little effect on the outcome of the battle.

After a short rest, the Versaillais moved forward during the early hours of 23 May for their attack on Montmartre, the principal objective for the day. 1st Corps was to encircle it from the north, and 5th Corps from the south. There was some resistance near the cemetery, on the north-western approach to the hill, which caused Abatucci's brigade to pass further to the north, but it did not last, and Pradier's brigade, following Abatucci, was able to take the Fédéré positions.[20] On the Versaillais right, the advance of 5th Corps was opposed by a mere handful of defenders, who none the less held up their progress. A large barricade in the Place de Clichy was held by only about thirty men, and that in the Place Blanche, at the southern foot of the hill, by a dozen – soon reduced to a woman and seven or eight men, all very old or very young.[21] Some important streets were not barricaded at all, and on the hill itself confusion reigned. The Fédéré gunners at the bastions were without orders and did not know what to fire at. Some were short of ammunition. Certain gun-crews, fearing encirclement, left with their guns for La Chapelle or La Villette; one went straight to the Père Lachaise cemetery, miles to the rear.[22] The Volunteers of the Seine, among the leading units of 1st Corps, took advantage of the defenders' confusion and advanced well ahead of the regulars, helped no doubt by their knowledge of the area. One of them, slightly drunk, ran into the Place des Abbesses, where the Fédérés had concentrated most of their men (mainly *sédentaires*) and, seizing their red flag, ordered them to surrender. Taken aback, 600 of them did so.[23] Commandant Durieu had led sixteen Volunteers to the top of the hill, where they met a superior force of Fédérés whose fire pinned them down behind a barricade, Durieu being fatally wounded.[24] At this time, about noon, 5th Corps began arriving from the south, having at last overcome the few Fédéré barricades by breaking through the nearby houses and firing down on the defenders. At first they mistook the Volunteers for Fédérés, and the scouts of the 14th *provisoire* were ready to shoot them.[25] At 12.50 Mont Valérien reported that the hill of Montmartre was covered with troops, a company of whom rescued Durieu's men in the Rue Fontanelle, on the far slopes.[26]

Although the capture of Montmartre was the main event of 23 May,

11   Fédérés defending Montmartre: a barricade in the Rue des Abbesses.

important advances were made too in the centre of Paris and on the Left Bank. 4th Corps moved slowly up to the Madeleine, which was occupied (by a half section of infantry under a second-lieutenant who shot all the defenders who continued to resist) and then temporarily abandoned,[27] and in the direction of the new opera house. On their left, they joined hands with Clinchant's 5th Corps near Notre Dame de Lorette (where Archibald Forbes, the war correspondant, narrowly escaped being shot by both sides).[28] Their right, however, supported by units of the Reserve Army in the Champs Elysées and Faubourg Saint Honoré, was still kept in check by Brunel holding the Rue Royale, Tuileries terrace and Place Vendôme with a few hundred men, solid barricades and cannon.[29] When Douay's men, as ordered, advanced by sapping through the houses and firing down on the defenders of the barricades, Brunel stopped them by setting fire to houses in the Rue Royale. The Versaillais were only able to occupy the Place Vendôme late that night after Brunel had withdrawn on orders from the Hôtel de Ville, under cover of the blazing Tuileries.[30]

On the Left Bank, where as yet there had been little resistance, units of 2nd Corps and the Reserve Army moved into the administrative quarter of the 7th *arrondissement*, occupying the Ministry of War, Public Instruction, and the Telegraph office. The fighting had already taken on a savage character. Under the personal command of General Bocher, who had gathered information concerning the Fédérés' whereabouts from local inhabitants, the Versaillais advanced rapidly through adjoining gardens and took the defenders, who were guarding only the streets, by surprise. They had no time to fight back and were 'all, and in great number, put to the sword'. Bocher's orderly officer, with a detachment of *chasseurs*, took a barricade in the Rue Bellechasse, and killed five Fédérés 'by his own hand'. Other *chasseurs*, under Commandant de Poussargues (a participant in the 18 March events at Montmartre), surprised the defenders of the Telegraph: 'The whole post . . . with its *cantinière* . . . were put to the bayonet without a single man being able to escape.'[31] Bocher occupied the area up to the Rue du Bac until relieved during the evening by two regiments of

12   The Rue de Rivoli barricade, defended by Brunel, 22–3 May.

Bruat's sailors, who ventured too far ahead and were caught in a crossfire, suffering 'heavy losses' – five killed and eight wounded.[32] In the centre, Lacretelle's division, advancing from the Babylone barracks, was held up by the Fédéré position at the Croix Rouge crossroads. Here, Varlin and Lisbonne held out until the night.[33] On the far right, Le Vassor-Sorval's division filtered through the little streets between the railway and the Avenue du Maine, swept by Fédéré cannon at the Place Saint Pierre and a mountain gun in the church tower; the second brigade moved along the fortifications to outflank this troublesome strongpoint. After several hours' exchange of fire, Boulanger led a charge against the remaining defenders, many of whom were killed. Those sniping from the church steeple were all shot, as were suspected deserters and a man accused of firing a shot from inside his shop. Several hundred prisoners were taken.[34] With the Avenue du Maine thus opened, the Versaillais were able to occupy the Montparnasse cemetery and the Place d'Enfer, and to move north into the small streets leading towards the Luxembourg gardens, the route to the Fédéré strongpoint at the Pantheon.[35]

On 24 May, Ladmirault asked MacMahon to halt his men's advance and allow them to rest the following day: 'for two days they have hardly been able to eat or sleep'. 5th Corps was in a similar state.[36] Progress had slowed to a crawl on the Right Bank. 'Clearly their policy was to take no risks, and to economise as much as possible in the matter of their own lives . . . fresh as the red-breeches were from their German captivity, their spirit was probably held not quite an assured thing.' In the Boulevard Haussmann, there remained only about twenty-five Fédéré defenders. 'Two minutes at the *pas de charge* would have given the regulars the boulevard from end to end; but they would not make the effort, and instead they were bursting their way from house to house, and taking pot shots out of the windows.' At the same time, the artillery was firing continuously along the boulevard. 'So scanty were the defenders that scarce any execution was done by all this expenditure of ammunition; but it probably tried the nerve of the few Communists left.'[37] 1st Corps had barely moved, in spite of the intervention of Montaudon's division, which marched round the outside of the fortifications with the Germans' permission, and entered Paris by the railway line on the morning of the 24th, occupying the Gare du Nord during the morning. The rest of the Corps remained in occupation of the hill of Montmartre and the surrounding streets.[38] 5th Corps, ordered to link up with 1st Corps on its left, was obliged to stop its advance as the latter held back: it merely occupied the south-western corner of the 10th *arrondissement,* and the north-eastern corner of the 2nd, reaching the Boulevard de Strasbourg and taking the Fédéré defences round the Porte Saint Denis, where, as in 1848, there was a flurry of fighting.[39] 4th Corps, a little further south, pushed a division as far as Les Halles. Vergé's division of the Reserve was unable to advance along the blazing Rue de Rivoli until the evening, when it occupied the area round the burning Hôtel de Ville. In the meantime, it helped put out the fires at the Louvre and the Palais Royal and save the records of the *rente* from the blazing Ministry of Finance.[40]

On the Left Bank too progress had slowed somewhat, though the day's objective, the Pantheon, was successfully occupied. Lacretelle's division had outflanked it from the south, reaching the Place Maubert. Le Vassor-Sorval's division had encircled it from the north. The Luxembourg Palace had been occupied shortly before when a battalion of Marines, exceeding their orders, advanced and found it undefended.[41] The 17th *chasseurs* charged across the gardens, supported by heavy fire, including that from mountain guns on the roof of the palace. The Fédérés held three barricades in the Rue Soufflot, the first of which they abandoned immediately. The Versaillais, however, were unable to advance any further than this, the men being 'tired' – surely a

13   Paturel's men attacking the Pantheon.

154

euphemism.[42] The brigade commander, General Paturel, and Colonel Biadelli of the 38th were wounded. Finally, the Pantheon was attacked from all sides. From the south, Susbielle's men advanced through the gardens of the Ecole Normale and the nearby convent, supported by guns and snipers in the Rue de l'Abbé de l'Epée, where there occurred a small engagement that gives a good idea of the character of the fighting. An army gun-crew remained an hour in the open cannonading a barricade, exposed to the fire of its defenders at 250 yards. But this proved 'more noisy than dangerous' and only two soldiers were wounded – bruised by ricochets.[43] The *chasseurs* and 38th *de marche*, unable to take the barricades in the Rue Soufflot by frontal attack, outflanked them by the parallel side streets, the Rues Cujas and Malebranche.[44] Realizing that they were in danger of being cut off on the other side by the Versaillais in the Boulevard Saint Germain and the Rue des Ecoles, many of the Fédérés retreated. Those who could not or would not were slaughtered: Biadelli claimed proudly that his regiment, the 38th, had killed 400; its own losses were one killed and twenty-seven wounded.[45] That night the Versaillais line stretched almost straight from the Gare du Nord to the Parc Montsouris.

At this time, halfway through the week, the fighting reached a climax. In slowing their advance after the first few hours, the army had allowed the Fédérés to recover their balance. The eastern half of Paris had been covered with barricades. Little of this was due to the leadership of the remnant of the Commune, which decided on 24 May to evacuate the Hôtel de Ville and its environs. The building was set on fire, and in spite of Delescluze's protests, headquarters withdrew to the *mairie* of the 11th *arrondissement*, far behind the lines.[46] The Commune as such no longer functioned, though some of its members were active as individuals. Responsibility for the defence came to rest on the shoulders of a few determined men, such as Lisbonne, a former *zouave* turned actor-manager and colonel of the 10th National Guard Legion; Vermorel, journalist and member of the Commune; Varlin, working-class militant and Finance Delegate of the Commune; and Brunel, ex-officer, Blanquist, Fédéré general and member of the Commune. Even more, perhaps, the defence depended on the wits and courage of a few hundred anonymous Fédérés, often defending their own quarter, even their own street.

Left to themselves, the Fédérés showed much strategic sense. Although many lives were thrown away defending small, isolated, badly constructed barricades that were nothing but death traps, the main effort was intelligently devoted to the defence of points in the city that the army was forced to take, but that it dared not approach directly, such as the Place de la Rotonde (now Place de Stalingrad), Place du Château d'Eau (now Place de la République) and Place de la Bastille. Haussmann's town planning worked to the insurgents' advantage, for their artillery was able to sweep the squares and avenues, which brought the army's cautious advance through side streets, courtyards and houses to a halt.[47] Other artillery was well placed on high ground at the Buttes Chaumont and the Père Lachaise cemetery. The Canal Saint Martin, covered over between the Bastille and the Rue du Faubourg du Temple, formed a ready made glacis along part of the front, and further north, where it lay open, formed a moat against the advance of 1st Corps. On the Left Bank, Wroblewski held the Butte aux Cailles with a strong force brought in from the southern forts. Here, just inside the city walls, high open ground above the River Bièvre covered by Fédéré artillery formed a serious obstacle to 2nd Corps. In attacking these strongpoints, the army's casualty figures reached their highest level, though remaining low in absolute terms.[48]

That the defenders were never able entirely to check the Versaillais advance or inflict heavy casualties was due to their tactical weaknesses – the instinctive reliance on barricades even when these had been made useless by the army's tactics of encirclement and sapping through buildings – and their lack of numbers and organization. A few hundred fought stubbornly, but many even of the genuine partisans of the Commune had had the fight knocked out of them. A Versaillais officer who lost his way and found himself alone in a Fédéré area, the Rues de Montmorency and Beaubourg, 'full of people coming back from the barricades', shouted out the order to surrender immediately, 'even threatening them with punishment if they disobeyed'. The bluff worked.[49] The 2nd Division of 5th Corps took ninety-three barricades during the week, but of these only ten were strongly defended and forty-one were not defended at all. The division, 6,000 strong, lost only 35 men killed and 272 wounded.[50] The defence, though patchy, was often sufficient to halt the cautious Versaillais. The 36th *de marche* (1st Corps), for example, took all day to capture a barricade defending the approaches to the Place de la Rotonde. Two battalions burrowed through walls and houses, left detachments to keep watch on the population, placed companies to distract the Fédérés with rifle fire, and only at 10.30 p.m. did they risk a charge against the surviving defenders, weakened by the concentrated musketry of two companies firing down from the roofs of adjoining houses. The regiment, 1,200 strong, lost only two killed, but evidently the fight was considered a hot one, for the next day the men were allowed to rest.[51]

Cissey on the Left Bank was more aggressive, and he took the first of the Fédérés' strongpoints, the Butte aux Cailles, on 25 May. The position was outflanked on both sides by Le Vassor-Sorval's division advancing along the fortifications and Susbielle's division moving on the Place d'Italie from the Pantheon. Lian's brigade attacked the main Fédéré positions round the Butte aux Cailles in the early afternoon. A few hundred of the defenders retreated across the Seine, but many others threw down their arms at the Place d'Italie, and about 700 negotiated their surrender at the Place Jeanne d'Arc, after which many were allowed to go home.[52] The rest of the Left Bank was occupied, including Forts Montrouge, Bicêtre and Ivry, and MacMahon was able to reassure Thiers, who had been worried that the Fédérés might still be able to attack Versailles, that this was no longer a danger.[53]

On the Right Bank, the objectives for the day were the Place du Château d'Eau and the Place de la Bastille. The former was taken by de Courcy's brigade of 5th Corps, in spite of courageous resistance by Lisbonne with about 300 men.[54] The Versaillais occupied the buildings on three sides of the square, and their musketry fire forced the defenders to abandon their barricades and retreat towards the Place Voltaire. Lisbonne and Vermorel were both seriously wounded and Delescluze, his despair completed by the distrust of some of the Fédérés,[55] walked down to the abandoned barricade at the end of the Boulevard du Prince Eugène (now Boulevard Voltaire), and was killed, probably by sharpshooters of the 15th *provisoire* in a house on the opposite side of the square.[56] The Fédérés had no means of halting the advance of 5th Corps, which occupied the area up to the Canal Saint Martin that night and the next morning, or of 4th Corps, on the right, which reached the line of the canal, the Boulevard Richard Lenoir, during the 26th.[57]

The Reserve Army, however, was unable to budge the Fédérés from their positions round the Place de la Bastille, where they held large barricades in the Rue Saint Antoine, and at the ends of the Rue du Faubourg Saint Antoine and the Rue de la Roquette. During 25 May, Vergé's division managed to advance through the Marais, filtering through the little streets on both sides of the Rue Saint Antoine and pushing small forces behind the Fédéré flanks during the night.[58] The leading units of Faron's division, marching along the *quais*, were held

14　A barricade at the Place du Chateau d'Eau, where Delescluze fell.

up by shell and rifle fire from the Bastille positions and the Père Lachaise cemetery, and by a huge blazing warehouse. Faron sent the 35th and 42nd *de ligne* over the Canal Saint Martin by an improvised footbridge, and they were able, with the help of supporting cannon fire from the gunboat flotilla and batteries on the Left Bank, to clear all obstacles as far as the Pont de Bercy, and occupy the Gare de Lyon and the Mazas prison. This enabled Derroja's brigade, which had advanced along the Left Bank, unable to cross the Seine because of the heavy fire from the other side, to cross the Pont de Bercy during the evening.[59]

The strong resistance at the Bastille may have decided MacMahon to encircle all the remaining Fédéré positions rather than press the attack in the centre. Vinoy was therefore instructed to move his leading units forward towards the Place du Trône (now Place de la Nation) and also to attack the Bastille from the rear.[60] 1st Corps, making very slow progress on the left, was to take the Place de la Rotonde. De la Mariouse's brigade of the Reserve Army, and that of Langourian, which had followed Derroja across the Seine, invaded the side streets between the *quai* and the Faubourg Saint Antoine, while Derroja's brigade made a wide detour along the fortifications just north of the Seine. The 109th *de ligne*, under Colonel Lespiau, seized the Bel Air railway station and the small barracks of the nearby bastion. The Fédérés, outnumbered and surprised, had hardly time to defend themselves: fifteen at the station and ten at the barracks were captured and killed, including, according to Pelletan, a *cantinière* and her daughter.[61] The 110th, under Derroja, then began to move along the railway viaduct from Bel Air towards the Bastille, supported by de la Mariouse's men in the streets below, and were able, not without difficulty, to reach the railway station overlooking the Place de la Bastille, forcing the Fédérés to retreat into the Faubourg Saint Antoine. Vergé's 1st brigade then charged down the Boulevard Beaumarchais and occupied the Place and the Fédéré barricades on its eastern side; the 37th *de marche*, leading the attack, lost only seven killed and forty-nine wounded in this, the most important action of the week.[62] The Place du Trône was occupied later in the day. On the Versaillais left, 1st Corps finally attacked the Place de la Rotonde. The 119th *de ligne* encircled its defenders, forcing them to abandon the domed customs building, at a cost of twelve killed and forty-eight wounded.[63]

The fighting ended in anti-climax. 4th and 5th Corps were ordered to hold their positions along the Canal Saint Martin; for them the fighting was practically over. 1st Corps and the Reserve were to march round the inside of the fortifications and take the Fédérés in the rear. The remaining obstacles in their path, the Buttes Chaumont and the Père Lachaise cemetery, were taken on 27 May, the former being surrounded as usual, then charged by a unit of the Foreign Legion, and

15   The Place de la Bastille after the battle.

the latter falling almost without resistance to a battalion of Marines who had advanced without orders. At both points, the defenders were much reduced in numbers and short of ammunition, although there were large stocks in the nearby church of Saint Ambroise.[64] The *mairie* of the 11th *arrondissement*, in the Place Voltaire, temporarily the centre of the resistance, had to be abandoned under concentrated artillery fire from batteries at the Places de la Bastille, du Château d'Eau and du Trône.[65]

During the night of the 27th, fighting was fierce on the northern approaches to Belleville, where the Volunteers formed the vanguard of 1st Corps, and near Père Lachaise.[66] The remaining Fédérés, combatants and followers, were crowded into a few streets adjoining the Boulevards de Belleville and de Ménilmontant, where, pressed hard on three sides, and with 4th and 5th Corps closing off the fourth, the defenders were incapable of halting the Versaillais advance.

Early in the morning of Sunday 28 May, 1st Corps and Derroja's brigade of the Reserve met near the Porte des Lilas and, forming a cordon inside the fortifications, turned west and marched down hill into Belleville, Ménilmontant and Charonne, trapping the remaining Fédérés between themselves and 4th and 5th Corps along the canal.[67] A few determined men held out to the last: Camélinat and the 209th battalion in the Rue d'Angoulême (now Rue Jean-Pierre Timbaud); the 191st with Vallès at the bottom of the Rue de Belleville; Varlin, Ferré and others in the Rue du Faubourg du Temple, a few hundred unknowns, 'the last remnants of the Commune', firing from windows.[68] The Versaillais replied with heavy gunfire, even from long range, MacMahon ordering the batteries at Montmartre to fire on the Fédéré position at the corner of the Rue Oberkampf, over two miles away.[69] As both sides blazed away with their cannon, Parisians not surprisingly took refuge in the cellars.

The last serious fighting took place at the bottom of the Rue de Belleville, whose barricade harboured 'all that is most resolute in the quarter'. The defenders answered the Versaillais summons to surrender with 'le mot de Cambronne', and so the 36th *de marche* charged and shot 'all those still offering resistance'. The Fédérés retreated to another barricade in the Faubourg du Temple, pursued by the 36th, and then again to the Rue Saint Maur, where they showed the white flag. A company of the 3rd battalion took 150 prisoner.[70]

Elsewhere, resistance had collapsed. De la Mariouse's brigade took 1,500 prisoners in the Rue Haxo, and then marched down through Ménilmontant without meeting opposition. Derroja took another 2,000 near Père Lachaise. At the Place Puebla, 800 Fédérés surrendered after a parley.[71] At the *mairie* of Belleville, a Foreign Legion soldier was 'calling on all those in sight to surrender and lay down their arms. I gave myself up as a prisoner of war, but had the advantage of seeing my name written down in the list of those taken without arms.'[72] Most fighting was over by early afternoon, though a few Fédérés continued to hold out near Ménilmontant church,[73] and hours later, at 6 p.m., Déroulède and a fatigue party of the 30th battalion of *chasseurs* collided with an occupied barricade in the Rue de Tourtille; he charged it, seized the red flag that flew over it, and was seriously wounded in the arm in this, the last skirmish of the civil war.[74]

Faith in the *levée en masse* was disappointed on 3 April, and again, far more disastrously, during the battle of Paris. The Parisian variant of the myth, in which the People, rifle in hand and cobblestones under foot, stand invincible behind their barricades, was shown to be quite unreal. Delescluze, whose rhetoric appealed to this myth at a decisive moment, may have hoped, with others, that the street fighting would neutralize the superiority of the Versaillais, which had grown irresistible in the fighting outside the walls. On the contrary, the street fighting of 1871 demanded greater coordination than had the siege operations, in which comparatively small numbers of Fédérés in the forts and bastions had been able to keep a visible enemy at a distance with artillery. Once inside the city, hidden among the buildings and filtering through the courtyards and gardens, the Versaillais, 110,000 strong, could only have been countered – at best a remote possibility – by a planned, concentrated, watertight defence. The scattered barricades the Fédérés threw up were easily by-passed, especially as the Versaillais showed greater ingenuity in street fighting than their opponents. As the latter, attached to their own quarters, could not be brought together, no defensible perimeter could be formed, though there were several suitable sites.[75] And although hundreds of unknowns died where they stood, there was no prepared last stand, for example on the Ile de la Cité, as several Blanquist members of the Commune had suggested.[76] Perhaps part of the explanation is that the Fédérés expected a rising of the whole people of Paris, making every street a fortress. This did not happen. Most of the population remained as spectators, unless forced into the action by one side or the other, as when forced by the Fédérés to build barricades, and then by the Versaillais to demolish them. Perhaps 20,000 fought,[77] but far fewer held on to the last.

The battle was therefore less testing for the army than might have been feared. No doubt they could have made faster progress had they been willing to take risks and accept higher losses, but MacMahon directed the operation cautiously, 'so as not to lose too many men'.[78] The casualty figures show his success: about 400 officers and men were killed and 1,100 seriously wounded.[79] Although the battle was tedious and fatiguing, it was rarely very dangerous for the troops. Most units spent only a day or two engaged in combat, and often took part in only one serious action. Thereafter they settled down to occupy captured areas.[80] The massacres that followed are therefore all the harder to explain.

10

Expiation

Expiation for the crimes of the Commune, said Thiers, would be complete; it would be so 'in the name of the law and by the law'.[1] As always, he was attempting to satisfy both the Right in the Assembly by promising 'complete' expiation, and the Left by resisting the extra-legal measures that had been proposed, such as mass transportation without trial. What actually happened bore little relation to Thiers's parliamentary phrase-making. The repression was enormous, striking at more people than had ever fought for the Commune, and yet it was incomplete in allowing the escape of many of those whom the Versaillais most wanted to punish. It tried to preserve the appearances of legality, setting up courts martial in Paris and at Versailles to try prisoners, but its excesses were so flagrant that no one was convinced that the laws of the land were being applied. Even Thiers, MacMahon and other Ministers and generals had to acknowledge the fact and condemn the excesses.[2]

Excuses and explanations had to be found. Versaillais apologists regretted what they claimed to be an accident, a sad consequence of human nature, stemming from the anger of the troops provoked by the crimes of the Commune.[3] The surviving Communards, while blaming the ferocity of the troops, wrongly supposed to be the 'armée césarienne' of soldiers 'mindless from seven years of service', were convinced that Thiers had willed the outcome to eliminate the 'reds'.[4]

The question of responsibility must be borne in mind. It concerns, of course, the relations between the government and the military authorities, orders given, the parts played by officers and men, the ancillary role of the police, the National Guard of Order and the population. But there is a more general question of causality, more difficult to answer. 'Why this bloodthirsty madness? Why?'[5]

At first there was little sign of what was to come. The entry into Paris, made without an assault and almost without bloodshed, was a relief to the soldiers and also to the inhabitants. Resistance was at first negligible. There were no counter-attacks or mines. The areas first occupied were not hostile, and even when there was some fighting, as in the Grand Boulevards, the population came out to watch, 'crying "Bravo!" and clapping their hands because they hoped and believed the Versaillists were winning'. When the troops arrived in force 'the excitement was hysterical. The inhabitants rushed from the houses with bottles of wine; from the windows money was showered into the streets; the women fell on the necks of the sweaty, dusty men in red breeches. . . . The soldiers fraternized warmly, drank and pressed forward. Their discipline was most creditable.'⁶ Some soldiers relaxed in response to the welcome. 'The soldier looks confident, good-natured', noted Rossel. Forbes saw a little soldier, alone, playing to the gallery by taking potshots at the Fédérés for the entertainment of the cheering crowd. But a few streets away, Vermeil de Conchard and his men of the 13th *provisoire*, though literally showered with gifts of money thrown from windows, remained suspicious: 'I had my sword drawn, my revolver loaded.'⁷ The Volunteers had strict orders at night to fire at any light.⁸ Outside the *beaux quartiers* the reception was less cordial. In the northern part of the 17th *arrondissement*, the inhabitants refused Vermeil a blanket or a mattress and would not give the men bread. He thought this typical of the Parisians' attitude.⁹ Such recalcitrance did not last: soon the inhabitants would not dare to refuse even if the soldiers troubled to ask.

When fighting took place not in the open spaces of the boulevards but within the confines of houses, courtyards and alleys, the atmosphere changed. Then the combatants on both sides, no longer in an arena watched by cheering crowds, became nervous of the presence of hidden enemies. Troops on both sides routinely ordered windows to be closed and shutters opened, to make sniping more difficult, and both issued stern warnings to the occupants of houses from which shots might be fired.¹⁰ Many ugly incidents took place, especially on the part of the Versaillais. It was accepted from the beginning that 'murderers' firing from concealment would be shot on the spot:

the crime must be punished and the murderer shot immediately. But there are ten men there, all swearing their innocence! Then each soldier must become supreme judge, must look to see whether the rifle has been recently fired, whether the hands are black with powder, whether the civilian overalls cover National Guard uniform! No one calls him to account over the right of life and death that he exercises among wives and children pleading on their knees; throughout the house one hears nothing but moans, cries and shots.[11]

It was the character of the fighting rather than its scale, and its imaginary rather than its real dangers, that increased the savagery of this 'tough, platoon-commanders' war'.[12]

The fighting itself was only the first phase of the restoration of 'order'. Searches of captured areas – demanding at least an equal deployment of force and causing many more deaths – were carried out by the army, eventually with the assistance of the police. The searches were considered a military necessity to eliminate the danger of hidden enemies being left in the rear, as well as a police operation to capture criminals. The many thousands of wrongful arrests and summary executions occasioned by these searches were later excused as the actions of troops exasperated by hard combat. But the fighting was rarely hard, and the repression that followed was not in general carried out by the fighting troops but by other units coming later.

The arrival of the army followed a pattern. First came a small section of scouts, sometimes without an officer, followed by a squad of engineers to clear barricades and, in case of fighting, to break passages through the walls of neighbouring buildings. Later came a battalion of the leading regiment of the brigade, a section of artillery and the rest of the engineers, followed eventually by the main body, which carried out the 'disarmament'.[13] There was therefore a delay between the occupation of an area and its searching, especially when there had been no fighting. Often several searches were carried out haphazardly by successive waves of troops. But though disorganized, arbitrary and violent, the 'disarmament' of Paris was not carried out by soldiers out of control, sacking the city in the tradition of the *soldatesque*. The troops remained under the direction of their officers, though Versaillais apologists implied the contrary when excesses were undeniable. This is indicated by the rarity of reports of looting, even in pro-Commune and neutral accounts of events. *The Times* (8 June), for example, knew of 'no instances of pillage . . . or of drunkenness'. While there were numerous thefts from houses being searched, from corpses, and even from living prisoners,[14] there was not the open, large-scale pillaging that would accompany a breakdown of discipline. Cases of rape are almost unheard of,[15] and drunkenness was restrained.[16] The officers did not trust the men sufficiently to permit laxity. 'Among us, at least, evil instincts were contained by discipline', claimed Hans.[17] The statement is absurd, but it contains a certain truth: whereas the Fédéré atrocities were unpremeditated outbursts of anger, the worst excesses of the army were committed on orders.

A leading part in the searches and the arrests was played by the police, detachments of which were attached to every army corps and division. They operated directly under the orders of the military commanders who, conscious of their superior knowledge of the city and its population, left them wide initiative. After the first fighting was over, they frequently directed the searches and arrests, and advised the military on the operations of the summary courts martial. These police detachments seem to have had little contact with the normal police hierarchy based at Versailles: police officers coming from there could not always circulate in Paris, where they had no 'constituted authority', martial law being in force.[18]

The second auxiliary of the army was the National Guard of Order, though its activities arose from personal zeal rather than the encouragement of the authorities. National Guard headquarters at Versailles had set up a clandestine network of commanders inside the city, attached officers to the army corps headquarters, and planned a rising to take place inside the city when the army arrived.[19] The rising came to nothing, but a number of pro-government National Guard officers installed themselves at their *mairies* and directed a petty reign of terror. Some were very dubious individuals, such as a Captain Robert, alias Suschki, who organized an amateur police force from the *mairie* of the 5th, consisting of a concierge named Texier and an ex-criminal named Marie. They directed the troops during house searches, and Robert was later prosecuted for theft during the course of them. So was Lieutenant-Colonel Lyoën, *'prévôt'* of the 17th *arrondissement*.[20] Usually local men, they knew (or thought they knew) the leading Communards in the district, and were helped by captured documents, such as the muster rolls of Fédéré battalions, which gave the names and addresses of participants.[21] Thousands of denunciations were received too, and at first acted upon. The Marquis de Forbin-Janson, for example, denounced several of his neighbours and tenants on his return to Paris, and one of them was shot at the Châtelet.[22]

The police and the National Guard of Order were more personally involved in paying off old scores than were the regulars, some of whom began by treating prisoners leniently. It was the combat unit of the National Guard of Order, the Volunteers of the Seine, which began the slaughter of prisoners at Montmartre. They were under the command of two local men, Commandant Durieu, a veteran of the counter-guerilla forces in Mexico and the *franc-tireurs* of the Vosges, who lived at La Chapelle, and Lieutenant Escolan de Grandpré, who had fought for the Confederate States of America, and lived in the 8th *arrondissement*. Arriving before the other troops, they began house searches and 'every man in National Guard uniform, having a rifle, or with the palm of his hand black with powder was shot. Commandant Durieu . . . carried out the executions personally, and killed a dozen in this way; only the young were taken prisoner.'[23] Escolan did the same. He had been chased out of Paris by the Fédérés and had 'sworn deadly hatred' against them; besides, 'there were definite orders'.[24] Whose orders these were it is hard to say. The Volunteers judged summarily, by appearance. Compiègne released one suspect who had 'a big sheepish face and looked so stupid that it seemed impossible that he could have done anything bad'. Sutter-Laumann, hiding a few streets away, took care to wash, comb his hair and brush his uniform, and to speak 'without a working-class accent in good French' when questioned by a Volunteer officer who finally let him go, saying 'I lived in this quarter a long time, I have not come to do harm', and warning that the regulars would be less 'soft'. Thirty-seven men had been shot outside in the Rue Lepic. Several army deserters captured by the Volunteers were shot too, as was a former naval petty officer serving the Commune as a gunner; Escolan blew out the man's brains with a revolver.[25]

The first regulars to arrive at Montmartre were in fact more gentle than the Volunteers. The men did not seem ferocious, and the officers looked displeased with their task. They were even reassuring. 'Do not be afraid', said one officer. 'We have come to rescue you.' One of the soldiers whispered, 'We are forced to march.' The peasant soldiers, however, recognizable by their accents, were less friendly, and the 10th battalion of *chasseurs* seemed worse than the Line. Whereas the Volunteers were merciless towards certain prisoners whom they considered more guilty than the rest, some of the regulars showed hostility towards the whole population; no doubt Montmartre was suffering from its reputation as the 'Aventine Hill' of the revolution. 'Parisian scum . . . good-for-nothing layabouts, you are not such loudmouths now. If you budge, off to Cayenne!' Other troops arriving later threatened to shoot all those in possession of rifles. Some helped themselves to household objects during the course of the haphazard searches. Those who bivouacked for the night were dangerously drunk, and arrested several men at random when they claimed to have been fired on.[26]

As the advance moved east into generally less friendly territory, and as the strain of the week's fighting grew, tension mounted. Even though casualties were low, the troops were aware of being constantly exposed to stray bullets and to shells fired at random from the Fédéré batteries on the eastern heights and in the forts. Food distribution was irregular, rest was scanty, and a hot sun added to the strain on minds and bodies, and must have increased the amount of wine drunk.

Fires broke out in the centre of the city, engulfing the Tuileries, the Ministry of Finance, the Hôtel de Ville, much of the Rues de Rivoli and de Lille, the Palais de Justice, the Grenier d'Abondance near the Arsenal, and eventually the huge La Villette warehouses. The spectacle affected everyone. 'Terrified, we are witnessing the end of a city, almost the collapse of a world.' The Fédérés felt the same: 'It is the end of everything.' 'I was often frightened during the Commune', recalled an American girl, 'but I do not remember anything more terrifying than the fires.'[27] Panic spread, for it seemed that the Fédérés were carrying out a plan to destroy Paris rather than surrender it; the myth of the fire-raising *pétroleuse* appeared. It was feared that whole areas of the city were mined, and might collapse into the limestone caverns upon which they were built. The troops searched the sewers, and mistakenly cut numerous telegraph wires thought to be the means of detonating explosive charges.[28] The collapse of burning houses in the Rue Saint Honoré caused a panic among soldiers and civilians alike: 'The quarter is mined! Everything is blowing up!' At the Pantheon, whose vaults were packed with gunpowder, there was the same panic: 'Women flee, dragging children behind them. . . . And everywhere the shout: The Pantheon is going to blow up!' With the fear came anger, even in areas sympathetic towards the Commune.[29] Many had been forced to leave their houses, and many more felt threatened with the same fate, or worse, for people had died trapped in the fires: seven were found suffocated in a house in the Rue Saint Honoré.[30] This was the prime cause of the increase in mob violence against Fédéré prisoners. Near the scorched ruins of the Ministry of Finance and the Rue Royale, women threw pieces of rubble at prisoners: 'the middle-class women, the tradeswomen, the passers-by of this well-to-do district . . . were pitiless. . . . The men looked on in silence.'[31]

The effect of this pressure and example on the troops, who throughout the campaign had been in contact with civilians hostile to the

16   The fire in the Rue de Rivoli.

Commune,[32] must have been enormous. The fraternization of the first days had the sinister result of uniting the troops and the now vengeful mob in the pursuit of real or supposed Fédérés and incendiaries. Forbes noticed soldiers 'hanging about the foot of the Rue Saint Honoré' – close to the most serious fires – 'enjoying the cheap amusement of Communard-hunting', helped by civilians who pointed out their hiding places. 'Very eager in this patriotic duty were the dear creatures of women.'[33] Outrage at the fires was increased for some by the feeling that they were a treacherous attack on the nation. General Du Barail reflected that 'while Frenchmen were burning Paris, Prussian officers were quietly watching . . . the dreadful culmination of their victory'.[34]

As well as fear and anger, the fires created an atmosphere of nightmare – to Lieutenant Vermeil 'a truly hellish scene'[35] – in which the emotions and inhibitions governing normal human conduct seemed no longer to have the same force.

All these fires, these crimes, produced in me a kind of drunkenness which took the form of a brutish insensibility. My feet touched wounded men and dead men, and I no longer felt anything . . . I know not how I escaped the dangers of fire and bullets; I hardly gave them a thought, so much had grief at the disaster taken hold of me. What was happening elsewhere? I do not know.[36]

Both sides were affected; on both sides savagery increased. Fédérés shot prisoners and suspects with as little compunction as did Versaillais: spies and suspected spies; 'traitors'; Gustave Chaudey and four gendarmes on the night of the 23rd; hostages at La Roquette, including the Archbishop, on the night of the 24th; the Dominicans of Arceuil on the 25th; fifty gendarmes, priests and policemen at the Rue Haxo on the 26th; suspected snipers and supposed enemies at random.[37] At the Belleville *mairie* on the 25th there came a procession of suspects to be shot. Trinquet, a Blanquist member of the Commune, killed one in the courtyard like 'swatting a fly'.[38]

On the Versailles side, similar atrocities occurred many times over: among others, the massacre of wounded at the Saint Sulpice hospital on 24 May by the 70th *de marche* under General Lacretelle;[39] the shooting of the Deputy Millière at the Pantheon on the same day;[40] massacres in the 13th *arrondissement* on the 25th, when Bocher's brigade searched the shanty town on the banks of the Bièvre, the haunt of ragpickers and *marginaux*, taking 'very large numbers of prisoners whom the angry soldiers shot without mercy'; and the liquidation of the officers and 'fanatical supporters of the Commune' among several hundred prisoners who surrendered at the Place Jeanne d'Arc, identified by one of their own number.[41] Examples could be multiplied endlessly. One may serve to suggest the atmosphere that reigned:

I saw four soldiers and an officer; two of the soldiers were half-dragging a man who was on his knees before the officer begging for his life. It made my blood run cold . . . to see that poor wretch on his knees, screaming to be spared, and the officer holding a pistol at his head. The soldiers kicked him to make him get up, and hit him on the head, so that you could hear the blows across the street. Someone from a window called out to the officer not to shoot him before so many women and children, so they pushed and kicked him until they came to the end of the street, and there they shot him. As he was being dragged past our house they stopped for a moment, and I saw a little boy about five years of age go up and kick the man while he was begging for pity . . .[42]

The worst atrocities of *la Semaine Sanglante*, however, cannot be explained as the result of growing bitterness during a week-long street battle. The shootings had begun immediately after the army entered

17 Prisoners at the Buttes Chaumont.

Paris, before resistance began, and the first organized executions took place on 22 May at the Parc Monceau, where the Volunteers saw fifteen men and a woman shot.[43] This was before anger had had time to seize the troops. On the other hand, they continued to take large numbers of prisoners at the very end of the week, in and around Belleville, when according to many accounts the savagery of the fighting had reached its highest pitch and the troops gave no quarter. On the contrary, they allowed the Fédérés to negotiate surrender. Certainly, there was appalling slaughter but much of it was carried out systematically and coldly. Prisoners taken in Belleville were marched to the Buttes Chaumont park and handed over to another regiment; only then were National Guard officers picked out and shot. Those shot in batches of 150 at the 'Mur des Fédérés', in the Père Lachaise cemetery, were taken from Mazas and La Roquette prisons, no doubt after being examined by the tribunals there.[44]

It would be wrong, moreover, to envisage the whole army as being at war with the whole population, however great the excesses committed. In hostile districts, certainly, when the fighting was barely over, the troops showed their tenseness in every movement. 'The officers keep their distance . . . They move nervously, jerkily, they speak violently.' In the taverns, the soldiers 'clash their glasses noisily on the bar, banging their rifles on the floor, throwing down their money'. But soon another mood appeared. The soldiers seemed sad. 'I saw the bivouacs during the campaign [against Germany]; they were more cheerful than this, even after a defeat.' 'The soldiers themselves are very silent. Although they are victors, they are sad; they do not drink, they do not sing. Paris might be a town . . . taken by dumb enemies; the irritation has worn off and the tears have not yet come.'[45] But other units in other parts of the city found the experience less of an ordeal. Parisians among the officers and Volunteers were able to visit relatives and be fêted by admiring neighbours. Others, when their units were stationed for a time in the same district, made haste to find comfortable quarters and a congenial café or restaurant and to establish reasonably good relations with the inhabitants, especially 'the *petites dames* of the district . . . Thus the hours went by agreeably.'[46] The average unit fought only once or twice during the week; the rest was routine.

More important in explaining the events of *La Semaine Sanglante* than the state of mind of the ordinary soldier was the predetermined policy of the High Command and the government. The killing of prisoners began on the first day of fighting, 2 April, on Vinoy's orders. It continued on 4 April at Châtillon, again on Vinoy's orders, and the same day written instructions were given for the immediate execution of deserters taken among the Fédérés. Other incidents involving the killing of prisoners occurred in which Galliffet, Boulanger and others were implicated.[47] In one case, however, when several prisoners were killed after the capture of Clamart station on 1 May,[48] evidence has survived which shows the involvement of higher authorities. Several of the prisoners taken there wore army uniform and one was foreign. Colonel Leperche held a court martial which condemned twelve soldiers and the foreigner, a Belgian named Peters, to death. But before the sentences were carried out, General Cissey's permission was sought and the Ministry of War was informed. The twelve deserters were shot the following day and the Belgian a day later, in the presence of the other prisoners.[49]

Rumours of this reached the public, producing 'a painful impression on the population, who claim that we are shooting *en masse* and without trial', and Cissey, following MacMahon's instructions, ordered his generals on 5 May to execute 'neither deserters nor any insurgent whatever' once the fighting was over. Instead, they were to be divided into categories: 'deserters, foreigners, ex-convicts or persons having a previous conviction, volunteers serving the Commune (men over forty years of age) etc.'[50] The significance is clear: these categories contained those the army considered its real enemies, for whom special treatment was reserved.

Although no more official executions appear to have been carried out for the time being, there were certainly occasions when this order was disobeyed by junior officers. Again, there exists a case for which evidence survives. On 7 May Commandant François (110th *de ligne*) had two men shot near Issy. The incident was reported to Thiers by a Deputy, de Tillancourt, and Le Flô ordered an enquiry into 'a savage act . . . deserving severe punishment . . . cold-blooded violence revolts me'. But excuses were found for François by his immediate superiors, and these again show the attitudes being adopted within the army: the two victims were not ordinary Fédérés, one being a Prussian on a special mission for the Commune; both had 'sinister faces' and powder-blackened hands, thus betraying their villainy and their participation in the fighting. The matter seems to have been dropped.[51]

When the army entered Paris the ban on the execution of prisoners was rescinded or ignored, and isolated cases occurred within the first few hours. But circumstances soon demanded that the treatment and disposal of prisoners should not be left to chance or the whim of junior officers. This was in part the result of the enormous number of prisoners taken, for whom no provision had been made. In Versailles there were problems of accommodation – 'we are overburdened', wrote Thiers – while in Paris commanders complained that they could not spare the men for guard duty.[52] The treatment of prisoners was therefore organized and to a degree centralized. The thousands captured or arrested daily were sent to the Ecole Militaire, the Parc Monceau, the Place Vendôme and other points where troops were assigned to guard them, and then to La Muette, from where they were marched in columns to Versailles escorted by cavalry and mounted gendarmes. Tribunals were set up to carry out a preliminary examination. On 23 May, Cissey wrote to MacMahon from his headquarters at the Ecole Militaire, 'I urgently need the military police section brought up to strength . . . every moment important prisoners are arriving who should be interrogated as soon as possible.'[53] The following day Berthe's brigade (which had not been engaged in any fighting in

Paris) arrived, and Cissey left the problem to him. As many prisoners were arriving, Berthe requested 'a gendarmerie officer to carry out the interrogations, and a few detectives'. The request was repeated in vain the next day, and so Berthe himself took charge. His troops 'gave assistance with . . . arrests and the executions at the Dupleix barracks'; firing squads there were provided by the 22nd battalion of *chasseurs*, and the police reported that 900 prisoners were shot.[54] Similarly at the Parc Monceau: when Clinchant moved 5th Corps headquarters, the 1st battalion of the 26th *de ligne* (4th Corps) was sent to police the area and guard prisoners, of whom 'some suffered the supreme penalty'. Executions continued there throughout the week.[55]

But if circumstances centralized the handling of prisoners, they did not determine how prisoners were to be treated. New orders were given. 'General Vinoy having given me the definite order to shoot deserters and foreigners arrested as insurgents, I had Zadunayski, Léon Henri, executed by firing squad this morning'; a note from the Municipal Police added, 'the orders of the Marshal and also those of the Minister of War are definite concerning deserters and foreigners who have served the Commune'.[56] These shootings were carried out in the garden of temporary police headquarters in the Rue Franklin (16th *arrondissement*) close to MacMahon's own headquarters in the adjoining Rue Vineuse. It was said that the victims were tied to a plum tree and shot by an old policeman with a revolver.[57] While it is conceivable that the police were merely assuming that these orders originated with MacMahon and Le Flô, it seems impossible that MacMahon could have been unaware of what was happening on his own doorstep. The reasons for this change of policy, whether ordered or only permitted by Le Flô and MacMahon, remain obscure, but probably included a belief that after the entry into Paris, when the defeat of the Commune was clearly inevitable, only a hard core of fanatics would continue to fight. Those who advocated a harsh policy may have been encouraged by the growing vehemence of anti-Commune opinion, and by the idea that during the fighting in Paris the army was its own master.

Far more serious in their consequences than the orders concerning foreigners and deserters were instructions dealing with prisoners taken carrying arms (*les armes à la main*). Long before the Commune, standing orders had laid down that they were to be shot on the spot.[58] Cissey had advocated 'an energetic repression' of those taken in arms.[59] Thiers had made offers of clemency, the wording of which takes on a special significance in this context. 'As for the insurgents, except for murderers, *those who lay down their arms* will have their lives spared'; 'We have repeated . . . that we will spare the lives of *those who lay down their arms.*'[60] MacMahon's later statements on the subject deplore specifically the killing of prisoners who did not resist the army and who were executed without trial. 'When men surrender their arms, they should not be shot. That was accepted [but] in some places [my] orders were forgotten.'[61] Ferry, in Paris, heard him condemn 'shootings without trial'.[62] But he at least tolerated the shooting of prisoners who had fought: 'I understood, without approving it, that in the heat of combat a man throwing away his weapon might be shot, but I could not accept that he should be executed in cold blood.'[63] Thus, neither Thiers nor MacMahon forbade or condemned the summary shooting of prisoners taken 'carrying arms'. Such careful ambiguity failed to restrain, if this was the intention, men like Vinoy or Cissey, who also demanded harshness in their subordinates. On 25 May, Cissey telegraphed to Du Barail, whose cavalry had formed a cordon south of Paris, 'no one is to be allowed to pass, men taken carrying arms are to be shot'. Colonel Leperche must have received similar instructions, for he replied 'Insurgents have been and will be treated as ordered.'[64] It seems impossible that Cissey would have sent such definite instructions to his equal in rank, Du Barail, unless he had been sure of the approval, or at least the acquiescence of his superiors, MacMahon, Le Flô and Thiers. There is no doubt that the government knew, for a copy of Cissey's dispatch is to be found among Thiers's papers, and the Minister of the Interior, Picard, read out an edited version of it to the Assembly – without the phrase quoted above.[65] Acquiescence on their part might have been enough for Cissey, who was a forceful character and an implacable enemy of the Commune. He was known to be next in line for the Ministry of War (to which he was appointed on 3 June), and had not been afraid to press his advice on MacMahon and Thiers, who had a high opinion of his abilities. MacMahon recommended him shortly afterwards for one of the Paris seats in the Assembly, and was later to appoint him prime minister. He might have taken matters into his own hands, confident of support within the army and the Assembly, where the government was sus-pected of softness towards the Communards, and the Right, reported *Le Soir* (27 May), was plotting to replace Thiers with MacMahon. Other commanders followed a quite different policy. Clinchant is reported to have tried to stop executions being carried out at the Parc Monceau when his headquarters were there, but the police, who were responsible, had orders 'from Versailles' that he could not overrule.[66] But he himself did not carry out such orders. According to his colleague Du Barail, 'the most lenient troops were those of General Clinchant [who] had given them very definite orders in this respect'.[67] Pelletan tells of an unnamed general who demanded written orders when told by his corps commander to carry out summary executions. After hesitating, the latter told him 'brusquely' to do as he liked.[68]

This difference between commanders suggests that instructions were given unofficially. There is evidence that instructions to execute those taken in arms were given, none the less, and generally carried out. The American Minister, Washburne, was told that 'the order was to shoot every man taken in arms'. General Bruat reported that National Guards in uniform 'taken carrying arms . . . were executed by firing squad on the very spot where they were arrested'. Captain Garcin told the Commission of Inquiry that 'all those who were taken carrying arms were shot . . . all who were Italian, Polish, Dutch, German were shot'.[69] Fortunately, Garcin was exaggerating: whether through accident, negligence or occasional humanity, many escaped. But sometimes even Garcin's sweeping categories were exceeded, and all those who could be presumed to have fought were treated as if taken 'carrying arms': men blackened as if with powder, in possession of a recently fired rifle or National Guard uniform, or even wounded, in which case they risked receiving (as the report to one of the military tribunals put it) 'the so-called *coup de grâce* with which wounded men taken carrying arms were finished off'.[70] It was in the degree to which these instructions were carried out or neglected that the individual attitudes of officers and even of ordinary soldiers were significant.

As well as those who had fought, many thousands were rounded up on the slightest suspicion, 'for they feared everyone, even the children', and some Versaillais thought that anyone seen in the streets was a Fédéré.[71] Many such suspects were shot in spite of lack of evidence. Generals who had the time and inclination, and little regard for appearances, constituted themselves judges. Galliffet was the most notorious, but he was not alone. Bounetou, of 2nd Corps, arriving well after the fighting, presided over an improvized court in a café at the Place Maubert. His immediate superior, Lacretelle, gave out orders for executions from his temporary headquarters at the Jardin des Plantes.[72] No doubt many other generals did likewise in parts of the city where journalists and memoir-writing witnesses were few. When decisions were not made on the spot because numbers were too great or when those responsible had qualms, suspects were generally sent to divisional or corps headquarters to be examined by the *prévôt* (military police commander) and his subordinates. Reported the *prévôt* of 4th Corps, 'I am often sent one or two (especially women) and the escort commander tells me that he does not know why they were arrested . . . These arrests are totally unjustified, nevertheless I take the people concerned until further order.'[73] In addition to the *prévôtés*, several tribunals functioned under area commanders. Colonel Leperche, commanding the southern forts, organized one, as did Colonel Vabre, Military Commander of the Hôtel de Ville. Others operated wherever a senior commander decided. The Code of Military Justice (1857), article 35, empowered corps and divisional commanders to nominate judges for *Conseils de Guerre* attached to their headquarters, and in emergencies permitted great latitude in their choice.[74]

Altogether, more than twenty military courts sat during the week. Little evidence of their procedure survives, but it is safe to say that few acted within the law. While military courts had jurisdiction under the

18 A *prévôté* at the Porte d'Italie.

state of siege, important requirements of the law, for example the right of appeal, were not respected. The *prévôtés*, whose role has been noted, could act legally only on foreign territory and in any case only on minor matters. A decree of the Government of National Defence (2 October 1870) provided for summary *cours martiales* empowered to pass death sentences on soldiers and civilians for a wide variety of offences, but for the duration of hostilities only. Nevertheless, this would probably be invoked as justification if necessary – an important point, for the appearance of legality must have been a powerful weapon in enforcing a systematic repression through the usual channels of the military hierarchy and in suppressing hesitation and doubt. It is clear that they were generally deemed to have a legal and official character. The Luxembourg tribunal, for example, made a show of formality. It had a chaplain, the Abbé Riche, who heard the confessions of the condemned and accompanied them to the place of execution, where they were shot in groups of ten; and one of the victims, Dr Tony Moilin, was permitted to regularize his common-law marriage in the presence of the mayor of the 6th *arrondissement* before being shot.[75]

Most of these tribunals, and certainly all the important ones, were established and supervised by the most senior commanders. The *prévôté* of 1st Corps was based with Ladmirault's headquarters at the Gare du Nord. The *prévôté* of 2nd Corps, the bloodiest, moved with Cissey to the Luxembourg Palace on 24 May. That of 4th Corps followed Douay's headquarters to the Place Vendôme. There is no record of Clinchant's 5th Corps *prévôté* having sat as a court. That of the Reserve Army remained in Versailles for most of the week, but Lieutenant Rascol's squad of *gendarmerie* attached to Le Vassor-Sorval's division performed its functions at the Ecole Militaire. In addition, Vinoy set up a *Conseil de Guerre* in the Rue de Grenelle, directed by National Guard Captain Ossude as *rapporteur* (prosecutor), with two officers and an NCO of the 113th *de ligne* as judges.[76] Later in the week Vinoy established a court martial at La Roquette prison, supervised by a Commissaire of Police, Noël; according to a press report, police officers acted as judges.[77] Douay, who had complained to MacMahon that he could not cope with the crowds of prisoners, made National Guard Colonel Vabre responsible for the *service des prisonniers* at the suggestion of General Borel, MacMahon's chief of staff.[78] Vabre's position as Military Commander of the Hôtel de Ville was probably deemed to give him some jurisdiction over the area, though owing to the destruction of the building he was obliged to use the nearby Châtelet theatre.

Prisoners were hastily examined and sentenced by these tribunals, to death if 'guilty', to Versailles if not proven; acquittals were rare, and reversible. 'Public notoriety' was considered to be sufficient evidence for summary courts martial, especially for supposed leaders of the insurrection: 'from the moment you say you are Millière, there is nothing else to be done', Garcin told the condemned man.[79] Obscure prisoners received less personal attention. The fact of being arrested was taken as a strong indication of guilt, and a few questions, 'always the same, rapid, inexorable', were enough to confirm it.[80]

Whether in an established tribunal or on a street corner, prisoners were judged according to a well established formula. The hard core of Communards – leaders, volunteers, foreigners, criminals and deserters – were marked down for special treatment, usually death. As leaders were counted members of the Commune and Central Committee, notables of radical politics and journalism, and National Guard officers. A surviving fragment of a list of men shot at La Roquette on 27–8 May gives twenty-six names, all National Guard officers, probably captured near the end of the fighting or handed over by the Prussians.[81] As volunteers were counted members of irregular Communard units – 'less deserving of pity', wrote Cissey – and those too old or too young for compulsory National Guard service; and, of course, it was particularly dangerous to be foreign, even if there were no other suspicious circumstances. Of eight men whom Leperche had shot on 27 May, six were outside the age of compulsory active service and one was Italian; of seventeen victims on 28 May, five were foreign, four were over forty, at least one was an official, and one was a deserter; of six victims on 30 May, four were over forty and one under twenty.[82] Attempts had been made throughout the campaign to identify criminals, but during the Paris fighting suspicious characters were picked out solely by appearance. Galliffet simply picked out the unusual, the dirty, the ugly. His exhibitionistic cruelty, which scandalized the foreign press, followed a certain method. 'You, step out of the ranks, you old scoundrel! And you . . . you are wounded! Well, we shall cure you . . . we have more than enough foreigners and scum here, we have to get rid of them.'[83] Thus were picked out volunteers, by age, known combatants, by their wounds, and, as always, foreigners. '"Ah! You are Italians," cries General Lian . . . "What the bloody hell are you doing here? . . . I have the right to have you shot.'''[84] The inability to account for his movements and presence in Paris might be enough to condemn a man:

What did you do during the Commune?
Nothing.
Nothing? You did not work? I see. Take him away.

The correct answer, of course, was 'I worked'; to have been without means of support during the insurrection aroused dark suspicions and was a recurring theme of interrogations.[85] Deserters received particularly harsh treatment. An example of the official and systematic way in which this was carried out is provided by the Paris fire brigade, technically an army regiment. Most of the men had stayed behind in Paris and had continued their service under the Commune, thus becoming 'deserters'. The Minister of War instructed the commanding officer, Colonel Willerme, to 'reconstitute' the regiment, and it was decided that 'subversive elements' who had cooperated with the Commune should 'disappear'. Lists of the guilty were drawn up, and those on the first list, the worst offenders, were handed over to the *prévôtés* on arrest and almost certainly shot. Of those taken to the Luxembourg, only one was spared.[86]

The sentences of the tribunals were carried out immediately: on a building site near the Gare du Nord (1st Corps), at the Ecole Militaire, Dupleix barracks and Champ de Mars (2nd Corps and Reserve), in the Place Vendôme and on the Tuileries terrace (4th Corps), at Mazas prison and the Père Lachaise cemetery (Reserve), and at many less important 'abattoirs'. The worst carnage took place at the Luxembourg, the Châtelet and La Roquette. Day and night from 24 to 28 May, crowds of men, women and children were brought to the Petit Luxembourg, and those condemned queued in the gardens to be shot. The total of victims ran into many hundreds.[87] Vabre and relays of assistants, including other National Guard officers, sat day and night at the Châtelet from 25 to 30 May. Centrally placed, they received prisoners from all over the Right Bank and attracted crowds of sightseers. The condemned were marched to be shot in 'batches' to the Lobau barracks, an annexe of the Hôtel de Ville. Two companies of the 10th battalion of *chasseurs* and part of the 26th *de ligne* were provided for the purpose. Three thousand may have died there.[88] The corpses, to the horror even of the anti-Communard mob, were thrown into ditches in the Square Saint Jacques, and later removed by the van load; some, it was rumoured, had been buried alive. At La Roquette prison, captured

19   The Luxembourg gardens, 24–8 May.

on 28 May, the police reported that 'a company of infantry is posted permanently behind the prison . . . Platoons of prisoners are brought to these soldiers, and at once they shoot them on the spot.' Inside the prison the Marines did the same. This continued with dreadful speed for over two days, for in eastern Paris thousands were rounded up as the fighting reached its close. The victims here may also have exceeded 3,000.[89]

These happenings were well known to the authorities. The senior generals who had set up the courts continued to supervise their operation. Cissey's headquarters were in the same building as the *prévôté*, and the *prévôt* was his direct subordinate. In the case of the Deputy Jean-Baptiste Millière, he himself passed sentence. Vinoy received reports from tribunals he had established and Ossude, *rapporteur* of the Rue de Grenelle court, wrote that he was sending prisoners to Vinoy after trial so that he could make the final decision.[90] Douay's staff kept an eye on Vabre. On at least one occasion an officer, possibly the *prévôt* of 4th Corps, accompanied prisoners sent from headquarters to the Châtelet, and reported to Douay's ADC that he was staying with

20   Inside La Roquette prison.

Vabre while they were 'sorted'; his note contains the sinister phrase, 'il n'y a plus à s'inquiéter de vos *deux recommandés, c'est fait*'.[91] MacMahon's headquarters were informed of progress. On 29 May Douay informed General Borel, the army chief of staff, that Vabre would no longer be needed, and that 'this officer whom you placed at my disposal will be sent back to the Marshal'.[92] On at least one occasion MacMahon intervened directly. Jourde, the Finance Delegate of the Commune, was arrested by the National Guard of Order and sent to Ossude's tribunal, where he was condemned to death. Colonel Corbin, chief of staff of the National Guard, was informed, and he wrote immediately to Borel to ask him to prevent the execution as Jourde might have valuable information. Borel noted, 'there is nothing to be done', perhaps because the case fell under Vinoy's authority. Nevertheless, an order did arrive from MacMahon to have Jourde sent to his headquarters, where he was questioned by Ansart, of the political police. From there he was sent to the Luxembourg, again sentenced to death (by his own account), saved to be interrogated by Cissey, and finally sent to Versailles on 1 June.[93] Not only the military authorities were aware of the activities of the military tribunals. Senior police officers accepted their jurisdiction, and reports to Versailles frequently mentioned them.[94]

There is no such clear documentary evidence concerning the smaller and seemingly less official tribunals. Reports of their existence come chiefly from non-official sources, and the links that can be established between them and the military hierarchy are circumstantial. For example, both Vuillaume and Da Costa mention the Mint as one place where prisoners were shot. A report records prisoners being taken there on 24 May. It was the site of Vinoy's headquarters by the 25th at the latest.[95] It is recorded that seventeen prisoners were shot at the Gare d'Orléans, which was General Bruat's headquarters.[96] It seems probable that most, if not all, of the tribunals acted on instructions from senior commanders, even though allowed latitude once in operation. For junior officers to take such responsibility upon themselves would have run against all the ingrained habits of the French army. The difference between Clinchant's area, where no systematic official massacres appear to have taken place, and those of Cissey and Vinoy, where they were multiplied, shows how much depended on the decision of the corps commanders.

MacMahon, however, seems to have taken no official decision until 26 May, when he instructed that if the insurgents offered to surrender they should be allowed to do so.[97] He claimed later to have given instructions that all prisoners were to be sent to Versailles, and not judged summarily, after Jules Ferry had warned him that executions were being carried out.[98] I have found no trace of such an order and, moreover, surviving orders from MacMahon are far less sweeping. On 25 May he ordered that military medical staff who had remained on duty in the Paris hospitals during the Commune were not to be treated like insurgents or deserters; this followed an incident in which one was shot and several others seriously ill-treated.[99] Had MacMahon indeed forbidden all shooting of prisoners, this order would have been superfluous, for the men concerned would already have been covered by it. Vinoy certainly interpreted the order narrowly, ordering Vergé not to shoot soldiers captured among the Fédérés 'without careful examination'.[100] MacMahon or Thiers or both may have given orders on about 27 or 28 May to stop summary executions once the fighting was over, for Vinoy ordered on 29 May that with the end of resistance 'there is reason . . . to suspend all summary executions', though he added a rider, perhaps on his own initiative, that nullifies the effect of the order.[101] *The Times* (2 June), in a dispatch dated 31 May, reported that summary executions had ended; 'now the executions are only to be inflicted after a legal trial'. Nevertheless, shootings continued in Vinoy's and Cissey's areas until June. Leperche shot an English student named Marx – an unfortunate name – on 9 June and a labourer named Léopold Dewen, no doubt another foreigner, three days later. There are reports of executions in Versailles itself on 27 May and 7 June.[102]

The circumstances in which the massacres ceased are obscure. Captain Garcin said that orders to stop came from Versailles,[103] and indeed the principal and most public tribunals halted their operations at about the same time. But the unevenness of the repression suggests that the control exercised by Thiers and MacMahon was at best incomplete. No evidence has come to light connecting Thiers directly with the repression in Paris, though he must have been aware of much that was happening.[104] It may be significant that on one notorious occasion Cissey tried to conceal the truth from MacMahon and Thiers. When the republican Deputy, Jean-Baptiste Millière, was arrested and brought to the Luxembourg, Cissey, who was lunching nearby at the celebrated Foyot's, immediately ordered his execution, 'entre la poire et le fromage', and sent Captain Garcin to carry it out on the steps of the Pantheon. Soon afterwards, a telegram arrived from MacMahon's chief of staff asking where Millière was. Cissey replied in ambiguous terms, concealing his own part in the matter and inventing an excuse for the shooting, asserting that Millière (who in fact had taken no part in the insurrection) had fired three revolver shots at the soldiers arresting him and seeming to imply that they themselves had shot him for this reason. This apparently was not enough, and Cissey had to admit his responsibility, which he justified on the grounds of Millière's 'crimes' and the desire for vengeance among the population.[105] Mac-Mahon claimed to have reprimanded him, though this had no noticeable effect on their relations. During the weeks and months that followed the military chiefs tried to avoid responsibility for the actions performed on their authority. Douay claimed to know nothing about Colonel Vabre's activities at the Châtelet, and in the case of the Dutchman Tribels, shot by Vabre, which became a diplomatic matter,[106] the army, in the person of Cissey, then Minister, stolidly denied knowledge of Vabre. The Ministry of the Interior tried to avoid paying him for the period after 18 March, in spite of what General Trochu called his 'important services to Marshal MacMahon [and] the cause of order after the occupation of Paris by the army'.[107]

Such evidence, while not conclusive, must call into question the view of Thiers as the director of the repression. His interest was in remaining in power. Exasperation with Paris took second place to the politician's concern with the Assembly, public opinion and the press, both domestic and foreign. While the Versailles mob was still literally shrieking for blood, a reaction had begun against the excesses of the repression. The foreign press, most notably *The Times*, had begun to condemn it.[108] Public opinion in Paris was turning against it.[109] Members of the government were unprepared for such carnage. Favre had asked Bismarck on 21 May not to turn back fleeing Communards, but to intern them and await requests for extradition. Had this been done, there would have been far less bloodshed.[110] Thiers's own vindictiveness has probably been exaggerated. He became quite willing to show leniency when it was expedient. He complained of those – 'heartless and lacking political sense' – who were arresting thousands of suspects, which he considered a serious problem. But during *la Semaine Sanglante* he did not care to intervene. Thinking, no doubt, that the Parisians had only themselves to blame for having opposed him, he abandoned them to the mercies of the generals. To have done otherwise would have been risky when feeling in the army and the Assembly ran so high. 'During the fighting we can do nothing', he wrote to Ferry, 'and it would be useless to wish to interfere.'[111]

La Semaine Sanglante was the work of the generals. MacMahon must have been broadly aware of events. He received reports and visited areas where mass executions were regularly carried out. The sound of shooting could be heard over long distances. He had a reputation for honesty and stupidity; both appear exaggerated, for his later statements were disingenuous. Probably he preferred, like Thiers, not to know too much and to interfere little in his subordinates' business. A stronger character would have been needed to stand up to Cissey, Vinoy and Douay and the widespread desire for a final solution to the problem of revolution. The worst atrocities were carried out on the orders of Cissey and Vinoy, and their personalities are important. Cissey was a man of limited vision but of great forcefulness. He had accepted the view of the Communards as rootless, dangerous scum, and urged 'the most energetic repression'. Harsh and overbearing in personality, he needed no encouragement to carry it to an appalling extreme. Vinoy, an ageing adventurer who had almost reached the summit, was harsh, unpopular and vain. Of all the generals, he had been the most insulted by the Parisians, and he extracted the bloodiest revenge.[112] Ladmirault, an elderly and benign Catholic gentleman, was said to have opposed the excesses of the repression;[113] he failed to impose his scruples on his subordinates, Galliffet among them. Clinchant, whether for personal reasons or out of concern for his popularity and reputation, won under the National Defence, or because he had less cause for resentment against Paris than certain of his colleagues, prevented his Corps, all former prisoners of war, from carrying out systematic massacres. The two leading Bonapartists, Douay and Du Barail, avoided personal involvement in the slaughter. For the latter, this was largely a matter of circumstance, and perhaps of choice, though he permitted Leperche to carry out a purge in the suburbs, where, with the help of twenty-seven policemen and a list of Fédérés found at Fort Bicêtre, he made 'valuable arrests'. A Commissaire of Police attached to Du Barail's headquarters was glad to report on 3 June that Leperche's court martial 'struck pitilessly' at some of the 'wretches', who were shot in the moat of the fort: 'no personality notable by his rank in the National Guard . . . can escape'.[114] Douay seems deliberately to have washed his hands of the Châtelet proceedings, having requested the assistance of an outsider, Vabre, to take charge. The Bonapartists had every reason to keep clear of the bloody mess created by the royalists and republicans of Versailles.

In the lower ranks there was every shade of fanaticism and doubt,

21 General de Cissey (*left*) and General Vinoy (*right*).

ruthlessness and humanity. Some sent hundreds to their deaths without compunction, some did so with a heavy heart. Some tried to stop the massacres, and a few even risked their own lives to protect prisoners. Nearly all, however, did as they were told. This is the main point: not that some were consciously lenient, or that many were unhappy with their duty, as so many observers noted, or even that only a small number were much involved in the treatment of prisoners, but that individual feelings mattered little. Throughout the civil war, there had been dissent within the army. After the entry into Paris there was no further sign of it.[115] Once the battle had begun, the soldiers had no way out, whatever their previous feelings, and the generals were careful never to push them to a point where a breakdown of morale and discipline became a danger, as on 18 March. Trapped in a war for which they had no taste, the soldiers' anger was by the end directed against the Fédérés, whose stubborn refusal to compromise or surrender, heroic in retrospect, seemed stupid and perverse. The propaganda of Versailles offered targets for this resentment, and the stereotypes of the true enemy – the foreigner, the traitor, the ambitious fanatic, the criminal – placed them beyond the pale of national, social, and almost of human solidarity. The animal imagery of Versaillais polemic is not mere name-calling, but a justification for inhumanity. The most ferocious Versaillais was therefore capable of kindness and even – or perhaps especially – of sentimentality when an enemy broke out of the stereotype, and therefore seemed no longer a 'real' Communard.[116] 'Unfathomable recesses of the human heart!'[117]

To resentment was added fear. Among the simple, fear of mines, petroleum and snipers; among the subtle, fear of international plots and a collapsing society. Overestimating the threat posed by the Commune, the army entered Paris expecting to find a formidable and determined army of thousands of Communards. This existed only in their imagination, and in attempting to destroy it, they killed and arrested far more people than had ever fought for the Commune. Probably most had no idea of the scale of the repression they were carrying out: 'My reason refused to believe such a thing', wrote Grandeffe; similarly, Albert de Mun denied the extent of the repression, as did MacMahon himself.[118] But however far reaching the repression, the imaginary enemy could not be extirpated. General du Geslin, commanding the Paris garrison, regretted that summary executions had not been more numerous at the time when they could be ordered, and General L'hériller, commanding the 3rd *arrondissement*, approached panic, reporting on 8 June that

the wretches we have just fought do not admit defeat. They announce themselves openly in the quarter . . . and their threats inspire such terror in peaceful men that they dare not denounce the guilty . . . a large number of insurgents are today living among us . . . The mayor, the commissaire of police and I can do nothing, absolutely nothing . . .[119]

Arrests in large numbers continued throughout June, all buildings in the city were searched, and all weapons, including antiques, confiscated. The National Guard of Order, so active in the repression, excited mistrust, and it was dissolved by decree on 30 May. It was feared that the force had been infiltrated by former Fédérés, and at best the 'Prudhommes' composing it were considered unreliable, having sworn, it was popularly said, 'to draw their swords only to defend our institutions, or if necessary to attack them'. Even corpses worried the soldiers. Cissey tried to prevent the body of Tony Moilin, shot at the Luxembourg, from being handed over to his widow, for fear that his grave might become a place of pilgrimage; he was overruled by the government. Similarly, Douay gave detailed instructions that Delescluze's body should be buried in a common grave so that it could not be identified or recovered.[120]

Most worrying of all was the attitude of the troops, whose ties with the population proved not to have been irrevocably broken by the events of *la Semaine Sanglante*, for the fighting had been less than terrible, and the repression, though far worse, had been concentrated in certain areas and against certain sections of the population, involving only a part of the army. On 29 May, Cissey warned MacMahon that soldiers were frequenting bars where the events of the day were discussed in 'veritable political meetings', and were forming undesirable contacts. He warned his officers that the men were drinking with 'people who could very well have fought them from behind the barricades'. Douay reported that the men were disobeying the order not to go out unarmed.[121] At Montmartre, La Villette and Belleville, the police noted a few days later that 'relations with the inhabitants [were] already beginning', and one of the Volunteers was surprised to find the people of Belleville 'charming'; being stationed there was like 'a rest period'. The garrison commander, du Geslin, reported that contacts between the troops and the population were becoming 'more and more dangerous'.[122]

There began a chorus of urgent requests that the troops should be withdrawn from Paris. On 3 June Faron asked that only one brigade be left to garrison the 19th and 20th *arrondissements*, and kept in the rampart barracks where they could be separated from the population. On the 6th, Derroja complained of the difficulty of supervising the men spread throughout the district, and warned of the bad effect on discipline of their relations with the population. Vinoy ordered that the men should be lodged apart from the public, 'in the interests of discipline', and he advised MacMahon to withdraw the bulk of the troops to Versailles, as longer contact with the Parisians could have 'the most undesirable results'.[123]

The military authorities, who had assumed responsibility for the government of the city, requested the assistance of the civilian police, being unable to rely on the zeal or thoroughness of their own men.[124] Occasional wrangles notwithstanding, they were eager to hand over their functions as soon as possible to the civil authorities, and the transition to more normal government for the city was swift: Ferry was sent to oversee the administration, provisional mayors replaced military commanders, and by 24 June the civilian police were functioning throughout the city. Most of the troops were withdrawn. Even outside Paris the men were not considered to be in safety. They visited taverns unarmed and without permission, fraternized with Fédéré wounded in the hospitals, and made contacts with the prisoners and their visitors.[125] The great Longchamps review, to celebrate the triumph of order and the rebirth of the French army, provoked repeated orders that the troops were to maintain silence during the march past. It was feared that agitators were urging the men to shout slogans.[126]

Expiation, then, had not been 'complete' to the satisfaction of the generals, and much Right-wing opinion agreed with them. The war was not regarded as over; it was suggested that forts should be built inside the city ready for the next battle.[127] But more insidious attacks on the social order seemed harder to guard against. The Parliamentary Commission of Inquiry was alarmed at the power of secret societies, especially the International, and was convinced that the moderate republicans, even those in power, favoured them by their weakness or complicity. These fears helped to shape the policies of the Right in the years that followed.

That the Right, and particularly part of the army, was dissatisfied with the scope of the repression shows the unreality of its views, for the repression had been crushing, and not fortuitously so. Little attempt had been made to spare the city, as if the whole population owed 'expiation' for the sin of having tolerated the Commune. Artillery was used widely, which enabled casualties to be kept low, but which must have caused immense damage, including some of the fires blamed on *pétroleuses*. The tactics of sapping through the houses must have wrecked countless homes – one cause, no doubt, of the anti-Versaillais reaction. But the main target of the repression was not Paris itself, which was seen as the 'trap' in which revolutionaries from all over France and Europe would be caught. To conservative soldiers, this was a chance not to be missed. The number of their victims is incalculable. A few lists survive, no doubt by accident. But they probably do not include those taken carrying arms, often shot on the spot, but only those who were given some sort of summary trial. The normal civil registration of deaths could not be carried out. An often mentioned estimate of 17,000 Fédéré casualties was only hearsay, and it is not clear to what it refers. A confidential report, by the highways department, of bodies removed from public places for burial in the city cemeteries gives a total of 5,517, but only for the ten outer *arrondisse-*

ments, and it is not clear whether or not this is intended to be the total for the whole city. Besides, some of the figures are hard to reconcile. Camille Pelletan, using his own sources for the numbers of burials, adds several thousand to the above total; moreover, he asserts that several thousand more were buried in common graves outside the city walls.[128] The total number of Parisians killed could therefore be anything between 10,000 and 30,000, with the most probable figure about halfway between. Of these several thousand had died in the fighting,[129] and at least half must have perished in the 'abattoirs' of the Luxembourg, the Lobau barracks, La Roquette and Mazas prisons, Père Lachaise, the Ecole Militaire, the Dupleix barracks and others.

About 38,000 prisoners were taken to Versailles. Most were released after a period of harsh detention – a way of punishing those whom the army suspected but against whom there was no evidence. Over 11,000 were tried by *Conseils de Guerre*; of these, nearly 5,000 were transported to penal colonies in New Caledonia. It was said that the judges feared an amnesty, and so increased sentences. Among the prisoners were

22   Young prisoners and their captors at Versailles.

5,000 soldiers. Most of these had not served the Commune, being from units disarmed at the armistice or left behind in the confusion of 18 March, on leave, or convalescent. No action was taken against them. Over a thousand were sent to Africa, 'as a disciplinary measure', joining many others sent during April and May. Another 1,400 were tried; three were executed. To some extent, the law restrained the judges' vengefulness.[130]

This had not been so during *la Semaine Sanglante*, when military authority had urged on and supplemented whatever resentment the troops had nursed against Paris. The most violent men were given full rein. The less violent found themselves thrust along the same path, and those whose consciences troubled them were able to stay clear of the massacres, except the men attached to units which quite arbitrarily were selected to man the 'abbatoirs'.[131] Of their reactions, nothing is known. 'I understand [summary executions]', one historian has written, 'because I have seen them.'[132] Such painfully won understanding is denied to most of his colleagues, who can only grope towards comprehension by the tedious methods of scholarship, trusting that reason is not wholly powerless to explain actions whose very authors were barely conscious of what they were doing.

La Semaine Sanglante ended in failure for all concerned. The hatred shown towards the Commune by much of the population, the destruction sown in Paris and the killing of the hostages seemed to show the moral bankruptcy of the workers' revolution as well as its impotence. Even among Communard prisoners, few were prepared to defend the 'excesses' of the revolution – a sign, surely, of a collapse of morale, not merely of a lack of courage. The monarchists, no more popular in Paris or any of the cities after the Commune than before it, had shown such mean-spirited tactlessness and aroused such determined opposition that the political future they proposed seemed impossibly dangerous to men of moderation. But the men of moderation themselves, middle-class republicans and liberals, whose precarious victory had been turned sour by the excesses of the 'expiation', seemed to some thoughtful men no more worthy of governing.[133] 'Cruel race; I am no longer part of it – the Republic is sick indeed, the monarchy is not viable. Finally, behold socialism in practice . . . the man who cannot read does not learn, he burns the alphabet . . . It is the fall of ancient Rome.'[134]

But France surmounted the catastrophe with astonishing ease, even though she never entirely recovered from it. Perhaps the Commune and its aftermath would have been pushed to the back of men's minds, along with the other violent outbursts of the century, and become nothing more than a distasteful memory of universal failure. But the vigorous polemic of the old Communards and their allies, especially that of Marx (less than wholly convinced by his own rhetoric), aided above all by the cruelties of *la Semaine Sanglante*, turned hopeless defeat into retrospective victory, creating the powerful image of the glorious harbinger of a new society, whose persecutors were nailed to the eternal pillory of history and whose martyrs were to rest for ever enshrined in the great heart of the working class.

11

Conclusions

The Army of Versailles was not a caste set apart from the rest of the nation by its social composition or its opinions. Among its members were peasants longing for peace and a return to the routine of farm and village; country gentlemen awaiting their Christian king and fighting the revolution as an embodiment of evil; small-town craftsmen as suspicious of the 'whites' as of the 'reds'; representatives of the *nouvelles couches sociales* opposing the insurrection in the name of a well behaved republic; government men putting aside their old loyalties to follow Thiers and the cause of order; men who feared for their property, their position and the liberty of their religion; men for whom the Fatherland meant unity, discipline and military strength. It would be a simple matter to find among even the small number of men who appear in these pages members and representatives of all these groups, and to show the links of shared opinion and common association between those inside and outside the army who opposed and defeated the Commune.

Yet these links, however important, were not in 1871 the determinants of the army's actions. The facts of background, belief and interest were constant; the behaviour of the army was not. Officers and soldiers who had no intention of fighting on 18 March fought a few days later. Many young peasants may indeed have feared the revolution and resented the superiority of Paris, but they fraternized with the crowds on 18 March like the rest. The changes in the army's conduct came about less because individual opinions changed (though many no doubt did so), than because circumstances did. There is no reason to suppose that in normal circumstances personal sympathies did any more than make soldiers more or less willing to do what they were compelled to do. There were very few who stepped out from the ranks to linger in the rear, to desert or – rarest of rarities – to disobey.

What held the army together was not conviction but discipline, which in the conditions prevailing in 1871 meant coercion. This required 'vigorous' leadership which many of the officers and non-commissioned officers of February, March and April could not or would not provide. Thus of all the reinforcements received by the army it was not the fresh troops from the National Defence armies or released prisoners from Germany that counted (for they too were far from eager to fight), but regular officers returning from captivity in April and May whose value lay not only in their political reliability but also in their professional ability and experience for organizing the campaign and enforcing discipline. Nevertheless, police reports and other evidence suggest that 'vigorous' leadership often remained a pious hope of the generals. It cannot be assumed that the army was thereby transformed in its attitudes, although the tightening of discipline, accompanied by a purge of Parisians and suspected sympathizers, certainly modified its actions.

Even less can it be assumed that the scanty measures of propaganda and persuasion taken by the government had a profound effect on the troops as a whole. To deny that they transformed the spirit of the army is not of course to deny them all importance. Everyday experience suggests that the main effect of propaganda is to confirm people in their original opinions, and this was no slight matter in 1871 when many had for a moment wavered in their views. It may also have heightened feelings, increasing hatred and violence. Almost certainly it had more effect on the officers than on the men. For some of those for whom evidence survives it can be seen that their views frequently coincided with those spread by certain newspapers whose influence can only have been magnified by the absence of other sources of news. If the personal opinions and sympathies of the rank and file had little impact on events, those of senior officers certainly did. The great power they wielded made the differences between them significant, as can be seen from the conduct of units under their command.

While the writings by and about senior officers help us to interpret their actions and opinions, for the ordinary soldiers there is no such assistance. It may be supposed that the major influence on opinion among the troops was the conversation they exchanged. Of this, all that has survived are the impressions of outsiders; from the men themselves there is nothing. This is undeniably a serious gap in the evidence. That which is available suggests strongly that the most common attitude was one of uncertainty about the political issues, lack of strong sympathy for either side and reluctance to participate in the conflict. This conforms with the view of France given by Weber:[1] a country far from unified in its loyalties and interests, in which remote events were regarded with passivity.

All that we know for certain of the troops is their actions, though if, as has been argued, their opinions were of secondary importance, it is their actions that demand most attention. It was said above that personal sympathies did not determine actions 'in normal circumstances'. The army commanders had therefore to ensure that normal circumstances prevailed as far as possible. This can be seen throughout the campaign. Discipline would hold, in the sense that few would openly disobey, unless outside circumstances destroyed the conditions in which discipline could be enforced, as they had done on 18 March. Discipline, of course, is relative: it may be said that the army never became sufficiently disciplined to be used without the greatest precaution.

It was not only that avoidance of defeat demanded the maintenance of discipline; it was also, and perhaps even more, the case that the maintenance of discipline demanded the avoidance of defeat. In consequence, no military risks were taken; indeed they were repeatedly forbidden. This involved the acceptance of other dangers, political and diplomatic, caused by the slow progress of the campaign, but there is no sign that Thiers ever tried to hurry the army. Before 18 March he (though not the generals) had underestimated the military difficulties. Afterwards, fear that their sword would again prove to be a lath obliged the government to follow a cautious, temporizing policy. It seems likely, as Marx later suggested, that a compromise would have been possible, and consequently that the Commune in fact had some room to manoeuvre.

In the event, the army avoided defeat with ease (and with it the possibility of German intervention) because of the inability of the Fédérés to mobilize their potential strength. Appeals to the brotherhood of the troops were not wholly unfounded in that many soldiers felt little hatred for the Parisians, at least at the beginning, and had no wish to fight them. But to be successful, such appeals would have needed to follow a victory, not an unbroken string of defeats which made the fall of the Commune seem certain. It may be that the respite provided by the second siege enabled certain bonds of comradeship to be formed among the soldiers, adding interior strength to a cohesion that had previously been dependent almost entirely on coercion.

The civil war should be considered in military terms. The troops performed their task when they were used in favourable conditions – in superior strength, with the advantage of surprise, and with artillery support; indeed they performed because they were used in such conditions. The failure of 18 March was first a military, not a moral or political failure: we may be sure that the troops would have removed the cannon, however much they may have grumbled, had the crowds and the National Guard not appeared in vastly superior numbers. Conversely, the recapture of Paris was a military success, rather than one of propaganda or politics. The same appears to be true of June 1848, when it was largely owing to purely military foresight that the unenthusiastic troops fought so well,[2] even though they had the benefit, denied to the Versaillais, of aid from the Garde Mobile and elements of the National Guard.

In 1871 the High Command was careful not to ask too much of its men. Their numerical superiority permitted troops in the front line to be relieved every few days. Casualties were kept low. Moments of crisis were as much as possible avoided. It might be said that the men were never given any excuse or opportunity to desert or disobey, but were manoeuvred into a position in which obedience was the easiest and least dangerous course. This is one aspect of the life of any army, but in 1871 it governed operations.

This can be seen in the strategy of the long campaign and in the tactics used outside and inside the city. There were no brilliant charges except in the newspapers; the bayonet was probably only used on prisoners. Instead there was endless trench digging, night surprises and long cannonades; and once inside the city, hours of waiting while enemy positions were outflanked and the defenders, overwhelmed with gunfire, withdrew. The low level of casualties testifies to the effectiveness of these tactics, whose cost was borne not by the army but by the population of Paris. The attackers were not helped by Haussmann's boulevards, however. This time the defenders too had cannon, and the new streets gave them an excellent field of fire. The army profited from the narrow streets to move under cover, and no serious resistance was encountered in the congested quarters of the city. However suitable their tactics – for the army adapted better than the insurgents to street fighting – it was numbers that were decisive, enabling the attackers to envelop the Fédéré positions, aided by the unplanned nature of the defence.

If the civil war is to be seen as a conventional military campaign rather than a spontaneous war of populations, fought by obedient, not

197

fanatical, soldiers, the ferocity of the repression, so out of proportion to its cause, 'like some appalling level-crossing accident that occurs at the end of a school outing to the seaside',[3] requires more than ever an explanation, while remaining of all matters the hardest to explain. Even some of those who took part in it were not aware of and refused to believe its scale. This is no doubt part of the explanation: no one at the time – not even MacMahon or Cissey, let alone the ordinary lieutenant or private – knew how many were being killed. Any one man would have seen perhaps two or three prisoners shot, sometimes a few dozen, or very rarely a few hundred. No one realized that the total reached tens of thousands. Certainly there was anger among the troops against the Fédérés: because they had not wanted to fight in someone else's war and were being forced to; because they were afraid, especially in the strange streets of a huge and hostile city; because they had been told that the Fédérés were savages, and the fires seemed to prove it. But this anger, where it existed, could have been and was held in check where there were officers who were content to take prisoners and not make victims. Even when prisoners were taken and sent to the rear, as happened far more often even at the climax of the Paris fighting than has usually been supposed, they were not safe. The generals and headquarters staffs decided whether they were to live or die. We have no sure way of penetrating the minds and hearts of those who took these decisions, and those who were ordered to carry them out and obeyed. Yet it was they who made the events of May 1871 of another order from those, otherwise similar, of June 1848. We may speculate that the recent disasters that had befallen France and her army had created in their minds the need to blame and punish, making them susceptible to reports of the anti-social and anti-French forces – the foreign adventurers, the professional agitators, the dangerous classes – who had fallen on Paris to complete the ruin of France. We may imagine their anger at the insults hurled at the *capitulards* and the humiliations inflicted by the Paris population on the army, the source of their own status and self-esteem. The number of their victims rose further in line with the unprecedented scale of the insurrection and the number of troops employed against it.[4] As for the troops who obeyed orders, it can only be noted, as so often in such circumstances, that it appears practically impossible for most men to preserve their individuality and normal standards of behaviour when they form part of a mass, especially when that mass is an army, whose uniformity is reinforced by the threat of punishment and in which personal responsibility is diminished by the pressure to obey. Even emotions seem to have been dulled. Many witnesses noticed the impassivity of the troops. Few showed either anger or kindness.

The part played by Thiers in the repression remains an enigma. He seems (like the other Ministers) not to have shared the irrational fears that gripped many on the Right. He was willing to moderate the repression when political expediency required it, and he preferred to leave the responsibility for the judicial repression to others. Perhaps in like manner he washed his hands of the events of *la Semaine Sanglante*: he could in any case have known only a part of what was happening in Paris, and controlled even less. Yet it seems likely that he had given at least tacit consent to the orders given to treat captured rebels harshly.

The repression was irrational but not random. It was aimed at certain groups believed to be at the centre of the revolt. It owed much to well established conservative myths of revolution, such as the fear of the rootless and criminal 'dangerous classes', making perhaps its last appearance on the stage of French politics. The fear, equally important, of cosmopolitan anti-French elements within the nation, supported by and aiding the interests of France's external enemies, was to have an enduring influence on Right-wing ideology.[5] Future nationalism was to seek to unite all classes in a popular movement against the internal and external enemies of the nation, and thus act as a bulwark of the social order, rather than trying to suppress the poorer classes and minimize their influence in political life.[6]

But in 1871, suppression was still the order of the day: suppression both of the urban working class and of the primacy of Paris in making and breaking regimes. Yet although the conflict of 1871 was in part one of class and of region, it was not primarily a spontaneous mass struggle. Enthusiasm on both sides was restricted to the few. Hordes of *ruraux* did not come to the aid of the Assembly; all the workers of Paris did not man the barricades. The struggle was one between institutions: government against government and army against army. This was the outcome of the policies pursued on both sides. Thiers did not want the aid of the few volunteers who did appear, while for its part the Commune tried to form a disciplined army of all able-bodied men irrespective of political opinion or class. As Philippe Riviale has pointed out, the Commune changed the insurrectionary movement into an organization representing the whole city; the revolution ended and became a war of secession.[7]

As such, it was fought out feebly, with neither side able to muster the physical or moral force to hasten a conclusion. The outcome was the inevitable one of such a war: a marked reduction in the political power of Paris and an increase in that of the provinces. This change was not, of course, to have the effect that the conservatives had hoped for, and the fruits of victory were not long to remain in their hands. That this was so seems to be in part a consequence of the limited nature of the civil war. Once it was over, as Saint-Valry pointed out, people could not be frightened as they had been after the June Days of 1848 by talk of more upheaval to come.[8] The population as a whole no longer felt threatened in its most vital interests, and the conservatives could not gather support for a sweeping programme of repression. Although measures were taken against the International and the press, there was no support for profound changes in the political system, as after 1848, or even for forts and more Haussmannism in Paris. On the contrary, the Left, including those accused of complicity with the Commune, made rapid gains, and pressure for an amnesty increased, prefigured by numerous remissions and reductions of sentence. The repression of *la Semaine Sanglante* had evidently gone too far.

The army had been brought into politics by the civil war, and for a time it continued to have responsibility for public order in those areas under a state of siege, including Paris. The extreme Right saw it as a bulwark of society and an instrument they hoped to use to impose a regime to their liking. But even with MacMahon as President, the army made no move to stem the tide of Left-wing advance, however much some of its officers would have liked to try. The lesson of 18 March seems to have been learnt: that the cohesion of the army itself was put at risk by involvement in internal disputes. MacMahon would not countenance illegality; General Berthaut, his Minister of War, refused to impose a state of siege after the *Seize Mai* for fear of compromising the army by putting political power in the hands of its commanders.[9] The army had won a military victory in 1871, but had been forced to realize the limits of military victory.[10] This was not the least of the consequences of the war against Paris.

APPENDIX 1

Order of battle (20 May)

ARMY OF VERSAILLES

Commander-in-Chief: Marshal de MacMahon
Chief of staff: General Borel

1st Army Corps

Commander: General de Ladmirault
Chief of staff: General Saget

1st Division: General Grenier

1st Brigade: General Abatucci
54th, 48th and 87th *regiments de marche*
2nd Brigade: General Pradier
10th bn *chasseurs*, 51st and 72nd *de marche*, Volunteers

2nd Division: General de Laveaucoupet

1st Brigade: General Wolff
23rd bn *chasseurs*, 67th, 68th and 69th *de marche*
2nd Brigade: General Hanrion
2nd bn *chasseurs*, 45th *de marche*, 135th *de ligne*

3rd Division: General Montaudon

1st Brigade: General Dumont
30th bn *chasseurs*, 39th *de marche*, *régiment étranger*
2nd Brigade: General Lefèbvre
31st and 36th *de marche*, 119th *de ligne*

Cavalry Brigade: General de Galliffet

9th and 12th *chasseurs à cheval*

Artillery, Engineers

2nd Army Corps

Commander: General Courtot de Cissey
Chief of staff: General de Place

1st Division: General Le Vassor-Sorval

1st Brigade: General Lian (replacing General Besson, killed 10 April)
4th bn *chasseurs*, 82nd and 85th *de marche*
2nd Brigade: General Osmont (replacing General Daudel)
113th and 114th *de ligne*

2nd Division: General Susbielle

1st Brigade: General Bocher
18th bn *chasseurs*, 46th and 89th *de marche*
2nd Brigade: General Paturel
17th bn *chasseurs*, 38th and 76th *de marche*

3rd Division: General Lacretelle

1st Brigade: General Noël
19th bn *chasseurs*, 39th and 71st *de marche*
2nd Brigade: General Bounetou (replacing General Péchot, killed 10 April)
41st and 70th *de marche*

Cavalry, Artillery, Engineers

3rd Army Corps (cavalry)

Commander: General Du Barail
Chief of staff: General Balland

1st Division: General Halna du Fretay

1st Brigade: General Charlemagne
2nd, 3rd and 8th hussars
2nd Brigade: General de Lajaille
7th and 11th *chasseurs à cheval*

2nd Division: General du Preuil

1st Brigade: General Cousin
4th dragoons, 3rd *cuirassiers*
2nd Brigade: General Dargentolle
8th and 9th dragoons

3rd Division: General Ressayre

1st Brigade: General de Bernis
6th *chasseurs*, 7th dragoons
2nd Brigade: General Bachelier
4th and 8th *cuirassiers*

Artillery

4th Army Corps

Commander: General Douay
Chief of staff: General Renson

1st Division: General Berthaut

1st Brigade: General Gandil
10th bn *chasseurs*, 26th *de ligne*, 5th *provisoire*
2nd Brigade: General Carteret
94th *de ligne*, 6th *provisoire*

2nd Division: General L'hériller

1st Brigade: General Leroy de Daïs (killed 25 May)
55th and 58th *de marche*
2nd Brigade: (incomplete)
a battalion of 27th *de ligne*

Cavalry, Artillery, Engineers

5th Army Corps

Commander: General Clinchant
Chief of staff: General de Brouillé

1st Division: General Duplessis

1st Brigade: General de Courcy
1st and 2nd *provisoires*
2nd Brigade: General Blot
3rd and 4th *provisoires*

2nd Division: General Garnier

1st Brigade: General de Brauer
13th and 14th *provisoires*

2nd Brigade: General Cottret
15th and 17th *provisoires*

Cavalry, Artillery, Engineers

RESERVE ARMY

Commander-in-Chief: General Vinoy
Chief of staff: General de Valdan

1st Division: General Faron

1st Brigade: General de la Mariouse
35th and 42nd *de ligne*
2nd Brigade: General Derroja
109th and 110th *de ligne*
3rd Brigade: General Berthe
22nd bn *chasseurs*, 64th and 65th *de marche*

2nd Division: General Bruat

1st Brigade: General Bernard de Seigneurans
74th *de marche*, 1st *de marche d'infanterie de marine*, 2nd *de marche de marins-fusiliers*
2nd Brigade: Colonel Le Mordan de Langourian
75th *de marche*, 2nd *de marche d'infanterie de marine*, 1st *de marche de marins-fusiliers*

3rd Division: General Vergé

1st Brigade: General Daguerre
26th bn *chasseurs*, 37th and 79th *de marche*
2nd Brigade: General Gremion
90th and 91st *de marche*

Cavalry, Artillery, Engineers, regiment of Gendarmerie

Total strength of the Army of Versailles

	Infantry	Cavalry	Artillery	Engineers	Total
1st Corps	19,934	1,246	2,068	667	23,915
2nd Corps	22,267	468	2,862	737	26,334
3rd Corps	—	6,024	481	—	6,505
4th Corps	9,944	683	1,196	736	12,559
5th Corps	12,857	529	1,402	444	15,232
Reserve	29,449	524	1,715	762	32,450
Total	94,451	9,474	9,724	3,346	116,995

APPENDIX 2

Officers and men accused of desertion or complicity in the insurrection

OFFICERS

Officers dismissed, court-martialled or reported for having sympathy with the insurrection, and of whom definite details can be traced

	Ex-ranks	Wartime promotion	'Advanced' opinions[a]	Parisian (or suburbs)
Arnaud	x	x		
Bosc	x	x	x	
Bourgogne	x		x	
Maluchet	x	x		x
Menuet	x		x	x
Savatier	x	x		
Serres	x	x	x	x
Sourdeau	x	x		x
Touiller	x	x	x	x

[a] based on their own admission or others' evidence.

The small number, the disappearance of evidence for others, deliberate concealment and changes of opinion make it necessary to reserve judgment. It is clear, however, that the authorities had some reason to suspect a certain type of officer, and it might well be that disaffection among officers of a similar background was common at the beginning of the insurrection.

OTHER RANKS

The surviving dossiers of sixty-eight men tried by the 2nd *Conseil de Guerre* in Paris preserved at the AHG constitute only a small sample of the 1,401 (according to the Appert Report) tried for offences connected with the insurrection. They appear, however, to contain a higher proportion of those convicted of serious offences: eight were sentenced to forced labour (out of twenty-nine receiving that sentence), one was sentenced to death (commuted) and sixteen to transportation to a fortified place.

The war against Paris 1871

As the documents give only the briefest indication of occupation, the simplest of divisions has been adopted in the following tables. For reasons of clarity and simplicity, the urban category refers only to the large towns.

Table 1. *All the accused (sixty-eight)*

	Military service record														
	Reserve			Less than 1 year			1–2 years			2–3 years			3 years plus			
Occupation	T	I	P	T	I	P	T	I	P	T	I	P	T	I	P	Total
Agriculture and assoc-iated	3	3	0	10	0	1	—			—			4	2	0	17
Rural trades	—			8	0	0	2	0	0	—			3	1	0	13
Urban pro-letariat	—			1	0	0	—			—			3	0	1	4
Urban trades	—			15	4	14	3	0	1	2	1	1	4	4	4	24
Domestic	—			2	0	0	—			1	0	1	1	0	0	4
Middle class	—			1	0	0	—			—			1	1	1	2
Other	—			1	0	1	—			—			3	0	0	4
Totals	3	3	0	38	4	16	5	0	1	3	1	2	19	8	6	68

Note: T = total, of which I = inactive units (administration, hospital, disarmed troops etc.) and P = Parisians.

Appendix 2

Table 2. *Those particularly compromised (twenty-eight)*

| | Military service record | | | | | | | | | | | | | | |
| Occupation | Reserve | | | Less than 1 year | | | 1–2 years | | | 2–3 years | | | 3 years plus | | | Total |
	T	I	P	T	I	P	T	I	P	T	I	P	T	I	P	
Agriculture and assoc-iated	2	2	0	6	0	1	—			—			2	1	0	10
Rural trades	—			3	1	0	1	0	0	—			2	1	0	6
Urban pro-letariat	—			1	0	0	—			—			2	0	1	3
Urban trades	—			5	2	5	1	0	0	—			1	1	1	7
Domestic	—			—			—			—			1	0	0	1
Middle class	—			—			—			—			1	1	1	1
Other	—			—			—			—			—			0
Totals	2	2	0	15	3	6	2	0	0	0	0	0	9	4	3	28

Note: T = total, of which I = inactive units (administration, hospital, disarmed troops etc.) and P = Parisians.

vv

The composition of army units

OFFICERS

Comparison of the 42nd *de ligne*, one of the surviving infantry regiments of the Imperial Army, with two regiments of wartime formation shows that the latter took a high proportion of their officers from the reserve or the ranks and among civilians having no pre-war experience. Also noteworthy is the arrival of regular officers released from captivity, and joining the 74th (and similar regiments) in April.

Table 1. *A regular regiment: the 42nd* de ligne

	Military service record						
	More than 1 year's commissioned service				Less than 1 year's commissioned service		
	From ranks		From schools[a]				No pre-war service
Arrival at regiment	A	B	A	B	Reserve	Ex-ranks	
Pre-war	9	—	3	3	—	8	—
Oct.–Dec. 70	1	—	—	—	—	—	—
Jan.–March 71	1	—	—	—	—	2	—
April–May	—	—	—	—	—	—	—

[a] i.e. military academies.
A = subaltern officers; B = field officers.

Table 2. *A regiment of wartime formation: the 74th* de marche

Arrival at regiment	Military service record: More than 1 year's commissioned service: From ranks A	From ranks B	From schools[a] A	From schools[a] B	Less than 1 year's commissioned service: Reserve	Ex-ranks	No pre-war service
Dec. 70 or before	4	1	—	2	14	8	7
Jan. 71	1	—	—	1	2	—	3
February	4	—	—	—	2	2	—
March	—	—	—	—	—	—	—
April	6 (POWs)		1 (POW)		—	—	—
May	—	—	—	—	—	—	—

[a] i.e. military academies.
A = subaltern officers; B = field officers.

Table 3. *A regiment of the Army of Paris: the 114th* de ligne

Arrival at regiment	Military service record: More than 1 year's commissioned service: From ranks A	From ranks B	From schools A	From schools B	Less than 1 year's commissioned service: Reserve	Ex-ranks	No pre-war service
Nov. 70 or before	16	1	2	2	3	27	4
December	—	—	—	—	2	—	—
Jan. 71	—	—	—	1	—	—	—
February	1	—	4	2	1	2	1
March–April	—	—	—	—	—	—	—
May	—	—	1	—	—	—	—

OTHER RANKS

Table 4. *A regiment of the Army of Paris: the 114th de ligne*

	Military service record													
	Reserve			Less than 1 year			1–2 years			2 years or over			Total		
Occupation	T	P	N	T	P	N	T	P	N	T	P	N	T	P	N
Agriculture[a]	4	—	2	325	8	9	9	—	—	39	1	17	377	9	28
Rural trades[b]	3	—	2	122	—	12	3	—	1	38	—	24	166	0	39
Urban trades	3	1	2	30	6	4	3	—	1	10	—	6	46	7	13
Industrial[c]	—	—	—	13	5	—	2	—	1	9	2	4	24	7	5
Domestic	2	1	—	30	1	—	1	—	—	2	—	2	35	2	2
Middle class[d]	1	—	1	18	5	4	1	1	1	4	2	4	24	8	10
Other[e]	—	—	—	23	3	2	1	1	—	14	—	7	38	4	9
Total	13	2	7	561	28	31	20	2	4	116	5	64	710	37	106

Note: T = total, of which P = Parisians and N = NCOs.
[a] Including *cultivateur, laboureur, jardinier* and *journalier.*
[b] Including *artisans* and *garçons.*
[c] Including miners.
[d] Including proprietors, professional men and students.
[e] Including military, transport and unspecified.

This random sample of 710 men was taken from volumes 1, 2 and 3 of the *Registre matricule de la troupe,* counting men noted as having taken part in the campaign. As noticeable as the preponderance of young recruits from rural areas in the total is the number of rural and urban artisans among the NCOs, no doubt for educational reasons, who were more likely to have opinions of their own. The small number of reservists is due to organizational factors.

Notes

ⅴⅴ

The following abbreviations are used in the notes:

AHG   Archives Historiques de Guerre
APP   Archives de la Préfecture de Police
AS   Archives de la Seine
BN   Bibliothèque Nationale
MAE   archives of Ministère des Affaires Etrangères
RHA   *Revue Historique de l'Armée*

1. Wars and rumours of wars

1. Louis Lazare, *Les Quartiers pauvres de Paris, le 20e arrondissement* (1870); David H. Pinkney, *Napoleon III and the Rebuilding of Paris* (1972).
2. Jacques Rougerie, 'Belleville', in Louis Girard (ed.), *Les Elections de 1869* (1960).
3. Jacques Rougerie, *Paris libre 1871* (1971), 39, quoting speaker in a middle-class political club.
4. Speech of de Belcastel, 10 March 1871. *Annales de l'Assemblée Nationale* (1871), I, 276.
5. Jules Simon, *Le Gouvernement de M. Thiers* (1878), I, 235.
6. *Ibid.*, 161, 167.
7. Gaston de Saint-Valry, *Souvenirs et réflexions politiques* (1886), 44.
8. A remark by the President of the court martial, the Duc d'Aumale. *Procès du Maréchal Bazaine, compte-rendu des débats du 1er Conseil de Guerre* (1874), 90.
9. A. Flamarion, *Le Livret du docteur, souvenirs de la campagne contre l'Allemagne et contre la Commune de Paris, 1870–1871* (1872), 125.
10. Jean-Baptiste Millière, quoted in Rougerie, *Paris libre*, 116. See also Rougerie, 'Notes pour servir à l'histoire du 18 mars 1871', in *Mélanges d'histoire sociale offerts à Jean Maitron* (1976), 234.
11. What the heroes of classical antiquity were to the revolutionaries of 1789, writes the artist Bernard Dufour, the Commune is to revolutionaries of the twentieth century, through 'cette stimulation de l'imagination révolutionnaire par l'échec de la Commune de Paris'. Note on his painting 'Holger Meins' in the exhibition *Guillotine et Peinture* (Centre Georges Pompidou, June–August 1977).

211

12. Jacques Duclos, interviewed in *Magazine Littéraire* (March 1971), p. 26. See also his own book, *La Commune de Paris à l'assaut du ciel* (1971).
13. Karl Marx, *The Civil War in France* (Peking 1966), 72.
14. Letter to F. Domela-Nieuwenhuis, 22 Feb. 1881, quoted in George Lichtheim, *Marxism, An Historical and Critical Study* (1964), 121.

2. A defeated army

1. MAE Papiers Gambetta, vol. 52, 'Notes politiques', p. 117.
2. See remark made by General Bourbaki, in Michael Howard, *The Franco-Prussian War* (1967), 29.
3. General François Charles Du Barail, *Mes Souvenirs* (1894–6), I, 69; dossiers DOUAY, Félix Charles, AHG GD (2e série) 1406, and de MACMAHON, AHG MF (2e série) 57; *Procès du Maréchal Bazaine*, 4–5; Pierre Chalmin, *L'Officier français de 1815 à 1870* (1957), 284.
4. François Kunzt *L'Officier français dans la nation* (1960), 48.
5. Du Barail, *Souvenirs*, II, 234–5, 238–41; Léonce Patry, *La Guerre telle qu'elle est* (1897), 61. For the state of the army before the war see also General J. Regnault, 'Les campagnes d'Algérie et leur influence de 1830 à 1870', *RHA* no. 4 (1953); Col. Eugène Carrias, *La Pensée militaire française* (1960), 225; and a recent detailed study, Richard Holmes, 'The road to Sedan, the French army 1866–70' (PhD thesis, Reading University, 1975).
6. General J. Regnault, 'Le haut commandement et les généraux français en 1870', *RHA* no. 1 (1971), 9.
7. Patry, *La Guerre*, 34, 44, 186.
8. Chalmin, *L'Officier français*, 360.
9. Translation of an official German report, 'Critiques et renseignements', AHG Lv 19.
10. Chalmin, *L'Officier français*, 370–1.
11. J. Monteilhet, *Les Institutions militaires de la France* (1932), 60–1.
12. *Ibid.*, 56.
13. Patry, *La Guerre*, 63; Paul Déroulède, *1870, Feuilles de route* (1907), 160.
14. General Sir Charles Beauchamp Walker, *Days of a Soldier's life* (1894), 297.
15. Déroulède, *Feuilles*, 86.
16. *Ibid.*, 187.
17. Lieut.-Col. Louis Alfred Meyret, *Carnet d'un prisonnier de guerre* (1888), 42.
18. Patry, *La Guerre*, 69.
19. L. de Narcy, *Journal d'un officier de turcos* (1902), 105.
20. Déroulède, *Feuilles*, 162.
21. Meyret, *Carnet*, 90 (entry of 1 Sept.).
22. General Barthélémy Edmond Palat, *Histoire de la Guerre de 1870–1871* (1898), VII, 394–5.
23. *Ibid.*, VII, 505–7; Du Barail, *Souvenirs*, III, 208.
24. Henri Choppin, *Souvenirs d'un cavalier du second empire* (1898), 236; Patry, *La Guerre*, 207.

25. Choppin, *Souvenirs*, 215.
26. *Ibid.*, 247, quoting a letter from Colonel Bilhau.
27. Du Barail, *Souvenirs*, III, 86.
28. Patry, *La Guerre*, 173; Déroulède, *Feuilles*, 42.
29. Arthur de Grandeffe, *Mobiles et volontaires de la Seine* (1871), 24; de Narcy, *Journal*, 151.
30. Letter of 8 Feb. 1871, quoted in Jacques de la Faye (ed.), *Souvenirs du général Lacretelle*, (1907), 270.
31. *Le Moniteur de l'Armée*, 26 March. See General Montaudon's outraged reaction, *Souvenirs militaires* (1900), II, 42.
32. Many letters written in the 1870s from officers of Gambetta's armies, complaining to him of mistreatment by the returning military establishment and asking for his intercession, may be found among his papers. MAE Papiers Gambetta, vol. 55.
33. Patry, *La Guerre*, 388.
34. Louis-Nathaniel Rossel, *Papiers posthumes* (1871), 231.
35. *Ibid.*, 66.
36. J. P. T. Bury, *Gambetta and the National Defence* (1936), 144. For details of the composition of the provincial armies, see AHG *Registres matricules* of units; officers and men who fought in the civil war are identifiable from the lists of their campaigns.
37. Following contemporary practice, *de ligne* is used to denote regular Line infantry regiments, as opposed to temporary *régiments de marche* and *régiments provisoires*. There were 104 Line regiments before the war; those numbered 105 and onwards were of wartime formation.
38. Howard, *Franco-Prussian War*, 344–7, 364–7.
39. Jacques Desmarest, *La Défense nationale* (1949), 423–8.
40. Du Barail, *Souvenirs*, III, 227.
41. Montaudon, *Souvenirs*, II, 42.
42. Quoted by Montaudon, *ibid.*, 260–2.
43. Patry, *La Guerre*, 73.
44. Quoted by Choppin, *Souvenirs*, 225.
45. Flamarion, *Livret*, 125.
46. De Narcy, *Journal*, 246–7.
47. *Le Moniteur de l'Armée*, 16 March; du Barail, *Souvenirs*, III, 458–94.
48. See his police dossier, APP Ba 1088.
49. Howard, *Franco-Prussian War*, 31.
50. Grandeffe, *Mobiles et volontaires*, 188.
51. De la Faye, *Lacretelle*, 270.
52. Paul Déroulède, *70–71, Nouvelles Feuilles de route* (1907), 329.
53. De la Faye, *Lacretelle*, 271.
54. Déroulède, *Feuilles*, 329.
55. Edith Thomas, *Rossel* (1967), 252, 257. He became colonel of the 17th National Guard Legion, then chief of staff to the War Delegate and finally War Delegate himself.

3. Insurrection

1. Archibald Forbes, *My Experiences of the War between France and Germany* (1871), II, 399.
2. The preliminary peace treaty, signed 26 February, permitted the Paris garrison to be increased to 40,000. For texts, see Michael Hurst (ed.), *Key Treaties for the Great Powers 1814–1914* (1972). II, 460, 464.
3. See Gen. Joseph Vinoy, *Campagne de 1870–1871*, II, *L'Armistice et la Commune* (1872), for the view of the authorities, and Prosper-Olivier Lissagaray, *Histoire de la Commune de 1871* (1972), first published in 1876, for that of the revolutionaries.
4. A P P Ba 497, dossier on 'Assassinat du sous-brigadier de police Vincensini'; Macé to *Enquête parlementaire sur l'insurrection du 18 mars*, no. 740, Assembée Nationale 1871 (Versailles 1872), II, 220; Vinoy to *Enquête*, II, 91.
5. Details in *Le Gaulois*, 1 March.
6. Vinoy to *Enquête*, II, 92; G H Q to Gen. Faron, 1 March, A H G Li 100.
7. Vinoy to *Enquête*, II, 95.
8. Statements to *Enquête*, by Col. Lambert, II, 244; de la Rochethulon, II, 408; and Gen. Appert, II, 251.
9. Vinoy to *Enquête*, II, 92–5; Simon, *Gouvernement*, I, 206.
10. See dispatch of 5 March from Jules Ferry, Mayor of Paris, to Thiers, in Louis Fiaux, *Histoire de la guerre civile de 1871* (1879), 43, and Jules Favre's correspondence in M A E Papiers Jules Favre, Guerre, vol. 5.
11. *Enquête*, II, 97.
12. Vinoy, *Campagne*, 187; Simon, *Gouvernement*, I, 206.
13. Vinoy, *Campagne*, 172; Le Flô to *Enquête*, II, 86.
14. Vinoy to *Enquête*, II, 90; Vinoy, *Campagne*, 180; Gen. Malroy to Gen. Susbielle, 15 March, A H G Lu 17.
15. Colonel of 120th to G O C 1st Div., 6 March, A H G Li 101; evidence of Capt. Fernandez, A H G 2nd *Conseil de Guerre*, dossier 356; Ordre Général, 10 Feb., A H G Lu 15; report of M O of 110th, 18 March, A H G Li 120; and Flamarion (M O of 67th *de marche*), *Livret*, 127.
16. A H G Li 90.
17. Lissagaray, *Histoire*, 107.
18. Le Flô to Vinoy, 3 March, A H G Li 120; Vinoy, *Campagne*, 183.
19. Reports from regiments, A H G Li 101; Patry, *La Guerre*, 259, 397.
20. Dossier SUSBIELLE, Baron Bernard (1808–93), A H G G D (2e série) 1512.
21. List of officers of 37th, 2 April, A H G Lu 34; A H G *Registre matricule des officiers* (74th *régiment d'infanterie*), vol. 2.
22. Gen. A. A. Devaureix, *Souvenirs et observations sur la campagne de 1870* (1909), 576; Patry, *La Guerre*, 255.
23. Vinoy, *Campagne*, 389–90; G H Q to Faron, 17 March, A H G Li 100.
24. Statements to *Enquête* by Roger, II, 441; d'Aurelle, II, 432; Picard, II, 54; Dubail, II, 335. See also *Le Figaro*, 10 March and *Le Gaulois*, 12 March.
25. Charles Yriarte, *Les Prussiens à Paris et le 18 mars* (1871), 152; Thiers to

Suzanne and Vinoy, 5 March (from Bordeaux), AHG Li 90; Favre to Thiers, 8 March, MAE Papiers Favre, vol. 5, fol. 306.

26. Ferry to *Enquête*, II, 64.
27. Fiaux, *Guerre civile*, 57; Yriarte, *Prussiens*, 148, 163, 191; statements to *Enquête* by Vautrain, II, 373, and Baudoin de Mortemart, II, 454.
28. Yriarte, *Prussiens*, 218; statements to *Enquête* by Vinoy, II, 97, Baudoin de Mortemart, II, 449, and d'Aurelle, II, 434.
29. Yriarte (who was serving on Vinoy's staff), *Prussiens*, 163–4, 183, 188–9; and see *Le Gaulois*, 18 March.
30. Jules Favre, *Gouvernement de la défense nationale* (1875), III, 209.
31. Yriarte, *Prussiens*, 174, 181; Vinoy to *Enquête*, II, 97; Simon, *Gouvernement*, I, 228
32. Simon, *Gouvernement*, I, 248, 242; statements to *Enquête* by Ferry, II, 65; Vinoy, II, 97–8; d'Aurelle, II, 434; Thiers, II, 11.
33. Le Flô to *Enquête*, II, 78.
34. D'Aurelle to *Enquête*, II, 432.
35. Yriarte, *Prussiens*, 183; Susbielle, report, AHG Lu 7. See also Du Barail, *Souvenirs*, III, 247, and Vinoy to *Enquête*, II, 98.
36. Statements to *Enquête* by Choppin, II, 117, and Picard, II, 55.
37. *Ordre de mouvement*, given in Vinoy, *Campagne*, 411–17.
38. Wolff's brigade (67th and 68th *de marche*) to occupy Bastille and Faubourg Saint Antoine; Hanrion's brigade (2nd bn *chasseurs de marche*, 45th and 69th de marche) the Cité and Luxembourg gardens; the 110th *de ligne* the Lobau barracks behind the Hôtel de Ville; the 120th, the Prince Eugène barracks (Faubourg du Temple); a battalion of the 109th, the Gare du Nord and Gare de l'Est; and other detachments the Tuileries, Ecole Militaire, and Louvre.
39. Paturel's brigade (17th bn *chasseurs*, 76th *de marche*), and Lecomte's brigade (18th bn *chasseurs*, 88th *de marche*).
40. De la Mariouse's brigade (35th and 42nd *de ligne*) and Derroja's brigade (part of 109th and 110th *de ligne*). Daudel's brigade (113th and 114th *de ligne*) were occupying the southern forts.
41. AHG MR 2151.
42. Reports, Gen. Susbielle. AHG Lu 7.
43. Vinoy, *Campagne*, 412.
44. Vinoy to Min. of War, 13 March, AHG Li 190; Gen. de Valdan (chief of staff) to Min. of War, AHG Li 120.
45. Suzanne to Vinoy, 3 March; Remount Bureau to Minister, 16 March, and to Vinoy, 18 March. AHG Li 90.
46. Reports by police commandant Vassal, 26 March, AHG Li 126; Gen. Susbielle, on events of 18 March, and by OC 76th *de marche*, AHG Lu 7.
47. Report of OC 88th *de marche*. AHG Lu 7.
48. Reports, Vassal, AHG Li 126, and Toussaint, AHG Lu 7.
49. Reports, Col. Allavène, AHG Li 123, and Capt. Kluber, AHG Lu 7.
50. Reports, OC 76th *de marche*, OC 17th bn *chasseurs*, and Gen. Susbielle. AHG Lu 7.
51. Report, Lieut. Toussaint. AHG Lu 7.
52. Statements of Pte Ligneley, Pte Giraudier and Cpl Lance, AHG 2nd

Conseil de Guerre, dossier 12; and statement of Cpl Bléry, dossier 352. This case concerned the trial for dereliction of duty of several soldiers, mostly of the 88th, who evidently had an interest in finding excuses for their conduct. Nevertheless, their evidence was not disputed and many were acquitted.

53. Reports, Vassal, A H G Li 126, Susbielle, A H G Lu 7, and Toussaint, A H G Lu 7; statements by Comm. Poussargues (9 May 1871) and Lieut. Franck (3 April and 16 Nov. 1871), both of 18th bn *chasseurs*, A H G Li 126.

54. Reports, OC artillery, Brig. Lecomte, A H G Lu 7; OC 2nd regiment *gendarmerie à cheval*, A H G Li 120; and police captain Berraz (22 March), A P P Ba 364–3.

55. Reports, Susbielle, A H G Lu 7; OC 88th *de marche*, A H G Lu 7; Poussargues, A H G Li 126; statement by Franck (3 April 1871), A H G Li 126. See also *Le Figaro*, 20 March.

56. Reports, Col. Lespiau (109th *de ligne*) and Col. Roblastre (110th). A H G Li 120.

57. Report, Col. Comte (42nd *de ligne*). A H G Li 120.

58. Yriarte, *Prussiens*, 236; note from 35th *de ligne* on events of 18 March, A H G Li 120; Macé to *Enquête*, II, 221.

59. MacMahon to *Enquête*, II, 22.

60. Telegrams quoted by Ferry, *Enquête*, II, 65–77.

61. Col. Vabre to *Enquête*, II, 537; reports, O C 120th *de ligne*, and from 35th *de ligne*, A H G Li 120.

62. Flamarion, *Livret*, 141.

63. Patry, said by his C O to have 'excellent principles', later became a lieutenant-colonel and was given diplomatic missions. Dossier PATRY, Marie Gabriel Léonce, A H G Pensions (3e série) 56338.

64. Nickname of Napoleon III.

65. Patry, *La Guerre*, 402–10.

66. Flamarion, *Livret*, 132.

67. Vinoy to *Enquête*, II, 99.

68. Le Flô to *Enquête*, II, 81.

69. See A H G MR 2151.

70. Le Flô to *Enquête*, II, 81, 87.

71. Thiers to Favre, 10 March. BN Papiers Thiers, n.a.fr. 20623, fol. 108.

72. This has led him to be cast in the role of agent provocateur: 'Vinoy précipitant sa défaite pour mettre Thiers face à face avec les rouges et faire comprendre aux Allemands que le retour de Napoleon III . . . serait plus sain pour eux que la révolution.' Armand Lanoux, *Une Histoire de la Commune de Paris* (1971), I, 54.

73. Instructions of Marshal de Castellane, 18 March 1858. A H G MR 2151.

74. Report by Vinoy. A H G Li 120.

75. There were 104 men of the 88th reported to have stayed behind in Paris (list, A H G Li 116); the 76th arrived in Versailles 150 men short (report by lieut.-col., A H G Lu 7); the 42nd reported only 25 missing (dossier of lists of men left in Paris, A H G Li 117). Most of the several thousand soldiers in Paris under the Commune belonged to disarmed units of the wartime

Army of Paris, or to the 120th *de ligne*, isolated in their barracks at the Place du Château d'Eau.

76. 'Guerres d'insurrection' (May 1839). A H G MR 2151.

4. Interlude

1. *Enquête*, II, 14.
2. The political calculations of the government are discussed in more detail in my article in the *Historical Journal*, xxiii, no. 4 (1980), 813–31.
3. Jeanne Gaillard, *Communes de province, Commune de Paris, 1870–1871* (1971).
4. *Enquête*, II, 14.
5. Vinoy to *Enquête*, II, 100; Daudel to Faron, 2.50 p.m., 18 March, A H G Li 101.
6. See dispatches, March, A H G Li 101, 120 and 128; police reports, 20 and 21 March, A P P Ba 364–3; and Du Barail, *Souvenirs*, III, 260.
7. *Journal de marche* (Mont-Valérien), A H G Lu 98; reports and dispatches, March, A H G Li 120 and 121.
8. Gen. de Galliffet, 'Mes souvenirs', *Journal des Débats*, 22 July 1902.
9. Comte d'Hérisson, *Nouveau journal d'un officier d'ordonnance* (1889), 113.
10. *Enquête*, II, 23.
11. Vicomte de Meaux, *Souvenirs politiques* (1905), 46.
12. Simon, *Gouvernement*, I, 292.
13. Report, Insp. Vauchelet, 24 March, A P P Ba 364–3; de Grandeffe, *Mobiles et volontaires*, 194.
14. Schoelcher to *Enquête*, II, 327.
15. Saisset to *Enquête*, II, 308; Galliffet, 'Mes souvenirs' (22 July 1902).
16. *Le Soir* (Versailles edn), 25 March.
17. E. B. Washburne, *Recollections of a Minister to France* (1887), II, 57, quoting a diary entry of 28 March; Lord Newton, *Lord Lyons, a Record of British Diplomacy* (1913), I, 380.
18. Tirard to *Enquête*, II, 343.
19. E.g. 'Soon the men were saluting smartly again and matters began to look less hopeless.' Stewart Edwards, *The Paris Commune 1871* (1972), 192.
20. Marseille to *Enquête*, II, 200; Hector Pessard, *Mes petits papiers, deuxième série* (1888), 7.
21. Correspondence, 22 March – 5 April, A H G Li 117, Li 120 and Lu 7.
22. G O C Evreux column to Vinoy, 27 March. A H G Li 120.
23. *Liste nominative*, 16th battery, 6th artillery regiment. A G H Li 120.
24. Report by police captain Berraz of conversation overheard, 22 March. A P P Ba 364–3.
25. E.g., reports of La Fontaine, 20 March, and Capt. Berraz, 22 March. A P P Ba 364–3.
26. Report, Service de la Presse, 29 March. A P P Ba 364–3.
27. A P P Ba 364–3.
28. Reports of Capt. Pignolet, 30 March, and Insp. de Nulley (my unlikely rendering of an illegible signature), 28 and 30 March, referring to the 89th, 136th and 70th regiments. A P P Ba 364–3.

29. Police reports, 31 March, APP Ba 364–3, and 5 April, Ba 364–4.
30. Police report, Brissaud, 21 March. APP Ba 364–3.
31. AHG Li 120.
32. *Ibid.*
33. Min. of War to Vinoy, 29 March (a report confirmed from other sources), AHG Li 120; Commissaire Spécial, Nevers, to Min. of Interior, 31 March, APP Ba 364–3.
34. Police reports, de Nulley (31 March), Brissaud (20 and 27 March), Pignolet (28 March) and La Fontaine (31 March), APP Ba 364–3; Le Flô to Vinoy, 29 March, AHG Li 120.
35. J.P.T. Bury, *Gambetta and the Making of the Third Republic* (1973), 12. See also *Le Gaulois*, 24 April and 9 and 10 May. Rossel probably thought this; he had written to Gambetta in February, 'La révolution est peut-être à refaire . . . j'espère que nous la referons.' Thomas, *Rossel*, 250.
36. Conversation of nine subalterns, overheard by Vinoy's secretary. Police report, Brissaud, 31 March. APP Ba 364–3.
37. Overheard by a policeman at Chantiers station on 27 March, Note from Prefect of Police, 30 March, AHG Li 120. The Minister of War ordered an immediate enquiry: Le Flô to Vinoy, 1 April, AHG Li 121.
38. Patry, *La Guerre*, 417–19.
39. *Ibid.*, 415.
40. De la Mariouse to Faron, 22 March. AHG Li 120.
41. GOC 5th *subdivision militaire* to C-in-C Cherbourg (Ducrot), 11 April. AHG Lu 34.
42. List of absent officers. AHG Li 117.
43. MacMahon to Minister, no. 139, 25 April, and no. 270, 3 May. AHG Lu 8, vol. 1.
44. *Réponses au rapport* (daily orders), 1st Corps, no. 42, 17 May. AHG Lu 10.
45. List of absent officers. AHG Li 117.
46. Faron to 2nd brigade, 2 April. Notebook, 'Correspondances diverses', AHG Li 128.
47. Gen. Faron, dispatch no. 492, 22 March, and 245, 1 May. AHG Li 128.
48. Patry, *La Guerre*, 415; dossier PATRY, M.G.L., AHG Pensions (3e série) 56338.
49. Report of his court martial on 12 April, *Le Gaulois*, 14 April.
50. GOC 4th Div. to Vinoy, 7 April, AHG Li 121; report, Gen. Derroja, March, AHG Li 120; list of absent officers, AHG Li 116.
51. Circular, 1 April.
52. President of the court martial trying the rioters of 31 October 1870, his sympathy with their frustration and anger at the supineness of the government led him to be remarkably lenient. Gustave Lefrançais, *Souvenirs d'un révolutionnaire* (1972), 349.
53. Du Barail, *Souvenirs*, III, 263.
54. Report of court martial, *Le Gaulois* 14 April.
55. Choppin, *Souvenirs*, 269.
56. Patry, *La Guerre*, 419.
57. Letter, 16 April, quoted in de la Faye, *Lacretelle*, 277.

58. Montaudon, *Souvenirs*, II, 265.
59. *Ibid.*, 295–7; de la Mariouse to Faron, 22 March, AHG Li 120; Patry, *La Guerre*, 419.
60. Police reports: Daniel, 23 March and de Nulley, 30 March, APP Ba 364–3; Service de la Presse, 1, 2 and 3 April, APP Ba 364–4; and de Nulley, 22 April, APP Ba 364–5: 'they don't fall for that sort of trick'.
61. Police reports, La Fontaine, 25 March, and de Nulley, 31 March. APP Ba 364–4.
62. Police report, Brissaud, 23 March, APP Ba 364–3; *Le Soir* (Versailles edn), 22 March, (Paris edn), 3 April.
63. Orders of 19 and 20 March, and Min. of War to Sous-Intendant Militaire, 26 March, AHG Li 120; *Réponses au rapport*, 4 April, AHG Li 114; *Le Moniteur de l'Armée*, nos. 57 and 58, Dec. 1871.
64. MO's report, 110th *de ligne*, 1 April, AHG Li 121; police report, 8 April, APP Ba 364–4; GOC 1st div. to GOC 5th Corps, 7 May, AHG Lu 71.
65. Vinoy to Faron, *ordre* no. 44, 24 March, and circular, 23 March. AHG Li 120.
66. AHG Li 120.
67. Circular and letter from Vinoy, 31 March; Pref. of Police to Gen. de Maud'huy, 25 March. AHG Li 120.
68. The chorus ran: 'Vaillants soldats rappellons-nous nos mères/Avec bonheur guidant nos premiers pas/ On nous appelle à mitrailler nos frères/ Ne tirons pas (bis).' Police report, Insp. Albert, 30 March. APP Ba 364–3.
69. See lists of addresses of officers of 75th and 91st *de marche*, AHG Li 116 and Lu 34.
70. Police reports, 26, 29 and 31 March, AHG Li 120; 26 and 30 March, APP Ba 364–3.
71. Police report, 5 April. AHG Li 121.
72. See *procès-verbal* of interrogation of a drinks seller, 6 April, AHG Li 121; and Thiers to *Enquête*, II, 14.
73. APP Ba 364–4, *passim*, and police report, 30 March. AHG Li 120.
74. Vinoy, *Campagne*, 247.
75. Daily *réponses au rapport*, AHG Li 114, and decree of 1 April, AHG Li 121.
76. Min. of War to Vinoy; report of provost-marshal – both 6 April. AHG Li 121.
77. Police report, Insp. de Nulley, 31 March. APP Ba 364–3.
78. Report on 110th *de ligne*, Insp. de Nulley, 30 March. APP Ba 364–3.
79. Report on 1st bn *chasseurs*, Brissaud, 27 March. APP Ba 364–3.
80. Police reports, 30 and 31 March. APP Ba 364–3.

5. Civil war

1. Report of 109th, and Vinoy to GOC Reserve, 26 March, AHG Li 120; Galliffet, 'Mes souvenirs' (22 July 1902); Du Barail, *Souvenirs*, III, 260–1.
2. Police report, Brissaud, 27 March. APP Ba 364–3.
3. Note, Prefect of Police, 29 March; de la Mariouse to Faron, 30 March. AHG Li 120.

4. Police informant's report from Paris, 29 March. APP Ba 364–3.
5. Three police reports, 30 March. APP Ba 364–3.
6. Lissagaray, *Histoire*, 179; intercepted letter from a Fédéré, APP Ba 364–3.
7. John Leighton, *Paris under the Commune* (1871), 85.
8. Henri Lefèbvre, *La Proclamation de la Commune* (1965), 336.
9. APP Ba 364–3.
10. *Le Gaulois*, 1 April (i.e. the edition appearing on 31 March).
11. AHG Li 117.
12. Report, 31 March. AHG Li 120. See also accounts by Galliffet, 'Mes souvenirs' (22 July 1902), and an officer of 12th *chasseurs*, in *Journal des Débats*, 12 June 1894.
13. Report, Lochner, 31 March. AHG Li 120.
14. Register of dispatches, Mont Valérien. AHG Li 117.
15. AHG Li 120.
16. AHG Li 121.
17. Lochner to Vinoy, 10.50 a.m., 1 April. AHG Li 118.
18. Galliffer to Vinoy, 1.10 and 4.40 p.m., 1 April. AHG Li 118.
19. Lochner to Vinoy, 1 April, and Galliffet to Vinoy, 7.40 p.m., 1 April. AHG Li 118.
20. GHQ to Faron, 1 April. AHG Li 121.
21. *Intérieur* to *Etat-major*, 1 April. AHG Ly 4.
22. Letter, 1 April, APP Ba 364–5; Rossel, *Papiers posthumes*.
23. Circular, 'Dispositions à prendre en cas d'attaque', 1 April. AHG Li 121.
24. Gen. C.M.R. de Sesmaisons (then a junior officer on Vinoy's staff), *Hier et aujourd'hui, les troupes de la Commune et la loi de deux ans* (1904), 7; Washburne, *Recollections*, 69.
25. *Le Soir* (Versailles edn), 25 March; Galliffet, 'Mes souvenirs' (19 July 1902).
26. Sesmaisons, *Troupes*, 7.
27. GOC artillery to Vinoy, 3 April. AHG Li 121.
28. Du Barail, *Souvenirs*, III, 267–8; register of dispatches, Mont Valérien, AHG Li 117.
29. Albert de Mun, 'Galliffet', *Echo de Paris*, 10 July 1909.
30. Sesmaisons, *Troupes*, 9.
31. Report, 1st *régiment de marche de l'infanterie de marine*, 2 April, AHG Li 121; de Mun, 'Galliffet'; Vinoy to Thiers, 1.15 p.m., 2 April, AHG Li 118; report, Gen. Appert, 3 April, AHG Li 121.
32. Report, 2 April. AHG Li 121.
33. He had made his officers sign a pledge of loyalty to the Assembly, and tried to impose iron discipline on his men; the police reported, however, that they hated him and were ready to surrender to the Fédérés. Report, Insp. de Nulley, 29 March. APP Ba 364–3.
34. Police report, 2 April. APP Ba 364–4.
35. Reports, 2 April, from La Fontaine, APP Ba 364–4, and Col. Jules Aronssohn (a Versaillais agent), AHG Li 121.
36. *Le Soir* (Versailles edn), 4 April. The theory was further developed in the number of 13 May.

37. Lissagaray, *Histoire*, 180. See also report, Aronssohn, AHG Li 121, and dispatch, Vaillant to Nat. Guard HQ [2 April], AHG Ly 4.
38. Circular, 4 April. AHG Li 121.
39. Dossier VINOY, Joseph, AHG GD (2e série) 1336.
40. Report, Aronssohn. AHG Li 121.
41. Vinoy to Thiers, 1.15 p.m., 2 April. AHG Li 118.
42. Lambrecht, Min. of Agriculture, quoted by Meaux, *Souvenirs*, 51.
43. Reports, OC 21st battery, 15th artillery regiment, 2 April, AHG Li 121, and Reserve Army engineers, AHG Li 116.
44. *Situations*, 1 April. AHG Li 116.
45. Police report, 2 April, APP Ba 364–4; *Le Gaulois*, 4 April; Washburne, *Recollections*, 72; Gustave Paul Cluseret, *Mémoires du général Cluseret* (1887), I, 152.
46. Report, 74th *de marche*, 4 April. AHG Li 121. The men of the 74th who arrived in Paris were billeted at La Courtille barracks (Faubourg du Temple); fourteen gave themselves up to the authorities on 29 May and were sent to a penal battalion in Africa, and twenty-three others had turned up by the middle of June, but I have found no record of their fate. See Min. of War to Vinoy, 18 June, AHG Li 126, and report on losses, 74th *de marche*, 28 June, AHG Lu 95.
47. The former Papal Zouaves, recruited in France to fight for the Papal States, were reformed as the Volontaires de l'Ouest in 1870 and fought for the National Defence under their chief, Charette. They were naturally particular objects of republican suspicion. Although permitted to recruit volunteers for Versailles, they were kept in Rennes and never used against the Commune.
48. Thomas, *Rossel*, 272.
49. Fédéré dispatches, AHG Ly 4.
50. Galliffet to Vinoy, 7.25 p.m., 2 April. AHG Li 118.
51. Police reports, 10 p.m. and 11.15 p.m., AHG Li 121; Vinoy to Lochner, 11.10 p.m., 2 April, AHG Li 118.
52. Order, 3 April, and GOC 2nd Div. to Vinoy, 3 April, AHG Li 121; *Journal des marches*, 1st Div., AHG Li 115; report, Brissaud, 3 April, APP Ba 364–4.
53. Sutter-Laumann, *Histoire d'un trente-sous* (1891), 245–6; Cluseret, *Mémoires*, I, 42.
54. *Le Gaulois*, 14 and 16 March; *Le Soir* (Paris edn), 5 April.
55. Howard, *Franco-Prussian War*, 334.
56. Lochner told them that 'quant à la défense du fort sujet duquel les gardes nationaux paraissent être soucieux, ils peuvent se tranquilliser le Mont-Valérien est à l'abri de toute attaque de quelque côté . . . (illeg.)'. Register of dispatches, 20 March. AHG Li 117.
57. Lochner to Vinoy, 6.34 a.m., 3 April. AHG Li 118.
58. Commune dispatch, *Place* to *Guerre*, 3.05 p.m., 3 April. AHG Ly 4.
59. Dispatches, Lochner to Vinoy, 3 April, AHG Li 118; *Journal des opérations* (Mont Valérien artillery), AHG Lu 98.
60. Dispatches of Vinoy, Galliffet, Lochner and OC artillery, Mont Valérien,

3 April, AHG Li 118; Camille Pelletan, *La Semaine de Mai* (1880), 13; *Le Gaulois*, 8 April.

61. Galliffet to Vinoy, 12.40 and 2.10 p.m.; Gen. Valdan to Galliffet, 1 p.m. AHG Li 118.
62. Sesmaisons, *Troupes*, 12–13.
63. Report, Boulanger to Daudel, 3 April. AHG Li 121.
64. Report, Comm. Poulpiquet (113th), 4 April. AHG Li 121.
65. For details see Gaston da Costa, *La Commune vécue* (1903), I, 367.
66. Report, Derroja, and GOC 2nd Div. (Susbielle) to Vinoy, 3 April, AHG Li 121; Lissagaray, *Histoire*, 184.
67. Intercepted letter from National Guard. APP Ba 364–3.
68. *Le Soir* (Paris edn), 6 April, 'Lettre d'un témoin'; (Versailles edn), 5 April, 'La journée du 3 avril'; Sutter-Laumann, *Trente-sous*, 259.
69. Cluseret, *Mémoires*, I. 44, 158.
70. *Le Soir* (Versailles edn), 5 April (Paris edn), 6 April; report, Gen. Faron, 2 p.m., 3 April, AHG Li 121.
71. Wickham Hoffman, *Camp, Court and Siege* (1877), 260.
72. GOC artillery to Vinoy, 3 April. AHG Li 121.
73. Vinoy to Thiers and Le Flô. AHG Li 118.
74. For example: Vergé's division (at Châtillon and Meudon, 3 April): 90th – two killed, seven wounded, and 91st – none killed, three wounded; Artillery: three killed, nineteen wounded; Gendarmerie: seventeen killed or wounded defending Meudon. These figures include the lightly wounded and those injured by accident. AHG Lu 35 and Lu 95.
75. *Intérieur* to *Place* (Paris), 3 April, AHG Ly 4; Sutter-Laumann, *Trente-sous*, 260; Lissagaray, *Histoire*, 184; Galliffet to C-in-C, and Thiers, circular, AHG Li 118.
76. Dispatches, 4 April. AHG Li 121 and Lu 34.
77. Letter from officers of 70th *de marche*, *Le Gaulois*, 17 May; Yriarte, *Prussiens*, 315; Cluseret, *Mémoires*, I, 160; Elie Reclus, *La Commune de Paris au jour le jour* (1908), 70.
78. Lissagaray, *Histoire*, 186; Fiaux, *Guerre civile*, 194; Pelletan, *La Semaine de Mai*, 14.
79. Police reports (Service de la Presse and 5th Brigade de Recherches) 4 April. APP Ba 364-4. See also *Le Gaulois*, 5 April, and Col. Lambert to *Enquête*, II, 246.
80. *Le Soir* (Versailles edn), 5 April.
81. Dispatches, 5 April. AHG Li 118 and 121.
82. Dispatches, 6 April. AHG Li 118 and 121.
83. Vinoy to Hanrion and Faron, 11.05 p.m. AHG Lu 34.
84. Dispatches, 9 April. AHG Li 118, Lu 17 and Lu 34.
85. Sub-Pref. to Min. of Interior, 10 April (annotated 'Urgent. Copie au Mal MacMahon'), AHG Lu 7; Du Barail, *Souvenirs*, III, 279.
86. *Journal de marche* of 37th *de marche*, 11–18 April. AHG Lu 34.
87. Valentin to MacMahon, 3 May. AHG Lu 93.
88. See, e.g., Sutter-Laumann, *Trente-sous*, 227; *Souvenirs d'un garde national*

pendant le siège de Paris et pendant la Commune, par un volontaire suisse (Neuchâtel 1871), II. 185,229,316.
89. Simon, *Gouvernement*, I, 325.

6. The Army of Versailles

1. The Commune's forces in the 3 April sortie have been variously estimated at between thirty and sixty thousand.
2. Note, 9 March. AHG Lo 67.
3. 'Volontaires de la Hte Seine pour combattre l'insurrection à Paris', AHG Lu 95; police reports, 2 April, APP Ba 364–4.
4. E.g. *Le Gaulois*, 29 March. MacMahon arrived on 11 April.
5. Adolphe Thiers, *Notes et souvenirs de M. Thiers, 1870–1873* (1901), 146.
6. Thiers's later references to him are invariably slighting, e.g. *Notes et souvenirs*, 139, 148. Both Thiers and the Minister of War, General Le Flô, had suffered personally in the *coup d'état*.
7. Speech to Assembly, quoted in *Le Soir* (Versailles edn), 29 April.
8. Even that stern critic Rossel approved on the whole of their capacities. Roger Stéphane (ed.), *Louis-Nathaniel Rossel: mémoires, procès et correspondance* (1960), 297.
9. Howard, *Franco-Prussian War*, 66.
10. Devaureix, *Souvenirs*, 598; *Le Gaulois*, 25 March. His career had lagged noticeably under the Empire, remarked *Le Gaulois* (1 June), and as Minister of War he was to be unfriendly towards Bonapartist officers. See dossier COURTOT DE CISSEY, E.L.O.,APP Ba 1021.
11. Du Barail, *Souvenirs*, I, *passim*. For an appreciative view of his capacities from a hostile source, see MAE Papiers Gambetta, vol. 52, 'Notes politiques', pp. 65–6.
12. Dossier DOUAY, Félix Charles, AHG GD (2e série) 1406; MAE Papiers Gambetta, vol. 52, 'Notes politiques', p. 43.
13. Dossier CLINCHANT, Justin, AHG GD (2e série) 1517; MAE Papiers Gambetta, vol. 52, 'Notes politiques', p. 1.
14. One division was commanded by a marine, Faron, another by a sailor, Bruat, and a brigade was commanded by a colonel, Langourian.
15. Letter from Bazaine, 8 March, BN Papiers Thiers, n.a.fr. 20621, fol. 54; letter to Palikao, 3 March, in Gaston Bouniols (ed.), *Thiers au pouvoir (1871–1873), texte de ses lettres* (1921), 19; see also Thiers, *Notes et souvenirs*, 145–6.
16. Thiers wrote that it was 'surtout ses prétentions' that excluded him – he wanted to be made a Marshal. *Notes et souvenirs*, 150.
17. 'Bien habile serait lui qui pourrait dire ce que pense au juste le général Ducrot.' MAE Papiers Gambetta, vol. 52, 'Notes politiques', p. 60.
18. MacMahon to Min. of War, no. 3, 9 April. AHG Lu 8.
19. Note, 12 April. AHG Lu 34.
20. E.g. MacMahon to Min. of War, no. 317, 8 May, AHG Lu 8; Min. of War to Vinoy, 19 May, AHG Li 124.
21. *Marches et opérations du 2e Corps* (11–30 April), AHG Li 115.

22. *Ibid.*; and see Cissey to MacMahon, 13 April. AHG Lu 92.
23. *Le Gaulois*, 7 May.
24. Thiers, *Notes et souvenirs*, 146.
25. Col. Théodore Fix, *Souvenirs d'un officier d'état-major* (1896), II, 98.
26. Ladmirault to MacMahon, 15 May, AHG Lu 92.
27. Reports, 1st brigade, Div. Bruat (Reserve), 1 April, AHG Li 116; and of Comm. de Sigoyer (26th bn *chasseurs*), 29 April, AHG Lu 34. See also Vinoy to Vergé, 12 April. AHG Lu 34.
28. Vinoy to Vergé, 12 April. AHG Lu 34.
29. Report of 74th *de marche*, 1 April. AHG Li 116.
30. Faron to Vinoy, 1 May, AHG Li 113; lists of officers, AHG Lu 34.
31. MacMahon to Min. of War, no. 504, 26 May. AHG Lu 8.
32. Order, 26 Dec. 1871. AHG Lu 98.
33. AHG Lu 92.
34. *Marches et opérations du 2e Corps* (11–30 April), AHG Li 115.
35. Appendix 2.
36. Testimony of Lieut. Canel, AHG 4th *Conseil de Guerre*, dossier 67.
37. Dossiers: TOUILLER, Louis L., AHG N/23595 (sentenced to sixty days' prison and allowed to resign); BOSC, Gustave, AHG N/46384 (dismissed from the army); BOURGOGNE, Alphonse, AHG N/20716 (sentenced to two months' prison and dismissed); MENUET, Félix Emile, AHG Pensions (3e série) 36837 and AHG 6th *Conseil de Guerre* no. 215 part 1 (two years' prison).
38. Dossier SERRES, AHG 4th *Conseil de Guerre* no. 67, testimony of Pte Dujardin.
39. Devaureix, *Souvenirs*, 595.
40. The Commission pour la Révision des Grades was set up in August 1871 under the chairmanship of General Changarnier. It examined all officers promoted during the war.
41. See letters to Gambetta from the aggrieved, MAE Papiers Gambetta, vol. 55, *passim*.
42. Berthaut to Ducrot, 8 April. AHG Lu 34.
43. Albert Hans, *Souvenirs d'un volontaire versaillais* (1873), 11.
44. A circular from Le Flô ordered these 'unmilitary' protests to stop, saying that they would in any case be ignored. 29 April, AHG Lu 34.
45. Patry, *La Guerre*, 419.
46. Déroulède, *Nouvelles Feuilles*, 317.
47. Dossier CLINCHANT, Justin, AHG GD (2e série) 1517.
48. Hans, *Souvenirs*, 30–2; Le Flô to Cathelineau, 31 May, AHG Li 124; *Le Gaulois*, 2 May.
49. Vinoy to Vergé, 12 April, AHG Lu 34.
50. See comments in dossier 'Citations . . . Propositions', AHG Lu 16.
51. For example, the 74th received seven officers in April who had been released from imprisonment, all holding pre-war commissions. There were fifty-eight officers in all with the regiment. AHG *Registre matricule des officiers*, 74th *régiment d'infanterie*, vol. 2.

52. Police report, Presse, 18 April. A P P Ba 364–5. See also various memoirs, such as those of Montaudon, Devaureix, Du Barail and Lacretelle.
53. Cluseret, *Mémoires*, I, 277, 279.
54. Simon, *Gouvernement*, I, 230.
55. Min. of Marine, note, 7 March. A H G Lo 67.
56. A H G Lo 67 *passim.*
57. Fix, *Souvenirs*, 87.
58. Vinoy to Vergé, 3 May, A H G Lu 35. See also dispatches from Faidherbe on 11, 25 and 26 April, A H G Li 114, and from Valazé to MacMahon, 2 May, A H G Lu 92.
59. Note (undated), A H G Lo 67; and note from Admiral . . . (illeg.), 14 April. A H G Lu 34.
60. Clinchant to Minister, 27 February. A H G Lo 67.
61. Howard, *Franco-Prussian War*, 451. The *Journal Officiel* of Paris (23 March) announced that the Germans had promised to maintain a 'friendly and passive attitude'; and on 25 March the Central Committee declared that 'the Prussians, who have judged us at our worth, have answered by recognizing that we are in the right'. Maurice Paz, 'Le myth de la Commune: relations avec les Prussiens', *Est et Ouest* no. 479 (Dec. 1971), 21.
62. M A E Papiers Jules Favre, vol. 6, fol. 45.
63. Gordon A. Craig, *The Politics of the Prussian Army, 1640–1945* (1968), 207–12.
64. For a fuller discussion of this question, see below, pp. 134–7, 140.
65. Min. of War to Faidherbe, 6 March, A H G Lo 67; Min. of War to Ducrot (G O C Cherbourg corps), 25 March, A H G Lu 34.
66. *Enquête*, II, 16.
67. Note from commander of Cherbourg camp, 11 April, and reports from divisions, 15 April. A H G Lu 34.
68. A H G Lu 34 *passim.*, and report of 6th *provisoire*, A H G Li 116.
69. 4th Corps, *Journal des opérations*, A H G Li 115, and 5th Corps, *Journal des opérations*, A H G Li 116.
70. Police reports, Brigade de la Presse, 2 April. A P P Ba 364–4.
71. Police reports by 5th Brigade de Recherches and Brissaud, 3 April. A P P Ba 364–4.
72. Police reports by Brigade de la Presse, 10 April, A P P Ba 364–4, and Insp. Féau, 16 April, Ba 364–5.
73. Police report, Brissaud, 29 April. A P P Ba 364–5.
74. Police report, Insp. de Nulley, 29 April. A P P Ba 364–5.
75. Police reports by Brigade de la Presse, 26 and 29 April. A P P Ba 364–5.
76. Maud'huy to Thiers and MacMahon, 14 April. A H G Li 118.
77. Police reports by 1st company, 4th bn, and Brigade de la Presse, 13 April. A P P Ba 364–4.
78. Police report, Brissaud, 26 April. A P P Ba 364–5.
79. Gen. de Pointe de Gevigny (G O C Subdivision) to Gen. Ducrot, 2 April. A H G Lu 34.
80. Report, 18 April. A H G Lu 92.
81. Report to Min. of War, 26 April. A H G Lu 92. In spite of efforts by

MacMahon, their grievances were never fully redressed. See long letter from MacMahon to Le Flô, *Correspondance* no. 575, 1 June. AHG Lu 8.

82. Dispatch to commanders of units at Cherbourg, 9 April. AHG Lu 34.

83. 'Notes sur la compagne contre la Commune', Vermeil de Conchard (second-lieutenant, 13th *provisoire*). AHG Li 116.

84. Report of Col. de Geslin (94th *de ligne*, 4th Corps), 16 May. AHG Lu 35.

85. Police report, Brissaud, 27 April, APP Ba 364–5, and MacMahon to Clinchant, 26 April, AHG Lu 71.

86. Report of colonel of 15th *provisoire*, 25 April, AHG Lu 93; and police report, 5th Brigade de Recherches, 5 April, APP Ba 364–4.

87. Police reports by Brissaud, 20 April, and by Féau, de Nulley and La Fontaine, 22 April. APP Ba 364–5.

88. E.g. police reports by Féau, de Nulley and La Fontaine, 22 April, and Brissaud, 20 April. APP Ba 364–5.

89. Appert to Vinoy, 3 April, AHG Li 121, and MacMahon to Minister, no. 47, 16 April, AHG Lu 8.

90. Fix, *Souvenirs*, 240–7. For details see Pierre Bathille, 'Petite histoire de Biribi', *Le Crapouillot*, no. 25 (n.d.), *Petite Histoire de l'armée française*, 78–83.

91. MacMahon to Minister, no. 30, 14 April. AHG Lu 8.

92. *Prescriptions du rapport journalier* (daily orders), AHG Lu 16, and letter from Col. Thiery, 2 May, AHG Lu 35.

93. *Ordres* (2nd Div., 2nd Corps), 14 May; Cissey to GOC 2nd Div., 18 May. AHG Lu 16.

94. Police reports, 4, 26 and 30 April, APP Ba 364–4 and 5. See also Léonce Dupont, *Souvenirs de Versailles pendant la Commune* (1881), 90.

95. *Ibid.*, 154; Min. of War to MacMahon, 7 April, AHG Lu 92; *Le Gaulois*, 6 April and 12 May; Montaudon, *Souvenirs*, II, 307; Patry, *La Guerre*, 419.

96. *Enquête*, II, 27.

97. Report to Leperche, 18–19 May. AHG Lv 10.

98. AHG Lv 10, *passim*.

99. Prefect of Police to MacMahon, 29 April, AHG Lu 93; police report, Brigade de la Presse, 31 March, APP Ba 364–3; *Prescriptions du rapport*, 10 May, AHG Lu 16.

100. Police report, 13 April. APP Ba 364–4.

101. *Ordres du Corps d'Armée* (3rd Corps), no. 18, 17 May. AHG Li 127.

102. See police reports 31 March, APP Ba 364–3; 20 April, APP Ba 364–5; and 17 May, APP Ba 365–1.

103. 1st Div., Reserve, *Correspondance* (30 April–8 September), no. 251, 3 May. AHG Li 128.

104. *Ibid.*, no. 295, 20 May.

105. *Réponse au rapport* (5th Corps), 8 May, AHG Lu 71; *Correspondance* (MacMahon to Min. of War) vol. 2, no. 631, 5 May, AHG Lu 8.

106. See, for example, the cases of Pte Pillet (41st *de marche*), *Correspondance* (MacMahon to Min. of War) vol. 1, no. 276 AHG Lu 8; Sgt-Maj. Tibaut (114th *de ligne*), *Réponse au rapport*, no. 19, AHG Lu 8; and three men of 6th *provisoire*, *Réponse au rapport* 17 May, AHG Lu 35, all of whom were sent to the *zéphirs* during May.

107. Appendix 2. In the pro-Commune rising at Lyons on 30 April, the insurgents were 'primarily working-class individuals skilled in a particular trade'. Julian P. W. Archer, 'The crowd in the Lyon Commune and the insurrection of La Guillotière', *International Review of Social History*, XVII (1972), 183–8.
108. Appendix 3.
109. AHG 2nd *Conseil [de Guerre]* (box marked in chalk, no serial no.), folders of 'temoignages contre les présents' – men of the 120th *de ligne* left behind in Paris after 18 March.
110. Report, 3 July, AHG Lv 10. The garrison was probably composed of men of the 82nd *de marche*, with a few gunners and sappers. They voted by their department of origin, the results being sent on by post. Gambetta and and Floquet received eight and seven votes, the other candidates two and one.
111. Gaillard, *Communes*, 165–9.
112. Police report, Brigade de la Presse, on opinions of men of the 30th bn *chasseurs*, 24 April. APP Ba 364–5.

7. Propaganda, myth and the army

1. Police report, Brigade de la Presse, 18 April, APP Ba 364–5; Min. of War to C.-in-C., 11 April, AHG Lu 92.
2. Police report, Brigade de la Presse, 16 May. APP Ba 365–1.
3. *Ibid*, 8 April. APP Ba 364–4.
4. E.g. letters concerning the taking of Neuilly bridge, Le Soir (Versailles edn), 12 and 15 April, and from officers of the 70th *de marche*, *Le Gaulois*, 17 May.
5. Claude Bellanger, Jacques Godechot, Pierre Guiral, and Fernand Terrou (eds.), *Histoire générale de la presse française* (1971), III, 194.
6. Pelletan, *La Semaine de Mai*, 19.
7. Opinions and attitudes changed enormously between March and May, especially during the last week of the war. Many of the examples of hysterical Versaillais propaganda commonly quoted in works on the Commune date from *la Semaine Sanglante* or after, and are not typical of the whole period.
8. *Le Soir* frequently criticized the Assembly (e.g. Versailles edn, 24, 25 and 27 March) but nevertheless expressed the fear that in rejecting 'popular sovereignty legally and universally exercised' France was destroying the foundation of her political organization (Paris edn, 27 March).
9. Simon, *Gouvernement*, I, 380–1.
10. Speech to the Assembly, reported in *Le Gaulois*, 16 May.
11. *Le Soir* (Versailles edn), 13 and 14 April.
12. *Le Gaulois*, 25 April. See also Gustave Lefrançais (a member of the Commune), *Souvenirs*. 411.
13. A crudely forged letter supposedly addressed by Rigault to Floquet was published by *Le Gaulois*, 17 May.
14. *Le Gaulois*, 29 April and 7 May (quoting a letter said to have been written to an émigré in Versailles by an acquaintance in Paris, dated 20 April).

15. *Ordre Général* no. 1, 11 April AHG Lu 16.
16. For a conservative view of 'l'invasion de la bohème', see E. Caro, 'La fin de la bohème', *Revue des Deux Mondes*, XCIV (1871), 241–55.
17. *Enquête*, II, 235.
18. Montaudon, *Souvenirs*, II, 281.
19. *Enquête*, II, 250.
20. Montaudon, *Souvenirs*, II, 266.
21. *Le Soir* (Versailles edn), 23 April, 3 and 13 May.
22. *Enquête*, II, 236.
23. Report to MacMahon, 4 May. AHG Lu 119.
24. Reports, 2, 3 and 4 May. AHG Lu 95.
25. *Enquête*, II, 222. Jacques Rougerie notes that 21% of those arrested and 28.9% of those convicted for participation in the insurrection had previous convictions, principally for crimes against property. *Procès des Communards* (1964), 132–4.
26. Montaudon, *Souvenirs*, II, 276; police report, Insp. Féau, 16 April, APP Ba 364–5.
27. *Ordre général de l'armée*, 10 April. AHG Lu 16.
28. Police report, Brissaud, 21 April. APP Ba 364–5.
29. *Le Soir*, 19 March and (Paris edn) 27 March, articles by Pessard.
30. See, for example, *Le Soir* (Versailles edn) 22 March, and Adm. Saisset's statement, *Enquête*, II, 315.
31. Devaureix (who was on Lian's staff), *Souvenirs*, 613.
32. *Enquête*, II, 238–9, and report on interrogation of prisoners, 20 May, AHG Lu 95.
33. Cissey to MacMahon, 1 June. AHG Lu 92.
34. *Ordre*, 18 May. AHG Lu 16.
35. *Le Soir* (Versailles edn), 19 May; *Le Gaulois*, 20 April.
36. *Le Gaulois*, 20 April. The references are to Dombrowski, a Pole who had served as an officer in the Russian army, and Cluseret, a former officer in the French army who had received American citizenship after having served the Union during the civil war. La Cécilia was French, though born of Italian parents.
37. 11 April. AHG Lu 16.
38. AHG Lu 95.
39. Police reports, Brigade de la Presse, 9 April, APP Ba 364–4, and Insp. Féau, 16 April, Ba 364–5.
40. Quoted by J. Dautry, 'Trois documents auvergnats concernant la Commune', *La Pensée* no. 82 (Nov.-Dec. 1958), 122. The reference is to Cluseret.
41. Reported in *Le Soir* (Versailles edn), 5 April.
42. *Ibid.*, 'Echos parlementaires'.
43. *Ibid.*, 13 May.
44. *Rapport d'ensemble de M. le General Appert sur les opérations de la justice militaire relatives à l'insurrection de 1871*, no. 3212, Assemblée Nationale, annexe au procès-verbal de la séance du 20 juillet 1875 (Versailles 1875), 8, describing the causes of the insurrection.
45. Devaureix, *Souvenirs*, 614.

46. *Enquête*, II, 237.
47. Cissey to MacMahon, 20 May. AHG Lu 92.
48. E.g. *Le Gaulois*, 7 and 23 May; *Le Soir* (Versailles edn), 13 May. For a more jaundiced account of the treatment of prisoners at this time see 'Two nights in a French prison during the civil war', by an English tourist arrested at Courbevoie, *Macmillan's Magazine*, XXIV (May-Oct. 1871) 209–16.
49. Min. of War to Pref. of Police, 21 April. APP Ba 364–5.
50. *Le Soir* (Versailles edn), 13 May.
51. Marquis de Compiègne, 'Souvenirs d'un Versaillais pendant le second siège de Paris', *Le Correspondant*, 10 Aug. 1875, 633.
52. Déroulède, *Feuilles*, 67.
53. Sesmaisons, *Troupes*, 17.
54. Compiègne, *Souvenirs*, 633.
55. 20 May. AHG Li 123.
56. E.g. *Le Soir* (Versailles edn), 23 March; *Le Gaulois*, 8 April, 23 April, 10 May.
57. E.g. *Le Gaulois*, 13, 15 and 20 May; concerning Mgr Darboy, *Ibid.*, 8 April.
58. E.g. *Le Soir* (Versailles edn), 8 April, 6 May, 17 May.
59. 'Runaways and those who stay in the rear individually will be sabred by the cavalry; if they are numerous, they will be cannonaded.' *Journal Officiel* of the Commune, 10 May. For Versaillais reactions, see Devaureix, *Souvenirs*, 605–6.
60. *Le Soir* (Versailles edn), 22 April; *Le Gaulois* expressed similar views on the same day.
61. This mythology of revolution as it later developed is discussed by J. M. Roberts, 'The Paris Commune from the Right', *English Historical Review*, supplement 6 (1973).
62. Foreign opinion tended to blame the French character for the disasters of 1871. The French reply, through both the press and diplomatic agents, was to blame foreign revolutionaries and Prussian meddling and present France as the bulwark of European order rather than its weak point.
63. Medical officer's report, 114th *de ligne*, 5 May, AHG Lu 92. A stock of the shells was captured at Fort Issy. Report, Artillery Dept to Minister, AHG Li 123.
64. Report, 5 April. AHG Li 121.
65. Report, Artillery Dept to Minister. AHG Li 123.
66. Susbielle, Divisional Order, 25 May, AHG Lu 16; Vinoy, Order, 26 May, AHG Li 124; Cissey, Circular, 25 May, AHG Lu 7.
67. Circular, 27 May. AHG Lu 95.
68. *Histoire de la Commune de Paris* (1871), 55; Pelletan, *La Semaine de Mai*, 123.
69. Reports by *aide-major de tranchée* and Colonel Leperche, 13, 14 and 15 May. AHG Lv 10.
70. *Guerre des communeux de Paris, par un officier supérieur de l'armée de Versailles* (H. Sarrepont, pseud. of Eugène Hennebert), (1871), 195.
71. Concerning Red Cross flag: report, Leperche, 12–13 May, AHG Lv 10, and Eugène Delessert, *Episodes pendant la Commune, souvenirs d'un délégué de la société de secours aux blessés des armées de terre et de mer* (1872), 4–10; concern-

ing army wounded: Cissey to MacMahon, 12 May, AHG Li 123, citing report by Lieut. Jecker of 14th *provisoire;* concerning flag of truce, report by Lieut. Pavot, 1 May, AHG Li 123; concerning drugging, report, 10 May, AHG Li 123, *Le Gaulois,* 12 May, and *Le Soir* (Versailles edn), 13 May.

72. 7 May. AHG Lu 92.
73. The ferocity of the Moulin Saquet attack shocked opinion in Paris and gave rise to some rather unlikely atrocity stories. Though the reality was horrible enough, a large part of the explanation lies probably in the circumstances of the fighting, when a picked force of Versaillais surprised a much larger number of Fédérés at night. Report, Gen. Lacretelle, 5 May, AHG Li 123. Burial certificates, AS VD 3 21.
74. Police report, Brigade de la Presse, 26 April. APP Ba 364–5.
75. Grandeffe, *Mobiles et volontaires*, 255.
76. See a series of reports and orders from Leperche, especially a draft report, 13–15 May. AHG Lv 10.
77. Reports, 2 and 4 May. AHG Li 123.
78. Reports to MacMahon, 12 May, AHG Li 123, and 19 May, AHG Lu 92.
79. Phrase used in a report on army deserters in Paris, AHG Lu 95.
80. *Rapport Appert*, 179; and see Grandeffe, *Mobiles et volontaires*, 284.
81. There was talk in the Assembly and the press of the need for radical repression. Mass transportation without trial was advocated. *Le Gaulois* (21 April) wrote of 'twenty thousand or so scoundrels' to be sent to Cayenne; *Le Soir* (Versailles edn, 22 May) urged the purging of Paris to give 'forty years of security' to France. Edmond de Goncourt wrote with satisfaction of the purge of the 'combative part of the generation' which would delay the next revolution by twenty years (journal, 31 May), G. J. Becker (ed.), *Paris under Siege* (Ithaca 1969), 312.
82. Quinel, an officer of the Legion of Honour, member of the National Guard of Order, had been appointed to command the National Guard of the 4th *arrondissement* when Paris was reoccupied. The letter is dated 17 May. AHG Lv 10.

8. The second siege

1. *The Times*, 27 and 29 March.
2. Report to Min. of Interior, 12 April (presumably passed to Min. of War). AHG Li 121.
3. The political commentator Gaston de Saint-Valry noted in his diary (3 May) that 'rien ne prouve que M. Thiers ne prête la main à une sorte de transaction *in extremis* qui a toutes les chances du monde d'amener un conflit avec l'Assemblée'. *Souvenirs et réflexions*, 30.
4. Below, pp. 134–5.
5. E.g. da Costa refers to 'ce plan férocement machiavelique'. *La Commune vécue*, III, 85.
6. Simon, *Gouvernement*, I, 471.
7. Gen. Sir G. S. Clarke, *Fortification* (1907), 56–61; and see maps, AHG Li 115.
8. Cluseret, *Mémoires*, I, 138.

9. Police reports, APP Ba 364–5 and 365–1, *passim*.
10. *Rapport sur les opérations* (Gen. de Cissey). AHG Li 115.
11. Du Barail, *Souvenirs*, III, 260.
12. *2e Corps d'Armée, Génie, Rapport sur les opérations*. AHG Li 115.
13. Reports, AHG Li 115; Montaudon, *Souvenirs*, II, 300–54.
14. Note, 18 April. AHG Lu 95.
15. AHG Li 127 ('Dépêches, instructions . . . succession L'Hériller'). For preparations for attack, see reports and correspondence between 11 and 27 April, AHG Li 121, Lu 8, Lu 34, Lu 92 and Lu 95.
16. Circulars, 12 and 16 April. AHG Lu 95.
17. The American Minister, Washburne, was privately given the same reasons. *Recollections*, II, 57.
18. Report, Lieut. de la Bédollière (O.C. Breteuil battery), 8 May. AHG Lu 35.
19. Ladmirault to MacMahon, 3 May, AHG Li 123. He reported that his Army Corps would have needed seven hours to cross the bridge. Other bridges were built later.
20. *2e Corps, Génie, rapport*, ahg Li 115. For MacHahon's support of this policy, see letter to Le Flô, 5 May, AHG Li 123, and J. Silvestre de Sacy, *Le Maréchal de MacMahon* (1960), 255.
21. Cissey to MacMahon, 1 May (2e Corps EMG, no. 281). AHG Li 123.
22. Cissey to Faron, 1 May. AHG Lu 35.
23. Leperche, *major de tranchée* (chief of staff for the trench operations) and so responsible for carrying out the negotiations, made the threat on 30 April ('Correspondance, depeches, rapports . . .'), and again suggested it to Cissey on 1 May if the Fédérés should blow up the fort, after he had complained that they seemed unable to make up their minds ('Télégrammes et correspondance', 30 April and 1 May). AHG Lv 10.
24. Report of Lieut. Pavot (the army's envoy). AHG Li 123.
25. Leperche to Cissey, 2 p.m., 2 May. 'Télégrammes et correspondance', AHG Lv 10.
26. Report, de la Bédollière, 3 May. AHG Lu 35.
27. Telegram, Thiers to Faron, 3.40 p.m., 7 May, AHG Li 119. For the Montrouge attempt, see Leperche, *Rapport sur les faits militaires*, 21–8 May; he reported that the defenders fired on the flag of truce. Lv 10.
28. *Rapport sur les opérations* (Cissey), AHG Li 115. For casualties, see MacMahon to Le Flô, 5 May, AHG Li 123; for rations etc., see, for example, *Ordre Général* no. 14, 8 May ('Armée de Versailles, ordres du général en chef'), AHG Lu 16.
29. *2e Corps, Génie, rapport*. AHG Li 115. These features may still be seen.
30. *Rapport sur les opérations* (Cissey); *2e Corps, Génie, rapport*; *Marches et opérations* (2nd Corps), 11–30 April. AHG Li 115. Telegram, Cissey to Susbielle, 11.43 p.m. 29 April, AHG Lu 16.
31. Captain Le Mulier to Leperche, 3 May. AHG Lv 10.
32. *Rapport sur les opérations* (Cissey). AHG Li 115.
33. Leperche to Cissey, 2 May; and *rapport du 1er au 4e mai* ('Enregistrement des rapports journaliers'). AHG Lv 10.

34. E.g. *Le Soir* (Versailles edn), 15, 18, 23 and 29 April; *Le Gaulois*, 20, 21, 22, 24, 25 and 27 April.
35. *2e Corps, Génie, rapport.* AHG Li 115.
36. *Le Gaulois*, 4 May.
37. Note, Rivière, 5 May, AHG Li 123; telegrams between Faron and Cissey, 5 May, AHG Li 123 and Lu 35; *2e Corps, Génie, rapport*, AHG Li 115.
38. Telegrams, 5–6 May. AHG Lu 35.
39. Cissey to MacMahon, 6 May; Faron to Vinoy ('Confidentiel'), 11 May. AHG Li 123.
40. Cissey to MacMahon, 6 May, AHG Li 123; Thiers to Faron, 3.40 p.m., 7 May, AHG Li 119.
41. Berckheim to Cissey, 5 May; Cissey to MacMahon, 6 May. AHG Li 123.
42. Dispatches and correspondence of Cissey and Faron with MacMahon, Thiers, Vinoy and others, 6–9 May. AHG Li 123, Lu 15 and Lu 35.
43. Colonel de la Haye to Favre, 14 April. MAE Papiers Favre, vol. 6, fols. 50–3.
44. *Ibid.*; Favre to Le Flô, 4 April, *ibid.*, fol. 38; Le Flô to *Enquête*, II, 86.
45. Jules Simon noted that rebuilding the army quickly was of fundamental importance in 'liberating the territory' and guaranteeing the independence and credit of France. *Thiers, Guizot, Rémusat* (1885), 47.
46. Albert Sorel, *Histoire diplomatique de la guerre franco-allemande* (1875), II, 286. Favre, in a memorandum to von Fabrice (29 April), referred to Bismarck's accusation that the French government had 'une sorte d'arrière pensée . . . de se préparer à recommencer la guerre', or 'après la rentrée à Paris, de renoncer à la paix, ou d'éxiger de la Prusse un changement dans les conditions'. He denied it. MAE Papiers Favre, vol. 6, fols. 57–70. Bismarck wrote to Fabrice on 27 April that the French demands at the Brussels negotiations showed that 'on se moque de vous' (*sic*). Moritz Busch, *Bismarck, Some Secret Pages of his History* (1898), II, 60.
47. Favre, *Défense nationale*, III, 313. See also Norman Rich and M. H. Fisher, *The Holstein Papers* (Cambridge 1955), I, 81–2.
48. Favre to Thiers, 7 May. MAE Papiers Thiers, fol. 6.
49. Memorandum to Fabrice, 29 April. MAE Papiers Favre, vol. 6, fols. 70–1.
50. Bismarck to Fabrice, 28 April, quoted by Paz, 'Le mythe de la Commune: relations avec les Prussiens' (Dec. 1971), 24.
51. Carole Witzig, 'Bismarck et la Commune', *International Review of Social History*, XVII (1972), 207. The Dreikaisarbund was the outcome of the negotiations thus begun.
52. According to Paz (citing Cahn, the intermediary, a Bavarian diplomat attached to the Swiss legation), the initiative came from the Germans. 'Le mythe de la Commune: relations avec les Prussiens' (March 1972), 23–4. Norman Rich states that the first approach was made by Cluseret. *Friedrich von Holstein: Politics and Diplomacy in the Era of Bismarck and Wilhelm II* (Cambridge 1965), I, 67.
53. Busch, *Bismarck*, II, 58–9.
54. Rich, *Holstein*, I, 69–70; Cluseret, *Mémoires*, II, 8–18.
55. Busch, *Bismarck*, II, 61.

56. Rich thinks that it ended the slim possibility of mediation; *Holstein*, I, 70. Paz, however, points out that Bismarck instructed Cahn to maintain relations with the Commune. 'Le mythe de la Commune: relations avec les Prussiens' (Dec. 1971), 24. Bismarck did suspect, nevertheless, that Cluseret's arrest was an 'anti-German intrigue'. Busch, *Bismarck*, II, 69.
57. Favre to Thiers, 7 May (2 dispatches) and 8 May. MAE Papiers Thiers, fols. 4–8 and 13.
58. Sorel, *Histoire diplomatique*, II, 276–7; Favre, *Défense nationale*, III, 313–17, 325–8.
59. Favre to Thiers (from Frankfurt), 7 and 8 May. MAE Papiers Thiers, fols. 8 and 13. Bismarck had approached Napoleon III, who had not been responsive. Witzig, 'Bismarck et la Commune', 197, citing diary of General von Waldersee.
60. Sorel, *Histoire diplomatique*, II, 299.
61. Favre to Thiers, 7 May; Thiers to Favre, 8 May. MAE Papiers Thiers, fols. 8, 10 and 12.
62. Favre to Thiers, 7 May, *ibid.*, fol. 6. He thought, however, that the Commune would not agree to disarm the National Guard, which they would have to insist on.
63. Pontécoulant to Favre [10 May], MAE Papiers Favre, vol. 6, fol. 78; Favre, *Défense nationale*, III, 375–6.
64. *Rapport sur les opérations du siège* (4th Corps). AHG Li 115.
65. *Rapport* (Douay), AHG Li 115; and see Ducatel's reports, AHG Li 114.
66. *Rapport sur les opérations du siège* (4th Corps), AHG Li 115; reports, 18–20 May, AHG Li 124.
67. Letter published in Paris press and reproduced in *Le Gaulois*, 19 May.
68. *Rapport* (Douay). AHG Li 115.
69. Cissey to Faron, 9.20 a.m. and 8 p.m., 10 May, AHG Li 119; Cissey to Leperche, 11 May, AHG Lv 10.
70. Leperche to Cissey, 16 May, and *général de tranchée* (Susbielle) to Cissey, 17 May, AHG Lu 15; Le Mulier to Leperche, 5 May, and dispatch, 28 April, AHG Lv 10.
71. Report, Lieut. Gance (*aide-major de tranchée*), 18–19 May. AHG Lv 10.
72. Thiers to Cissey, 8.15 p.m., 10 May. AHG Lu 15.
73. Dispatch to Cissey, 17 May. AHG Lv 10.
74. *Rapport* (Cissey); *2e Corps, Génie, rapport*. AHG Li 115.
75. MacMahon to Min. of War, no. 487, 21 May ('Correspondance du Mal Ct en chef avec le Ministre'), AHG Lu 8; note from Barthélémy Saint-Hilaire (To Gen. Borel?), 21 May, AHG Lu 95; Thiers, *Notes et souvenirs*, 161.
76. Assuming that the Auteuil and Passy gates were surrendered, it had envisaged the deployment of 1st and 5th Corps on the Right Bank, 4th Corps on the Left, and 2nd Corps and the Reserve Army in support. Order, 18 May. AHG Lu 71.
77. *2e Corps, Génie, rapport*, AHG Li 115; casualty lists, AHG Lu 95. The worst losses had been on 11 April (132 casualties), 6 May (118) and 14 May (113).
78. De la Haye to Pontecoulant, 9 May; Favre to Thiers, 10 May. MAE Papiers Thiers, fols. 17 and 20.

79. De la Haye to Pontecoulant, 10 May, and Favre to Thiers, 21 May, *ibid.*, fols. 19 and 26; de la Haye to Favre, 15 May, M A E Papiers Favre, vol. 6, fols, 92–3. See also Busch, *Bismarck*, II, 75–7.

80. Favre to Pontecoulant, 20 May, M A E Papiers Favre, vol. 6, fol. 115. Favre did not mention a blockade when describing his interviews with Bismarck on 20 May, *ibid.*, and on 21 May, M A E Papiers Thiers, fols. 25–6. De la Haye, however, took it for granted, 'not of course to starve [Paris] but to close the mousetrap'. Dispatch to Pontecoulant, 10 May, *ibid.*, fol. 19.

81. Favre to Thiers, 21 May, *ibid.*, fol. 25; Thiers to Favre, 21 May, M A E Papiers Favre, vol. 6, fol. 119.

82. See correspondence of de Gabriac, *chargé d'affaires* at St Petersburg, especially the dispatches of 5 April and 24 May, saying that the government would be judged on its ability to repress the insurrection. M A E *Correspondance politique*, new series, vol. 245, 'Russie 1871', fols. 136 and 176.

83. Favre to Thiers, 21 May. M A E Papiers Thiers, fol. 23.

84. Lissagaray stated that 20,000 men assembled on the Right Bank and 17,000 on the Left. *Histoire*, 182.

85. Estimates of the number vary greatly. Benoît Malon, in *La Troisième Défaite du prolétariat français* (Neuchâtel 1871), 337, thought they suffered 20,000 casualties in April alone. Dr John Murray, of the British Ambulance, thought 12,000 during the whole siege ('Four days in the ambulances and hospitals of Paris under the Commune', *British Medical Journal* (Jan.–June, 1871), 541). A captured document gives a list of casualties at Neuilly for 15–30 April totalling 688, which seems more reasonable: A P P Ba 364–4. On such a basis of comparison, my own estimate would be roughly 6,000–8,000 casualties in all between 2 April and 21 May. The *Rapport Appert*, 180, states that 3,500 prisoners were taken during the same period.

86. Cluseret, *Mémoires*, I, 76. Da Costa gives a similar figure in *La Commune vécue*, II, 166.

87. Cluseret's order appeared in the *Journal Officiel* of the Commune, 9 April. For prisoners' morale, see reports on the interrogation of those captured near Issy, A H G Lu 95, and *Le Soir* (Versailles edn), 6 May, 'Les prisonniers du Moulin Saquet'.

88. Faron to Cissey, 8 May, A H G Lu 15, and *Le Gaulois*, 15 May, quoting a captured Fédéré dispatch.

89. There are many accounts of the Fédérés' prodigality with ammunition, which Cluseret tried to restrain. *Mémoires*, II, 28. For the generally innocuous yet intimidating effect of their spectacular cannonades, see A H G Lu 35, *passim*. By 2 June, the army had collected 640 cannon and 320,329 rifles inside Paris. Reports, A H G Lu 93. J. Bourelly states that fewer than half the cannon were used. *Le Ministère de la guerre sous la Commune* (1913), 109.

90. E.g. Cissey to Faron, 3 May, A H G Li 123; Cissey to Thiers and MacMahon, 4.10 p.m., 14 May, A H G Li 119; *2e Corps, Génie, journal de marche*, A H G Lu 15.

91. Thiers to Cissey, 8.50 p.m., 10 May, AHG Lu 15; and to *Enquête*, II, 18.
92. Bourelly, *Ministère de la guerre*, 140.
93. *Ibid.*, 183, 190; Marcel Dessal, *Un Révolutionnaire jacobin, Charles Delescluze* (1952), 384.
94. See, for example, Leperche's correspondence, AHG Lv 10, *passim*.
95. Cluseret, *Mémoires*, I, 139–40, 249; II, 8–18.
96. *Enquête*, II, 15.
97. As Dombrowski reported on 21 May. Bourelly, *Ministère de la guerre*, 200. Many others noticed the weakness of the defences, e.g. Lefrançais, *Souvenirs*, 416; Louis Barron, *Sous le drapeau rouge* (1889), 171; Pierre de Lano (ed.), *Journal d'un vaincu* (diary of M.-A. Gromier), (1892), 31.
98. Report, de la Bédollière, 1 May. AHG Lu 35.
99. Faron to Cissey, 6 May. AHG Lu 35.
100. *Aide-major de tranchée* to Cissey [7 May]. AHG Lu 15.
101. Even had the first attempt to 'buy' a gate on 2 May succeeded, 1st Corps would not have been able to get there in time. Ladmirault to MacMahon, 3 May. AHG Li 123.
102. Report, Col. Vanche (35th *de ligne*), 6 April. AHG Li 121.
103. *Le Gaulois*, 4 May.
104. Dispatch from Ladmirault, 5.20 p.m., 29 April. AHG Li 118.
105. *Souvenirs par un volontaire suisse*, 279.
106. Lefrançais, *Souvenirs*, 396.
107. Flamarion, *Livret*, 147.
108. Flamarion states that the Fédérés fired first, but Ladmirault seems to have decided to recommence firing himself because he believed that they were using the truce to strengthen their defences. Dispatch, 6.10 p.m., 30 April. AHG Li 118.
109. Circular no. 749, 20 May. AHG Lu 71.

9. The battle of Paris

1. Press cutting of letter from Douay's staff, and *Rapport sur les opérations du siège* (4th Corps). AHG Li 115.
2. *Ibid.*, and report by 3rd Div., Reserve Army, 21–8 May, AHG Li 116.
3. Lt de la Bedollière reported on 4 May that the ramparts were deserted (AHG Lu 34), as did *Le Gaulois* on 10, 11, 12, 15 and 21 May.
4. Archibald Forbes, 'What I saw of the Paris Commune', pt 1, *Century Magazine* XLIV (new series XXII) (1892), 807–9.
5. *Ibid.*, 812.
6. Dessal, *Delescluze*, 390–1.
7. *Rapport* (Douay), AHG Li 115, and telegrams, 21 May. AHG Li 119.
8. Intelligence report of defences of 16th *arrondissement*. AHG Lu 35.
9. Report, 90th *de marche*, AHG Li 116; report of police captain Rochut (21–7 May), *Journal de marche* of Gremion's brigade (3rd Div., Reserve), report of Gen. Gremion (23 May) and report of O. C. artillery, Vergé's division (23 May), AHG Lu 35. Also Flamarion, *Livret*, 158.

10. *Journal de marche* (2nd Corps engineers), 10 April–27 May, A H G Lu 15, and *Journal des opérations* (5th Corps), A H G Li 116.

11. Compiègne, 'Souvenirs', 611; Lissagaray, *Histoire*, 315–16; Jacques de la Faye, *Le Général de Ladmirault* (1901), 286. From a military view, such prudence was arguably correct. See Gen. Edmond Ruby, 'Quelques aspects militaires de la Commune de Paris', *Ecrits de Paris* (Sept. 1971), 47.

12. Vermeil de Conchard, 'Notes', A H G Li 116; Malglaire to MacMahon 5.50 a.m., 22 May, A H G Li 119; police report, 22 May, A P P Ba 365–1.

13. De la Faye, *Ladmirault*, 286.

14. Forbes, 'What I saw', pt 1, 814; and see circular from MacMahon, 23 April, A H G Li 127 ('Dépêches, instructions . . . succession L'Hériller').

15. Dessal, *Delescluze*, 392.

16. See, e.g., de Lano (ed.), *Journal d'un vaincu*, 34 (entry of 22 May), and Sutter-Laumann, *Trente-sous*, 301.

17. Tristan Rémy, *La Commune à Montmartre, 23 mai 1871* (1970), 37–44.

18. *Ibid.*, 50–1.

19. Proclamation to the people of Paris and the National Guard by Delescluze and the Committee of Public Safety. *Journal Officiel* of the Commune, 22 May.

20. *Opérations militaires* (1st Corps). A H G Li 115.

21. Sutter-Laumann, *Trente-sous*, 304–6.

22. Rémy, *La Commune à Montmartre*, 53.

23. Hans, *Souvenirs*, 100.

24. Compiègne, 'Souvenirs', 619–21.

25. Hans, *Souvenirs*, 98.

26. Col. Lochner to Thiers and Le Flô, 12.50 p.m., 23 May. B N Papiers Thiers, n.a.fr. 20649, fol. 13. Compiègne, 'Souvenirs', 621.

27. Report, 6th *provisoire*, A H G Li 116.

28. By the Fédérés for refusing to help defend the barricade, and then by the Versaillais, who took him for a Fédéré. His clean hands (i.e. not blackened by powder) secured his release. Forbes, 'What I saw', pt 1, 817.

29. Lissagaray, *Histoire*, 330–1.

30. *Ibid.*, 320, 330, 335. M. E. P. M. de MacMahon, *L'Armée de Versailles, depuis sa formation jusqu'à la complète pacification de Paris* (1871), 27.

31. Report, 2nd Div., 2nd Corps (Susbielle), 22–27 May. A H G Lu 7.

32. *Ibid.*

33. Lissagaray, *Histoire*, 336; MacMahon, *L'Armée de Versailles*, 24.

34. *Le Gaulois*, 29 May, quoting *La Patrie*.

35. MacMahon, *Armée de Versailles*, 24–5; and see operational reports of 2nd Corps, A H G Li 115 *passim*.

36. Ladmirault to MacMahon, 24 May. A H G Li 124.

37. Forbes, 'What I saw of the Paris Commune', pt 2, *Century Magazine* XLV (new series XXIII) (1892), 49, 51.

38. Montaudon, *Souvenirs*, II, 376–9; *Opérations militaires* (1st Corps), A H G Li 115.

39. *Journal des opérations* (5th Corps). A H G Li 115.

40. Report, 3rd Div., Reserve Army, A H G Li 116, and *Journal de marche*, Gremion's (2nd) Brig., (21–30 May), A H G Lu 35.
41. Report, 2nd *régiment de marche, inf. de marine*. A H G Li 116.
42. Report, 2nd division, 2nd Corps (22–7 May). A H G Lu 7. The 17th battalion of *chasseurs* and 38th *de marche* had spent the last two days merely guarding prisoners, and on 24 May had had only about two miles to march to their objective.
43. Report, 2nd division artillery, 24 May. A H G Lu 7.
44. Report, 2nd division, 2nd Corps. A H G Lu 7.
45. Report, 2nd bn, 38th *de marche*. A H G Lu 7.
46. Lissagaray, *Histoire*, 336–7.
47. Eugene Schulkind has argued the opposite in an unpublished thesis, 'Le rôle des travaux d'urbanisme du second empire dans les batailles de rue de la Commune de 1871' (Paris, June 1951), but seems to have been misled by the published accounts of MacMahon and Vinoy, which give a simplified version of the operations. The detailed military reports in the A H G show that wide streets held up the army, whereas the side streets and alleys that had traditionally been their bane enabled them to advance out of sight of the Fédéré guns.
48. E.g. 2nd Div., 5th Corps, lost three killed on 22 May, six on the 23rd, four on the 24th, sixteen on the 25th, three on the 26th, one on the 27th and one on the 28th. Folder 'Tués et blessés' (5th Corps), A H G Lu 95.
49. Vermeil de Conchard, 'Notes'. A H G Li 116.
50. Six of the ten well defended barricades were in the area round the Arts et Métiers building (3rd *arrondissement*) and were taken during the afternoon of 25 May. List of barricades taken, A H G Li 116.
51. Report, 36th *de marche*. A H G Li 116.
52. Cissey to MacMahon, 3.10 a.m. and 7.35 a.m., 26 May, A H G Li 119; and see dossier of Jules Quesnot (CO of 120th National Guard bn), 6th *Conseil de Guerre* no. 229, in A H G Ly 132.
53. MacMahon to Thiers and Le Flô, 6.30 a.m., 26 May, A H G Li 119; and Thiers to *Enquête*, II, 18.
54. Da Costa, *La Commune vécue*, III, 104.
55. When leading a small delegation to try to persuade the Germans to intervene he was refused passage by the Fédérés guarding the Porte de Vincennes, who suspected him of trying to escape the battle. Lissagaray, *Histoire*, 351, Maxime Vuillaume, *Mes Cahiers rouges au temps de la Commune* (1971), 294–6.
56. Report, 2nd Div., 5th Corps. A H G Li 116.
57. *Journal des opérations* (5th Corps), A H G Li 116; MacMahon, *Armée de Versailles*, 32.
58. Dispatch from G O C 1st Brig., 25 May, and reports from 37th and 91st *de marche*. A H G Lu 35.
59. *Registre de marche* (Faron's Div.) 21–8 May. A H G Li 116.
60. MacMahon to Cissey, 26 May. A H G Lu 15.
61. *Registre de marche* (Faron's Div.) 21–8 May, and report of 109th *de ligne* (signed Lespiau), A H G Li 116; Pelletan, *La Semaine de Mai*, 309.

62. *Registre de marche* (Faron's Div.) and report of 3rd Div. (Vergé), Reserve Army, 21–8 May. A H G Li 116.
63. Montaudon, *Souvenirs*, II, 398–9.
64. *Ibid.*, 408; *Journal de marche* (Div. Bruat), A H G Li 116; Lissagaray, *Histoire*, 367–8.
65. A H G Li 119, *passim*.
66. Hans, *Souvenirs*, 143–62; Report, 109th *de ligne*, and *Registre de marche* (1st Div., Reserve), A H G Li 116.
67. Movement order, Reserve Army, 28 May. A H G Li 124.
68. Jules Vallès, *L'Insurgé* (1972), 317–18; Lissagaray, *Histoire*, 369; report, 36th *de marche*, A H G Li 116.
69. Dispatch to Vinoy, 27 May. A H G Li 124.
70. Report, 36th *de marche*, A H G Li 116; Vallès, *L'Insurgé*, 319.
71. Report, Gen. de la Mariouse, and *Registre de marche* (Faron's Div.). A H G Li 116.
72. 'A victim of Paris and Versailles', *Macmillan's Magazine*, XXIV (1871), pt 2, 487.
73. *Registres de marche* (Faron's and Bruat's Divs.), A H G Li 116; Clinchant to MacMahon, 3.30 p.m., 28 May, A H G Li 119.
74. *Journal de marche*, 30th bn *chasseurs*, A H G Li 115; Camille Ducray, *Paul Déroulède, 1846–1914* (1914), 95.
75. Wroblewski had wanted the defensive effort transferred to the Left Bank, resting on the Pantheon, the Butte aux Cailles and the remaining forts. Lissagaray, *Histoire*, 328.
76. Frank Jellinek, *The Paris Commune of 1871* (1937), 319.
77. Da Costa's estimate, possibly slightly high. *La Commune vécue*, III, 81.
78. MacMahon to Thiers, 1.50 p.m., 26 May. A H G Li 119.
79. MacMahon gives a total (almost certainly inexact) of 877 killed and 6,454 wounded for the whole campaign. *Armée de Versailles*, 44. But probably less than half of these occurred in Paris: 2nd Corps, for example, lost 149 killed before 21 May, and only 89 afterwards in Paris. Casualty lists (folder '2e Corps'), A H G Lu 95. Detailed 1st Corps casualty lists show that over 70% of wounds were light; during the street fighting most were caused by bullets rather than shells, with many in the right shoulder, exposed when firing from windows. See lists (folder '1er Corps'), A H G Lu 95, and Murray, 'Four days in the ambulances', 596, and supplementary letter dated 31 May, *ibid.*, 622.
80. As again the casualty figures show. The 94th *de ligne* (4th Corps), for example, lost fifteen men killed during the week, but eight of these died at Les Halles on 24 May, five of them in the steeple of Saint Eustache. Lists (folder '4e Corps'), A H G Lu 95, and report from regiment, 24 May, A H G Lu 35. Similarly, the 37th *de marche* (Reserve) lost 96 of its 159 casualties in the attack on the Bastille on 26 May, whereas its total losses for 23, 24 and 27 May were eleven wounded. Report, 37th *de marche*, A H G Lu 36.

10. Expiation

1. Speech to Assembly, 22 May. *Annales*, III, 110. He repeated this on 24 May.
2. E.g. Thiers, *Notes et souvenirs*, 166; MacMahon to *Enquête*, II, 26; Simon, *Gouvernement*, I, 472; Montaudon, *Souvenirs*, II, 414.
3. E.g. Jules Simon, *Thiers, Guizot, Rémusat*, 64–5, who wrote that 'an army of philosophers' would have been required for the tragedy to be averted.
4. E.g. Da Costa, *La Commune vécue*, III, 83.
5. Adrien Dansette, *Les Origines de la Commune de 1871* (1944), 10.
6. Forbes, 'What I saw', pt 2, 52.
7. Rossel, *Papiers posthumes*, 184; Forbes, 'What I saw', pt 2, 52; Vermeil de Conchard, 'Notes', AHG Li 116.
8. Compiègne, 'Souvenirs', 613.
9. Vermeil de Conchard, 'Notes', AHG Li 116.
10. See orders from the Committee of Public Safety and the War Commission of the Commune in the *Journal Officiel* of the Commune, 24 May; and, for example, General Gremion's report to General Vergé on 27 May, saying that he had 'let it be known' that the inhabitants of houses from which shots were fired would be executed. AHG Lu 35.
11. Compiegne, 'Souvenirs', 615.
12. Ruby, 'Quelques aspects militaires', 47.
13. Order of march of 1st brigade, 1st division, 4th Corps, AHG Li 114; Vermeil de Conchard, 'Notes', AHG Li 116; Stéphane, *Rossel*, 279; Forbes, 'What I saw', pt 2, 52.
14. Some very large sums of money found on prisoners disappeared. See Col. Gaillard to *Enquête*, II, 247; Pelletan, *La Semaine de Mai*, 248; P. Angrand, 'Un épisode de la répression versaillaise, l'affaire Tribels', *La Pensée* no. 68 (July–Aug. 1956), 126–33. Some soldiers had 'du linge, des chaînes, des montres et beaucoup d'argent'. Edgar Monteil, *Souvenirs de la Commune* (1883), 204. Le Flô and MacMahon ordered complaints to be investigated and a number of men were court-martialled for theft. AHG Lu 9 and Li 126, *passim*.
15. The only one I have come across is an unlikely story related by Jules Bergeret in *Le Dix-huit mars, journal hebdomadaire* no. 1, 21 Aug. 1871.
16. For a few cases of drunken killings, see Pelletan, *La Semaine de Mai*, 259. A Corporal Dennetières (91st *de marche*) was sentenced to eight years' hard labour for drunkenly killing a comrade. AHG 2nd *Conseil de Guerre*, dossier 357.
17. Hans, *Souvenirs*, 160.
18. Report, 24 May. APP Ba 365–1.
19. Colonel Corbin (chief of staff of National Guard of the Seine) to General Borel (MacMahon's chief of staff), 15 May. AHG Lu 95.
20. *La Gazette des Tribunaux*, 27 August 1871 and 26 April 1872.
21. Colonel Corbin set up a bureau to scrutinize captured documents for such evidence. Corbin to MacMahon, 30 May. AHG Lu 93.
22. *La Gazette des Tribunaux*, 5 May 1872.

23. Hans, *Souvenirs*, 23, 68, 104; Compiègne, 'Souvenirs', 617–18, and Grandeffe, *Mobiles et volontaires*, 267.
24. Compiègne, 'Souvenirs', 593, 617.
25. *Ibid.*, 618, 625; Sutter-Laumann, *Trente-sous*, 312–21.
26. Sutter-Laumann, *Trente-sous*, 322–9.
27. Pessard, in *Le Soir* (Versailles edn), 26 May; Sutter-Laumann, *Trente-sous*, 326; 'What an American girl saw of the Commune', *Macmillan's Magazine*, XLV (new series XXIII) (1892), 66.
28. *Journal de marche* (2nd Corps engineers), A H G Lu 15; *Journal des opérations* (5th Corps), A H G Li 116; G H Q to Vinoy, 24 May, reporting complaints of inspector of telegraphs, A H G Li 124.
29. Gaston Cerfbeer, 'Une nuit de la semaine sanglante', *La Revue Hebdomadaire*, VI (May–June 1903), 422; Vuillaume, *Cahiers*, 307; Vallès, *L'Insurgé*, 292–3.
30. H. Pellaton, *Les Sapeurs-Pompiers et les volontaires de l'Eure aux incendies de Paris* (Evreux 1873), 70. There were various reports of similar incidents.
31. Cerfbeer, 'Une nuit', 424.
32. The suburban population had blamed the Commune for the shells they received from the forts and ramparts, and the Sceaux gendarmerie reported that this had completely turned public opinion against the Fédérés. Report, 11 May, A H G Li 123. The colonel of the 2nd hussars wrote that his men were angry with the Fédérés for firing on a suburban hospital, whose inmates asked the troops for 'help and protection'. A H G Li 123. For letters on the subject and reports on public opinion, see *Le Gaulois*, 23 April.
33. 'What I saw', pt 2, 54.
34. Du Barail, *Souvenirs*, III, 287.
35. Vermeil de Conchard, 'Notes'. A H G Li 116.
36. Gaston de Pressac in *Le Gaulois*, 26 May.
37. See, for example, Lissagaray, *Histoire*, 337, 339; Vuillaume, *Cahiers*, 67–144; Vallès, *L'Insurgé*, 285, 306.
38. Vallès, *L'Insurgé*, 312.
39. Pelletan, *La Semaine de Mai*, 84–6, refers to a 'Captain L—' as being responsible; but General Lacretelle claimed responsibility, stating that the Fédérés were pretending to be wounded. De la Faye, *Lacretelle*, 287.
40. Pelletan, *La Semaine de Mai*, 134-48; Garcin to *Enquête*, II, 239.
41. Report, 2nd Div., 2nd Corps, A H G Lu 7; Cissey to MacMahon, 7.35 a.m., 26 May, A H G Li 119. See also Pelletan, *La Semaine de Mai*, 78, 98.
42. 'What an American girl saw', 66.
43. Compiègne, 'Souvenirs', 613; Hans, *Souvenirs*, 72. See also Ulysse Parent, *Une Arrestation en mai 1871* (1876). For other shootings that day see J. Bruhat, J. Dautry, and E. Terson, *La Commune de 1871* (1970), 281, and G. Bourgin, *La Guerre de 1870–1871 et la Commune* (1939), 350.
44. 'A victim of Paris and Versailles', pt 2, 488; d'Hérisson, *Nouveau journal*, 351–3; report of 22nd bn *chasseurs*, A H G Li 116.
45. Sutter-Laumann, *Trente-sous*, 327; Vuillaume, *Cahiers*, 11; *Le Soir*

(Versailles edn), 26 May (quoting *Le Temps*); Leighton, *Paris under the Commune*, 350.

46. Grandeffe, *Mobiles et volontaires*, 283.
47. Above, pp. 78–9, 84, 86, 88.
48. Above, p. 133. Marx refers to the incident in *The Civil War in France*, 63.
49. AHG 2nd *Conseil de Guerre*, dossier 12, Corporal Lance; Leperche's correspondence, 2–4 May, AHG Lv 10; Faron to Cissey, 3.25 a.m., 1 May, AHG Lu 15, and Ministry of War copy of dispatch annotated in red, 'les sous-officiers et caporaux vont être fusillés', AHG Li 119.
50. Cissey to divisional commanders, 5 May. AHG Li 123.
51. Letters and reports. AHG Li 124.
52. Thiers to Lochner, 23 May, AHG Li 117; Douay to MacMahon, 23 May, AHG Li 127.
53. AHG Li 119.
54. Berthe to Faron and Faron to Vinoy, 24 May, and Berthe to Vinoy, 25 May, AHG Li 124. A note in the police archives reads 'Reçus les nommés Koreski, Gaugeois (fusillés) et les nommés Roche, Junker et Chalmaudray. Ecole Militaire, le 26 mai 1871, [signed] Le Général de Brigade, Berthe', APP Ba 365–1. See also *Journal des opérations*, Brigade Berthe, and report, 22nd bn *chasseurs*, AHG Li 116; and police report, Brig. de la Presse, 26 May, APP Ba 365–1.
55. Report of commanding officer, 24 May. AHG Li 124. And see *Le Gaulois*, 30 May.
56. Report of police captain Dufour, 24 May; note dated 11 a.m., 24 May. APP Ba 365–1.
57. Pelletan, *La Semaine de Mai*, 168.
58. Part of Marshal Vaillant's instructions for dealing with insurrection reads: 'Tout homme pris les armes à la main sera fusillé sur place' (June 1858). A later unsigned instruction reads: 'Les insurgés qui auront capitulé seront constitués prisonniers', but only if their surrender were unconditional. AHG MR 2151, 'Dispositions à prendre en cas d'émeutes'.
59. Cissey to MacMahon, 6 May. AHG Lu 92.
60. Circular, 12 April, and proclamation, 8 May. AHG Lu 95. My italics.
61. *Enquête*, II, 26.
62. *Ibid.*, III, 409.
63. Jacques Silvestre de Sacy, *Le Maréchal de MacMahon* (1960), 261, quoting from unpublished memoirs.
64. AHG Li 119 and Lu 15.
65. BN Papiers Thiers, n.a.fr. 20649 fol. 152; *Annales de l'Assemblée Nationale*, III (13 May–11 Oct. 1871), 135 (25 May).
66. Pelletan, *La Semaine de Mai*, 40.
67. *Souvenirs*, III, 390.
68. Pelletan, *La Semaine de Mai*, 18.
69. Washburne, *Recollections*, II, 157; Bruat to Vinoy, 14 June, AHG Li 125; Garcin to *Enquête*, II, 241.
70. Rapport, 6th *Conseil de Guerre*, dossier Pascal, AHG Ly 132.

71. Leighton, *Paris under the Commune*, 328; Devaureix, *Souvenirs*, 688.
72. Stéphane, *Rossel*, 281–2; Pelletan, *La Semaine de Mai*, 95.
73. *Prévôt* to chief of staff, 4th Corps, 24 May. AHG Lu 35.
74. A. Champoudry, *Manuel des tribunaux des armées de terre et de mer* (1878), 243.
75. Statement of Abbe Riché and *rapport*, AHG Ly 120; Pelletan, *La Semaine de mai*, 208–9. For the legal question, see 'Loi sur l'état de siège, 9 aout 1849', *Bulletin des lois de la République française*, 10th series, IV, 147–8; *Code de Justice Militaire*, arts. 51–2, 204–8, 249–54 in Champoudry, *Manuel*, 219–313; A. Champoudry, *La Justice prévôtale aux armées* (1895); decree of 2 Oct. 1870, AHG Lhs 4.
76. Report, Ossude, 29 May. APP Ba 365–1.
77. Report, Noël to Vinoy, 19 June, AHG Li 126; Vinoy to MacMahon, 2 June, AHG Li 125; Pelletan, *La Semaine de Mai*, 339.
78. Douay to MacMahon, 6.45 p.m., 25 May. AHG Li 127.
79. Garcin to *Enquête*, II, 239.
80. Vuillaume, *Cahiers*, 29.
81. AHG Li 125.
82. Cissey to MacMahon, 4 May, AHG Li 124; list of names, AHG Ly 14, marked 'Succession Leperche', and apparently provided by him in reply to a solicitor's letter sent some years later requesting information concerning a man believed to have been shot at Fort Bicêtre; he does figure on the list, as do the thirteen known to have been shot on 2–3 May.
83. Galliffet addressing prisoners, quoted in 'A victim of Paris and Versailles', pt 2, 489.
84. Devaureix, *Souvenirs*, 673.
85. Vuillaume, *Cahiers*, 27; and see records of police interrogations, *cahier* 309, AHG Ly 35.
86. Willerme to MacMahon, 2 and 13 June, AHG Lu 93; statement of Abbé Riche, AHG Ly 120.
87. Vuillaume, *Cahiers*, 15–46; Pelletan, *La Semaine de Mai*, 394; statement from Abbé Riche, AHG Ly 120.
88. Letter, d'Arnouville, AHG 5th *Conseil de Guerre*, dossier 76 (Walter, A.); report, General Gandil (4th Corps), 29 May, AHG Li 114; *Le Gaulois*, 29 May; Pelletan, *La Semaine de Mai*, 394.
89. Police report, 28 May, APP Ba 364–1; Monteil, *Souvenirs*, 205; *The Times*, 2 June; Lissagaray, *Histoire*, 496.
90. Report, Ossude, 29 May. APP Ba 365–1.
91. Note to de Fayet, 26 May. AHG Li 124.
92. AHG Lu 92.
93. Corbin to Borel, 30 May, AHG Lu 93; F. Jourde, *Souvenirs d'un membre de la Commune* (Brussels 1877), 94–8; police report, 1 June, APP Ba 365–2.
94. APP Ba 365–1, *passim*.
95. Report, 75th *de marche*, 22–8 May, AHG Li 116; order, Vinoy, 25 May, AHG Lu 35.
96. Louis Gallet, *Guerre et Commune, impressions d'un hospitalier* (1898), 237; *Journal de marche*, div. Bruat, AHG Li 116.

97. AHG Li 124.
98. Silvestre de Sacy, *MacMahon*, 260.
99. MacMahon to Vinoy, no. 241. AHG Li 124.
100. 'Recommandations' (Reserve GHQ), 26 May. AHG Lu 35.
101. Circular, 29 May. AHG Li 124.
102. A police report, 1 June, stated that many of those arrested in the 20th *arrondissement* were being shot at the Père Lachaise. AHG Li 125. Pelletan claims that this continued at least until 7 June. *La Semaine de Mai*, 348–9. Leperche was doing the same at Fort Bicêtre. Report of Commissaire of Police, 3 June, APP Ba 497, and list of names and dates, AHG Ly 14. A certain Lescure was reported to have been executed in a Versailles barracks on 27 May. Police reports, Captain Lombard and Presse, APP Ba 365–1. A number of *pompiers* were said to have been shot there on 7 June. A. Arnaud, *Pompiers de Paris* (1958), 124.
103. *Enquête*, II, 241.
104. A special telegraphic section monitored dispatches and sent copies to the Presidency. An example of this operating on an important occasion for which evidence survives concerns Cissey's telegram about the shooting of prisoners, mentioned above p. 175.
105. Borel to Cissey, 12.55 p.m., and Cissey to MacMahon and Thiers, 1.07 p.m., 26 May, AHG Lu 15; Cissey to MacMahon, 26 May, AHG Li 124.
106. Angrand, 'Une épisode de la repression', 128, 133.
107. Douay to MacMahon, 14 June, AHG Lu 92; dossier Vabre, AS D.2 R⁴225.
108. Henri de Blowitz, *My Memoirs* (1903), 44.
109. *The Times*, 1 and 3 June; *Le Gaulois*, 2 and 9 June; police report, 15 June, APP Ba 365–2.
110. Favre to Thiers, 21 May. MAE Papiers Thiers, fol. 25.
111. Henri Malo, *Thiers 1797–1877* (1932), 514–15.
112. Dossier COURTOT DE CISSEY, APP Ba 1021, and for hints concerning his character, AHG Lu 16 and 93, and Du Barail, *Souvenirs*, III, 291, 323. Dossier VINOY, AHGGD (2e série) 1336, and for an unflattering account of his character, MAE Papiers Gambetta, vol. 52, 'Généraux . . . hors cadres', fol. 79.
113. Rossel had heard this. Stéphane, *Mémoires*, 296. See also de la Faye, *Ladmirault*, 287–8.
114. Report, Commissaire de Police at Villebon. APP Ba 497.
115. Other than Pelletan's mention of two soldiers being shot for firing at their officers. *La Semaine de Mai*, 28–9. I have been unable to verify this.
116. Captain Kiener, 2nd Corps *prévôt*, had Ulysse Parent fed after his reprieve and sent him to Versailles in a carriage with expressions of goodwill. Parent, *Une Arrestation*, 48–53. See also de Lano, preface to *Journal d'un vaincu*.
117. Vuillaume, *Cahiers*, 39, referring to the sentimentality of a police agent attached to the Luxembourg *prévôté*.
118. Grandeffe, *Mobiles et volontaires*, 259; de Mun, preface to de la Faye, *Ladmirault*, xxiii; MacMahon to *Enquête*, II, 27.

119. L'Hériller to Douay, 8 June. AHG Lu 36.
120. Cissey to MacMahon, 4 June, AHG Lu 92; L'Hériller to Douay, 29 May, AHG Lu 35.
121. Cissey to MacMahon, 29 May, AHG Lu 92; *Prescriptions du rapport*, 31 May, AHG Lu 16; report (4th Corps) 3 June, AHG Li 125.
122. Minister of War to MacMahon, 10 June (folder 'Cabinet, correspondance générale . . . juin 1871'), AHG Lu 92; Grandeffe, *Mobiles et volontaires*, 293–4; Du Geslin to MacMahon, no. 84, 15 June (folder 'Rapports des commandants des forts'), AHG Li 126.
123. Faron to Vinoy, 3 June; Derroja to [Faron], 6 June; Vinoy to MacMahon, 3 June. AHG Li 125.
124. Faron to Vinoy, 1 June, AHG Li 125; Douay to MacMahon. 6 June, AHG Lu 92; MacMahon to Thiers no. 1087, 1 June, AHG Lu 9.
125. Du Barail to MacMahon, 5 June, AHG Li 125; police reports, 9–11 June, APP Ba 365–2.
126. Cissey to MacMahon, 16 June, AHG Lu 92; MacMahon to Vinoy, 28 June, AHG Li 126.
127. *The Times*, 3 June; Grandeffe, *Mobiles et volontaires*, 280.
128. Mention of 17,000 casualties, in *Enquête*, II, 26–7; Rapport de l'ingénieur en chef, 8 June 1871 (folder 'Inhumations . . .'), AS VO (NC) 234; Pelletan, *La Semaine de Mai*, 372–98.
129. Da Costa thought 10,000. *La Commune vécue*, II, 121. Malon thought about 3,000. *La Troisième Défaite*, 474.
130. *Rapport Appert*, 213–19; AHG 2nd *Conseil de Guerre*, passim. A number of death sentences were commuted by the appeal tribunals.
131. Berthe's brigade, used for this purpose at the Ecole Militaire and the Père Lachaise cemetery, was probably chosen because it was under strength and so unsuitable for ordinary operations.
132. Ruby, 'Quelques aspects militaires', 49.
133. E.g. *The Times*, 29 May: 'Where above all are the signs of that combined generosity, firmness and foresight in statesmen and soldiers . . .? we know not where to look for hope or consolation.'
134. Letter from Jules to Paul Cambon (n.d.), MAE Papiers Jules Cambon, vol. 19, fol. 7. He had accompanied Ferry into Paris during *la Semaine Sanglante*.

11. Conclusions

1. Eugen Weber, *Peasants into Frenchmen, the Modernization of Rural France 1870–1914* (1977), especially chapters 7 and 15.
2. Frederick A. de Luna, *The French Republic under Cavaignac 1848* (Princeton 1969), 164, citing an unpublished dissertation by W. Zaniewicki.
3. Richard Cobb, *Tour de France* (1976), 129.
4. Perhaps even with the increased power of weapons: it was often alleged that *mitrailleuses* were used to execute prisoners *en masse*.
5. It is worth recalling that leading figures of important new political movements of the future – Déroulède, Boulanger and de Mun – served in the

Army of Versailles, and de Mun made no secret of the effect of that experience on him.

6. It was suggested that the 1850 suffrage should be reestablished. Roger Price, 'Conservative reactions to social disorder: the Paris Commune of 1871', *Journal of European Studies*, I (1971), 341–52.

7. Philippe Riviale, *La Ballade du temps passé* (1977), 337–8.

8. Saint-Valry, *Souvenirs et réflexions*, I, 216. He was commenting on the political situation following the 'Seize Mai', the attempt in 1877 by MacMahon, as President, to use his powers to bolster a conservative regime.

9. Daniel Halévy, *La Fin des notables*, II, *La République des ducs* (1937), 295–6. Berthaut went to the length of imprisoning a Right-wing journalist of *Le Figaro* (who happened to be a reserve officer) for attacking his decision.

10. Gambetta's informant concluded that by 1875 the army would not support the government or the man 'qui essaierait d'engager une nouvelle lutte fratricide'. M A E Papiers Gambetta, vol. 52, 'Notes politiques', p. 117.

Bibliography

vvvvvvvvvvvvvvvvvvvvvvvvvvvvvvvvvvvvvvvvvvvvvvvvvvvvvvvvvvvvvvvvvvvvvvvvvvvvvvvvvvvv

MANUSCRIPT SOURCES

Archives Historiques de Guerre (AHG)

The sub-series used principally were Li, 'Guerre de 1870–1871: Armée de Paris' (which later became the Reserve Army), and Lu, 'Guerre de 1870–1871: Armée de Versailles'. The relevant parts are Li 90 – Li 128, and Lu 7 – Lu 98. The following were used from other sub-series:

Lhs 4 'Guerre 1870–1871: cours martiales'

Lo 67 'Guerre 1870–1871: rentrée des prisonniers'

Lv 10 'Succession Leperche'

Lv 19 'Critiques et renseignements'

Ly 2 and 4 'Commune de Paris' (orders and telegrams)

Ly 9 'Commune de Paris 1871, informations contre les soldats du 88e de marche et du 120e de ligne'

Ly 14 'Commune de Paris 1871, incendies et pillages'

MR 2151 'Dispositions à prendre en cas d'émeutes et de troubles à Paris'

Registre matricule des officiers, 42nd *de ligne*, 74th *régiment d'infanterie* (vol. 2), 114th *de ligne* (vol. 1)

Registre matricule de la troupe, 114th *de ligne* (vols. 1–3)

'Commune de Paris 1871: Conseils de Guerre' – documents from various dossiers

Individual dossiers were also used from the series GB (Généraux de Brigade), GD (Généraux de Division), MF (Maréchaux de France), N (nominatif), Réformés, and Pensions

Archives de la Préfecture de Police (APP)

Of primary importance was the Correspondance (of the Prefect) from March to June, Ba 364 and 365, which includes a wide variety of reports and official correspondence. Also of use were the personal dossiers of military figures in the series Ba. Other items of interest were:

Ba 497, dossiers on 'Assassinat du sous-brigadier de police Vincensini' and 'Envoi d'un commissaire de police spécial à Villebon'

Ba 511 'Mission de Mr Saget, Commissaire de Police, à Gretz et à Villebon' (with reports of other officers detached on special missions connected with the insurrection)

Bibliography

Ministère des Affaires Etrangères, Archives Diplomatiques (MAE)

From the section *Papiers d'agents*:
Papiers Thiers, 'Traité de Francfort, armée d'occupation, 1871–73'
Papiers Jules Favre, Guerre, vol. 5 (16 Feb.–10 March 1871) and vol. 6 (11 March–15 June)
Papiers Gambetta, vol. 52 ('Notes politiques' on officers) and vol. 55 (concerning army personnel)
Papiers Jules Cambon, vol. 19 (letters to and from Paul Cambon, 1869–1922)

From the section *Correspondance politique*:
'Angleterre', new series, vol. 756
'Russie', new series, vol. 245

Bibliothèque Nationale (BN)

Papiers A. Thiers: 'Correspondance', 1871, n.a.fr. 20621–20623
'Siège de Paris en 1871' (dispatches received), n.a.fr.20646–20650

Archives de la Seine (AS)

VD 3 21 (Gardes Nationaux tués) and VO(NC) 234 (Voie Publique)

PRINTED SOURCES

Official publications

Enquête parlementaire sur l'insurrection du 18 mars, no. 740, Assemblée Nationale, 1871. 3 vols. Versailles 1872.
Rapport d'ensemble de M. le General Appert sur les opérations de la justice militaire relatives à l'insurrection de 1871, no. 3212, Assemblée Nationale, annexe au procès-verbal de la séance du 20 juillet 1875. Versailles, 1875.
Annales de l'Assemblée Nationale, 1871.
Bulletin des lois de la République française, 10th series, vol. IV. 1850.

Newspapers

Le Figaro
La Gazette des Tribunaux
Le Gaulois
Le Journal Officiel (of the Commune)
Le Moniteur de l'Armée
Le Soir (Paris and Versailles editions)
The Times

Bibliography

Memoirs and correspondence

Books

Unless otherwise stated, French books were published in Paris and English books in London.

Amigues, Jules (ed.), *Papiers posthumes* (of L. N. Rossel). 1871

Barron, Louis, *Sous le drapeau rouge.* 1889

Becker, George J. (ed.), *Paris under Siege, 1879–1871, from the Goncourt Journal.* Ithaca, 1969

Blowitz, Henri Stephan de, *My Memoirs.* 1903

Bouniols, Gaston (ed.), *Thiers au pouvoir (1871–1873), texte de ses lettres.* 1921

Busch, Moritz, *Bismarck, Some Secret Pages of his History.* 3 vols. 1898

Choppin, Capt. Henri, *Souvenirs d'un cavalier du second empire.* 1898

Cluseret, Gustave Paul, *Mémoires du général Cluseret.* 3 vols. 1887–8

Costa, Gaston da, *La Commune vécue.* 3 vols. 1903–5

Delessert, Eugène, *Episodes pendant la Commune, souvenirs d'un délégué de la société de secours aux blessés des armées de terre et de mer.* 1872

Déroulède, Paul, *1870, Feuilles de route, des bois de Verrières à la forteresse de Breslau.* 1907

Déroulède, Paul, *70–71, Nouvelles Feuilles de route, de la forteresse de Breslau aux allées de Tourny.* 1907

Devaureix, General Anne Albert, *Souvenirs et observations sur la campagne de 1870.* 1909

Du Barail, General François Charles, *Mes Souvenirs.* 3 vols. 1894–6

Dupont, Léonce, *Souvenirs de Versailles pendant la Commune.* 1881

Favre, Jules Gabriel Claude, *Gouvernement de la défense nationale.* 3 vols. 1875

Fix, Colonel Théodore, *Souvenirs d'un officier d'état-major.* 2 vols. 1896

Flamarion, Dr Alfred, *Le Livret du docteur, souvenirs de la campagne contre l'Allemagne et contre la Commune de Paris, 1870–1871.* 1872

Forbes, Archibald, *My Experiences of the War between France and Germany.* 2 vols. 1871

Gallet, Louis, *Guerre et Commune, impressions d'un hospitalier.* 1898

Grandeffe, comte Arthur de, *Mobiles et volontaires de la Seine pendant la guerre et les deux sièges.* 1871

Gromier, Marc Amadée. See Lano, Pierre de

Guerre des communeux de Paris, par un officier supérieur de l'armée de Versailles (H. Sarrepont, pseud. of Eugène Hennebert). 1871

Hans, Capt. Albert, *Souvenirs d'un volontaire versaillais.* 1873

Hérisson, Maurice d'Irisson, comte d', *Nouveau journal d'un officier d'ordonnance, la Commune.* 1889

Histoire de la Commune de Paris (18 mars–31 mai 1871). 1871

Hoffman, Wickham, *Camp, Court and Siege.* 1877

Jourde, François, *Souvenirs d'un membre de la Commune.* Brussels, 1877

La Faye, Jacques de (pseud. of Marie de Sardent) (ed.), *Souvenirs du général Lacretelle.* 1907

Lano, Pierre de (ed.), *Journal d'un vaincu* (dairy of Marc Amadée Gromier). 1892

Bibliography

Lefrançais, Gustave, *Souvenirs d'un révolutionnaire*. 1972

Leighton, John, *Paris under the Commune, or The Seventy-three Days of the Second Siege*. 1871

MacMahon, Marshal M.E.P.M. de, *L'Armée de Versailles, depuis sa formation jusqu'à la complète pacification de Paris*. 1871

Malon, Benoît, *La Troisième Défaite du prolétariat français*. Neuchâtel, 1871

Meaux, vicomte Camille de, *Souvenirs politiques, 1871–1877*. 1905

Meyret, Lieutenant-Colonel Louis Alfred, *Carnet d'un prisonnier de guerre*. 1888

Montaudon, General Alexandre, *Souvenirs militaires*. 2 vols. 1898–1900

Monteil, Edgar, *Souvenirs de la Commune, 1871*. 1883

Mun, comte Albert de, preface to La Faye, J. de, *Le Général de Ladmirault*. 1901

Narcy, L. de, *Journal d'un officier de turcos, 1870*. 1902

Parent, Ulysse, *Une Arrestation en mai 1871*. 1876

Patry, Captain Léonce, *La Guerre telle qu'elle est, Metz, Armée du Nord, Commune*. 1897

Pellaton, H., *Les Sapeurs-Pompiers et les volontaires de l'Eure aux incendies de Paris*. Evreux, 1873

Pessard, Hector, *Mes petits papiers, deuxième série, 1871–1873*. 1888

Reclus, Elie, *La Commune de Paris au jour le jour*. 1908

Rossel, Louis Nathaniel. See J. Amigues and R. Stéphane

Saint-Valry, Gaston de, *Souvenirs et réflexions politiques*. 1886

Sardent, Marie de. See La Faye, Jacques de

Sesmaisons, General comte Claude Marie Rogation de, *Hier et aujourd'hui, les troupes de la Commune et la loi de deux ans*. 1904

Simon, Jules, *Le Gouvernement de M. Thiers, 8 fevrier 1871 – 24 mai 1873*. 2 vols. 1878

Simon, Jules, *Thiers, Guizot, Rémusat*. 1885

Souvenirs d'un garde national pendant le siège de Paris et pendant la Commune, par un volontaire suisse. 2 vols. Neuchâtel, 1871

Stéphane, Roger (ed.), *Louis-Nathaniel Rossel, mémoires, procès et correspondance*. 1960

Sutter-Laumann, *Histoire d'un trente-sous (1870–1871)*. 1891

Thiers, Adolphe, *Notes et souvenirs de M. Thiers, 1870–1873*. 1901

Vallès, Jules, *L'Insurgé*. 1972

Vinoy, Gen. Joseph, *Campagne de 1879–1871, II, L'Armistice et la Commune*. 1872

Vuillaume, Maxime, *Mes Cahiers rouges au temps de la Commune*. 1971 (facsimile of 1909 edn)

Walker, General Sir Charles Beauchamp, *Days of a Soldier's Life*. 1894

Washburne, Elihu B., *Recollections of a Minister to France, 1869–1877*. 2 vols. 1887

Yriarte, Charles, *Les Prussiens à Paris et le 18 mars*. 1871

Articles and pamphlets

'A victim of Paris and Versailles', *Macmillan's Magazine*, XXIV (1871), pt 1, 384–408; pt 2, 487–96

Bibliography

Bergeret, Jules, *Le Dix-huit mars, journal hebdomadaire*, August and September 1871 (three issues), London and Brussels

Caro, E., 'La fin de la bohème', *Revue des Deux Mondes*, XCIV (1871), 241–55

Cerfbeer, Gaston, 'Une nuit de la semaine sanglante', *La Revue Hebdomadaire*, VI (1903), 417–24

Compiègne, Marquis de, 'Souvenirs d'un Versaillais pendant le second siège de Paris', *Le Correspondant*, 10 Aug. 1875, 589–633

Forbes, Archibald, 'What I saw of the Paris Commune', *Century Magazine*, XLIV (new series XXII) (1892), 803–17; and XLV (new series XXIII) (1892), 48–61

Galliffet, General Gaston de, 'Mes souvenirs', *Journal des Débats*, 19, 22 and 25 July 1902

Mun, comte Albert de, 'Galliffet', *Echo de Paris*, 10 July 1909

Murray, Dr John, 'Four days in the ambulances and hospitals of Paris under the Commune', *British Medical Journal* (Jan.-June 1871), 541–2, 596–7, 622

'What an American girl saw of the Commune', *Macmillan's Magazine*, XLV (new series XXIII) (1892), 61–6

Secondary works

Books

Arnaud, Comm. Aristide, *Pompiers de Paris*. 1958

Bellanger, Claude, Godechot, Jacques, Guiral, Pierre and Terrou, Fernand (eds.), *Histoire générale de la presse française*. 3 vols. 1971

Bourelly, General Jules, *Le Ministère de la guerre sous la Commune*. 1913

Bourgin, Georges, *La Guerre de 1870–1871 et la Commune*. 1939

Bruhat, Jean, Dautry, J., and Terson, E., *La Commune de 1871*. 2nd edn, 1970

Bury, J. P. T., *Gambetta and the National Defence, a Republican Dictatorship in France*. 1936

Bury, J. P. T., *Gambetta and the Making of the Third Republic*. 1973

Carrias, Colonel Eugène, *La Pensée militaire française*. 1960

Chalmin, Pierre, *L'Officier français de 1815 à 1870*. 1957

Champoudry, Alphonse Joseph, *Manuel des tribunaux des armées de terre et de mer*. 1878

Champoudry, Alphonse Joseph, *La Justice prévôtale aux armées*. 1895

Clarke, Sir George Sydenham, *Fortification*. 1907

Cobb, Richard, *Tour de France*. 1976

Craig, Gordon A., *The Politics of the Prussian Army, 1640–1945*. 1968

Dansette, Adrien, *Les Origines de la Commune de 1871*. 1944

De Luna, Frederick A., *The French Republic under Cavaignac 1848*. Princeton, 1969

Desmarest, Jacques, *La Défense nationale, 1870–1871*. 1949

Dessal, Marcel, *Un Révolutionnaire jacobin, Charles Delescluze, 1809–1871*. 1952

Ducray, Camille, *Paul Déroulède, 1846–1914*. 1914

Edwards, Stewart, *The Paris Commune 1871*. 1972

Bibliography

Fiaux, Louis, *Histoire de la guerre civile de 1871, le gouvernement et l'assemblée de Versailles, la Commune de Paris.* 1879

Gaillard, Jeanne, *Communes de province, Commune de Paris, 1870–1871.* 1971

Girard, Louis, *La Garde nationale, 1814–1871.* 1964

Halévy, Daniel, *La Fin des notables.* 2 vols. 1930 and 1937

Howard, Michael, *The Franco-Prussian War.* 1967

Hurst, Michael (ed.), *Key Treaties for the Great Powers 1814–1914.* 2 vols. 1972

Jellinek, Frank, *The Paris Commune of 1871.* 1937

Kunzt, François, *L'Officier français dans la nation.* 1960

La Faye, Jacques de (pseud. of Marie de Sardent), *Le Général de Ladmirault, 1808–1898.* 1901

Lanoux, Armand, *Une Histoire de la Commune de Paris.* 3 vols. 1971

Lazare, Louis, *Les Quartiers pauvres de Paris, le 20e arrondissement.* 1870

Lefèbvre, Henri, *La Proclamation de la Commune.* 1965

Lichtheim, George, *Marxism, An Historical and Critical Study.* 2nd edn. 1964

Lissagaray, Prosper-Olivier, *Histoire de la Commune de 1871.* 1972 (taken from the Dentu edn, 1896, revised from the original 1876 edn)

Lucas-Dubreton, J., *Aspects de Monsieur Thiers.* 1948

Malo, Henri, *Thiers, 1797–1877.* 1932

Marx, Karl, *The Civil War in France.* Peking, 1966 (compiled from *Selected works of Karl Marx and Frederick Engels.* Moscow, 1951, and *Archives of Marx and Engels*, Moscow, 1934)

Monteilhet, J., *Les Institutions militaires de la France (1814–1924), de l'armée permanante à la nation armée.* 2nd edn. 1932

Newton, Thomas Wodehouse Leigh, Baron, *Lord Lyons, a Record of British Diplomacy.* 2 vols. 1913

Palat, General Barthélémy Edmond, *Histoire de la Guerre de 1870–1871.* 15 vols. 1893–1908

Pelletan, Camille, *La Semaine de Mai.* 1880

Pinkney, David H., *Napoleon III and the Rebuilding of Paris.* 1972

Procès du Maréchal Bazaine, compte-rendu des débats du 1er Conseil de Guerre. 1874

Rémy, Tristan, *La Commune à Montmartre, 23 mai 1871.* 1970

Rich, Norman, *Friedrich von Holstein, Politics and Diplomacy in the Era of Bismarck and Wilhelm II.* 2 vols. Cambridge, 1965

Rich, Norman and Fisher, M. H., *The Holstein Papers.* 4 vols. Cambridge, 1955–63

Riviale, Philippe, *La Ballade du temps passé, guerre et insurrection de Babeuf à la Commune.* 1977

Rougerie, Jacques, *Procès des Communards.* 1964

Rougerie, Jacques, *Paris libre 1871.* 1971

Silvestre de Sacy, Jacques, *Le Maréchal de MacMahon, duc de Magenta, 1808–1893.* 1960

Sorel, Albert, *Histoire diplomatique de la guerre franco-allemande.* 2 vols. 1875

Thomas, Edith, *Rossel, 1844–1871.* 1967

Valfrey, Jules, *Histoire du traité de Francfort et de la libération du territoire français.* 2 vols. 1874–5

Bibliography

Weber, Eugen, *Peasants into Frenchmen, the Modernization of Rural France 1870–1914*. 1977.

Articles

Angrand, P., 'Un épisode de la répression versaillaise, l'affaire Tribels', *La Pensée* no. 68 (July–Aug. 1956), 125–33

Archer, Julian P. W., 'The crowd in the Lyon Commune and the insurrection of La Guillotière', *International Review of Social History*, XVII (1972), 183–8

Bathille, Pierre, 'Petite histoire de Biribi', *Le Crapouillot* no. 25 (n.d.), *Petite Histoire de l'armée française*, 78–83

Dautry, J., 'Trois documents auvergnats concernant la Commune', *La Pensée* no. 82 (Nov.–Dec. 1958), 122

Paz, Maurice, 'Le mythe de la Commune, relations avec les Prussiens', *Est et Ouest* no. 479 (Dec. 1971), 20–4; and no. 485 (March 1972), 22–4.

Paz, Maurice, 'Le mythe de la Commune, les deux reproches majeurs', *Est et Ouest* no. 482 (Feb. 1972), 23–28

Price, Roger, 'Conservative reactions to social disorder: the Paris Commune of 1871', *Journal of European Studies*, I (1971), 341–52

Regnault, General J., 'Les campagnes d'Algérie et leur influence de 1830 à 1870', *Revue Historique de l'Armée* no. 4 (1953), 23–37

Regnault, General J., 'Le haut commandement et les généraux français en 1870', *Revue Historique de l'Armée* no.1 (1971), 7–22

Roberts, J. M., 'The Paris Commune from the Right', *English Historical Review*, supplement 6. 1973

Rougerie, Jacques, 'Belleville', in Girard, Louis (ed.), *Les Elections de 1869* (Bibliothèque de la Révolution de 1848, XXI). 1960

Rougerie, Jacques, 'Notes pour servir à l'histoire du 18 mars 1871', in *Mélanges d'histoire sociale offerts à Jean Maitron*. 1976

Ruby, General Edmond, 'Quelques aspects militaires de la Commune de Paris', *Ecrits de Paris* (Sept. 1971), 37–52

Tombs, Robert, 'The Thiers government and the outbreak of civil war in France, February–April 1871', *Historical Journal*, XXIII, no. 4 (1980), 813–31

Witzig, Carole, 'Bismarck et la Commune', *International Review of Social History*, XVII (1972), 191–221

Wright, Gordon, 'The anti-Commune, Paris 1871', *French Historical Studies*, X (1977), 149–72

Unpublished dissertations

Holmes, Richard, 'The road to Sedan, the French army 1866–70'. PhD thesis, Reading University. 1975

Schulkind, Eugene, 'Le rôle des travaux d'urbanisme du second empire dans les batailles de rue de la Commune de 1871', Paris, June 1951

Index

Index